AS I RECALL

As I Recall

Calvin L. Rampton

Edited by
Floyd A. O'Neil and Gregory C. Thompson

University of Utah Press
Salt Lake City
1989

Second printing, 1990

Library of Congress Cataloging-in-Publication Data

Rampton, Calvin L., 1913–
    As I recall / by Calvin L. Rampton ; edited by Floyd A. O'Neil and
Gregory C. Thompson.
        p.   cm.
    ISBN 0-87480-334-9
    1. Rampton, Calvin L., 1913–   . 2. Utah–Governors–Biography.
3. Utah–Politics and government.   I. O'Neil, Floyd A.
II. Thompson, Gregory Coyne.   III. Title.
F830.R36A3   1989
979.2'033'092 – dc20   89–22669
                                                            CIP

CONTENTS

FOREWORD

Calvin Rampton of Utah was a remarkable governor. He had a deep concern for people, was a champion of education, and he finished his long stay in the governor's office knowing that he had made a substantial difference in the lives of the people of his state.

I have known Calvin Rampton since he was first elected governor of Utah. I was at the time fresh out of the North Carolina governor's office and was engaged in studying the governorship and federalism under foundation grants at Duke University. "The Study of American States" made me a professional governor-watcher. My staff and I immediately identified Utah's governor as a model of what states ought to be doing. One of the chief projects of the study was the creation of the Education Commission of the States. Governor Rampton helped me in getting this idea quickly accepted by the governors, and later served as chairman. He was one of a few governors at the time betting the future of his state on improved education.

The fact that he endured was a political feat. First he ran with Lyndon Johnson, and that was easy. Then he ran with Humphrey when Nixon won his first term, and his win was impressive. Finally he won when McGovern was beaten in a landslide, and that was remarkable. He had a Democratic legislature his first two and last two years, with eight years of Republicans in between, and that was, or might have been excruciating. He was a durable, well-liked, and creative governor who accomplished much. Not only did he survive the Republican sweep of the decade, but he saw his Democratic choice elected as his successor, and reelected. This book tells something about how he achieved it all.

He had developed a keen sense of the possible, the knack of surefootedness, the flexibility to contain his opposition, when in 1966 he was engulfed by a Republican flood that changed the comfortable Democratic margin in the legislature to an overwhelming Republican presence, with the speaker personally hostile. Rampton, as prophets of old, was sorely tested. He wrote: "Even though I had opposed them I was faced with the practical problem that they were there, and if the state was going to avoid a period of deadlock, I had to take the first step toward making sure that we would have the proper cooperation."

Maybe he got that flexibility to adjust from his father, who was quick enough, as Rampton recounts, to change his elder son's name from Hollis, the mother's choice, to Calvin as he walked down the chapel aisle for the christening. The new name was spontaneously suggested by an uncle who happened to have his hymnal open at a John Calvin hymn.

He demonstrated that sense of the situation, that ability to recover rapidly, in the first grade. The governor remembers the first day when he wore patent leather shoes and a yellow pongee shirt with ruffles, which got him and the shirt bloodied in a fight. The next day he wore hobnail shoes, a work shirt, and blue jeans.

In a conservative climate he was a leader in promoting education with bonds and new taxes, and took firmly and repeatedly to task the Republicans who challenged the food tax that supported education.

Facing the Republican legislature, he was pragmatic: "I wanted to . . . present to what was obviously a conservative Utah electorate a very sparse budget, a very conservative budget . . . I was determined to move ahead with the school program that we had set in motion two years previously, because I'd made a promise that I would take a number of annual or biennial steps to bring the Utah student expenditure up to the mountain states' average." He succeeded.

Rampton is candid. A public official can afford to be candid after he has run the course so well. "After the legislature left," he writes, "I vetoed some twenty-two bills. One day, in exasperation and frustration, I said something . . . I regretted almost immediately — that in some twenty-five years of watching the state legislatures, this house had been the worst legislative body I had ever seen." The governor, however, had the capacity to make them want to do better.

This is a warm story of personal struggle in the days of the Great Depression; of a young man determined to succeed, innovative, hard working always at several jobs, determined to hold family together after the sudden death of his father; of the support he gave and received from his mother, who was a remarkable woman; of the courtship of his wonderful first lady; of his war service. It will have lasting utility for political scientists, and will be a special treat for Utahans.

Governor Rampton, who has devoted his life to public service, has added another public service by writing this book. History needs it. Such a written record is not an exercise in vanity. It is a service to posterity. These were productive, creative years for Utah. How did a forward-looking governor wend his way through the booby traps and obstacle courses of a conservative population to move them to progress and new aspirations? That is leadership. Reading the story is an inspiration to would-be political leaders. How did he do it with constant honor and dignity? That is a lesson for would-be leaders.

Whenever the history of modern Utah is considered, the Rampton years will be essential to that study. It would have been too bad if the central player had not recorded his memories.

Calvin Rampton was an influential leader in a period when there was a considerable move in American federalism that saw the states emerge from the underfunded, ineffective, subordinate, and dependent subgovernments they, or most of them, had been for fifty years. They have become, or most of them, sources of creative and innovative leadership, staffed with a professional civil service, vigorous in advancing the opportunities of their people. It was a time when education was moved to the top of the public agenda in most states. It was a time of revival of federalism. Those who will be concerned in the future with making state governments more effective, with strengthening American life by enhancing our unique concept of federalism, will find Governor Calvin Rampton's own account of these times a rewarding source for their understanding.

Terry Sanford
United States Senate
September 1988

EDITORS' COMMENTS

Governor Calvin L. Rampton's *As I Recall* was initially dictated from his own remembrances. Lucybeth Rampton, his wife, provided compilations of materials and gave strong encouragement to the work. Both were of immense value to the success of the project.

The University of Utah Library Special Collections Department and the University of Utah American West Center cooperated in the preparation of the tape-recorded transcripts. The Everett L. Cooley Oral History Project paid for the transcription costs of the approximately nine hundred pages transcribed and presently available in the library's manuscript division. The editors selected the material included in the book. Size limitations dictated that many important and interesting events in Governor Rampton's life, including the Ramptons' many travels, be omitted. The events centering on his Utah public career were emphasized.

We extend our thanks to David Catron, Norma Mikkelsen, Scott Engen, and the University of Utah Press for their dedication to this project. Special gratitude is expressed for the contribution of Margery W. Ward for her careful reading of the manuscript. We also extend our thanks to the staff of the American West Center.

The publishing of *As I Recall* was made possible in part by a generous contribution from the law firm of Jones, Waldo, Holbrook & McDonough.

Our gratitude is expressed to Governor and Mrs. Rampton for their constant support.

ACKNOWLEDGMENTS

This project did not start out to be a book. It had been suggested by a member of the American West Center at the University of Utah that I should record some recollections on electronic tape to then be transcribed by personnel at the center. I undertook this beginning several years ago. Almost all of the recording was done during trips between our condominium in St. George and our Salt Lake City home. Lucybeth would drive the car while I dictated. She often supplemented or corrected my own recollections. The only source materials were my own memory, a journal which I kept during World War II, and a voluminous scrapbook of newspaper clippings that Lucybeth maintained during the time I served as governor.

Some thirty hours of recording were transcribed into approximately nine hundred typewritten pages of transcript. Both my sympathy and appreciation go to Ann Curtis, Jeanie Reynolds, Judy Robertson, and Madelyn Wormald of the American West Center, who performed the tedious job of listening to my often disjointed ramblings and typing them into a coherent text.

Dr. Floyd A. O'Neil, director of the American West Center, and Dr. Gregory C. Thompson, director of special collections, Marriott Library, approached me with the idea of editing the transcript down into a manageable size and publishing it as a book. I was pleased to participate in this project, and the editing process began. Editing was done by David Hoehner, Susan McKay, and Winston P. Erickson, who were employed by the American West Center; however, the principal work was done by Drs. O'Neil and Thompson. I am grateful for the patience and skill they exhibited in this task. The book covers the events of my life as I remember them; whether they are accurate, the reader will have to judge. These, however, are the events as I recall.

Calvin L. Rampton

CHAPTER • ONE

A Bountiful
Beginning

I was born at Bountiful, Utah, on November 6, 1913, the first child of Lewellyn S. Rampton and Janet Campbell Rampton. Mother and Dad had been married for about five years before I was born, and they felt some concern as to whether they would have children. And so when Mother was pregnant with me, they were pleased. They were later to have two more children: my brother Byron, who is approximately four years younger than I, and my sister Virginia, who is just about eleven years younger. I was born in a house on North Main Street, and I do mean born in a house, because at that time children were generally not born in hospitals but in the home, either in the bedroom or on the kitchen table.

I remember the house very well because, although we moved away from there when I was three years old and I have very few recollections of living there, it wasn't torn down until around 1940. My Aunt Nell and Uncle Jeff Haley later lived in part of the house for a period of time. The house was generally known in the community as the Mitchell House, and I'm sure at the time it was built that it was a very fine place.

I have only one clear recollection of living in the Mitchell House. I remember standing out on Main Street and watching teams of horses moving the building which was my father's blacksmith shop back from Main Street to a place on First North. Dad and Uncle Jim Rampton were later to build a brick garage where the old blacksmith shop had stood. I remember vividly those horses pulling that big building. I'm sure that it was before my fourth birthday because sometime in my fourth year we moved out of the Mitchell House and into a white frame house on East Center Street where my brother Byron was born.

This second house was on a lot approximately half an acre in size. We had no lawn. The entire yard, front and back, was planted with alfalfa. In the backyard we had a potato pit that was entered by a stairway. It had sloping roofs on each side, with sod on top. The inside where the potatoes and other vegetables were stored was cool even in the summertime. I had quite a number of rabbits, as many as a dozen, which lived in pens made of chicken wire. I remember pulling the alfalfa and then putting it on the sloping sod roof of the potato cellar to dry. I then put it in sacks so it would keep, and we could feed it to the rabbits. Then, when I was about seven years old, we moved from the house on East Center Street into a new house on West First North.

Mother and Dad had lived part of their married life in Centerville, a smaller town located about two miles north of Bountiful. Their homes, before they were married, were located within about two hundred yards of each other. My Grandfather Rampton ran a blacksmith shop on the corner of First North and Main Street, and his home was about fifty yards east of the shop. The blacksmith shop is now gone but the home is still there, as well as the old granary behind the home where my father was born. My Grandfather and Grandmother Campbell lived on the corner of Second East and Center Street. Mother and Dad began courting when she was about seventeen or eighteen. Dad was some six years older than Mother. He had finished a year at LDS College after graduation from high school, and then went to Canada to work in some mines that were being developed by his brother-in-law, Ernest Woolley. He came back from the mines periodically, and it was during those times that he and Mother courted and finally were married.

I think Mother was always disappointed that her first child was not a girl. Even though I was a boy, she was going to name me Hollis. Plans were made to give me that name. We went over to the church, and when it was time to bless the children, Dad got up to take me to the front of the chapel. About the only time Dad went to church was when he had a child to christen. My mother's sister Florence and her husband Harold Roberts had come over for the occasion and were sitting near us in the chapel. As Dad passed by him, Uncle Harold said, "You can't call that boy Hollis." Dad said, "Then what shall we call him?" The story goes on to say that Uncle Harold had a hymnbook open on his lap, turned to the page of a hymn written by John Calvin, and he said, "Call him Calvin." I can't vouch for the truth of that story, but I can vouch for the results.

I remember all four of my grandparents quite well. My Grandfather Henry Rampton had been a blacksmith all his life, as had his father before him. Grandfather was a big man—I would say six foot one or two—and probably weighed two hundred and thirty pounds. He had no fat on him: he was all muscle as a result of working daily in the smithy. From the time I knew him Grandfather was hard of hearing; you really had to shout at him. He was a mild-mannered, pleasant sort of man, and I always used to like to visit the blacksmith shop where I'd turn the bellows and watch him work. Sometimes he shoed horses and sometimes he made iron implements of various kinds for the people in Centerville.

Grandmother Luna Smith Rampton was a very handsome woman. She wasn't tall, but she was stately in her appearance and not as easy to approach as Grandfather, although she was certainly not an unloving grandmother. She had a stroke when she was around sixty, and that's how, unfortunately, I remember her most. She just declined and died three years later.

After Grandmother Rampton died, my grandfather continued to live in their home and to run the blacksmith shop until near the time of his death. One of my most vivid memories of this period concerns one night when we received a telephone call telling us that Grandfather Rampton's house was on fire. Dad and I jumped in his automobile and drove frantically to Centerville. When we got there the house was enveloped in flames. The volunteer fire department was not motor driven; it was a handcart company. The flames were well beyond its capacity by the time it arrived. When we got there, we couldn't find Grandfather, and Dad just assumed that he was in the house. Of course, he could very well have been, because he was hard of hearing and might have been trapped in there. I remember Dad's frantic effort to get into the house to find his father—efforts that were unsuccessful because the fire was too hot. It had pretty well subsided, not through the efforts of the fire department, but because it had consumed what was consumable, when the streetcar from Salt Lake came along and Grandfather got off. He was shocked to see what had happened to his house, but all the rest of us who'd believed that he might have been burned in there were greatly relieved. He did have the house rebuilt, and he lived in it until he died.

My Campbell grandparents were a little younger than my Rampton grandparents. Grandfather Alexander Campbell was a shorter and stockier man than Grandfather Rampton, but equally as strong. He worked as a section hand on the railroad right up until he reached about sixty-five years of age. He was a difficult man to know, not as warm and friendly as Grandfather Rampton, although in later years, after he was widowed and came to live with us, we became much closer. Grandmother Betsy Ellen Schofield Campbell became ill when she was around fifty years old, with an ailment that at that time was called creeping paralysis. Remembering the symptoms as the disease progressed, I think it was either muscular dystrophy or multiple sclerosis. She lost her power of movement, but it never affected her mind. For the last two or three years of her life she was confined either to a wheelchair or to bed. She was a sweet and affectionate person, and I and all the rest of the grandchildren loved her very much. Both of my grandfathers lived to their midseventies and died within a short while of each other; Grandmother Campbell lived to fifty-nine years of age; and Grandmother Rampton lived to sixty-three.

Of my four great-grandfathers, all of them except Great-grandfather Campbell were polygamists. The three served time together for unlawful cohabitation in the Utah territorial prison, although I have no way of knowing whether they knew each other. My Great-grandfather Campbell and his children lived in Beaver, where my grandfather met grandmother and they were married. Grandfather was working on the railroad even at that time. He would commute from Beaver to Milford on weekends. They continued living in Beaver until Mother was about twelve or thirteen, when they moved to Centerville. Mother was the second of four daughters: Aunt Laura was two years older, Aunt Floss two years younger, and Aunt Nell four years younger.

My father grew up in a family that was not active in church affairs. I was told that sometime in the 1890s an event had occurred that dampened their enthusiasm for the church. My Grandfather Rampton, in spite of his congenial exterior and friendly manners, was somewhat of a freethinker and objected violently to being told what to think. He made some public utterances that were critical of some of the church doctrines—not necessarily of the leaders, but of the doctrines themselves. He was charged in a church court and threatened with excommunication. Largely because of the intervention of Brigham H. Roberts, his close friend and brother-in-law, he was not excommunicated but was "disfellowshipped." I think you're permitted to apply for readmission after being disfellowshipped. But being disfellowshipped didn't particularly seem to bother Grandfather, who never made application for reinstatement. So Dad grew up in a family where the Mormon religion was not practiced, although there was no hostility toward it. Dad was, as I learned from looking at the records, ordained into the priesthood of the church and held the three ranks in the Aaronic Priesthood: deacon, teacher, and priest, but he didn't go beyond the Aaronic Priesthood. Although Dad was never a religious man, he was a man of high moral standards.

I, however, was very active in LDS church activities. A great deal of our social life at that time was built around the Bountiful First Ward chapel. It still stands, and I had some hand in preventing its demolition in the 1970s. I explored every inch of that old building when I was a boy, even climbing into the attic above the hall where the joists and rafters were of unhewed timber. That building predates the Salt Lake Temple and the Tabernacle. At the time demolition was threatened, it was, next to the Assembly Hall on Temple Square, the oldest Mormon structure in continuous use in the state of Utah.

The relationship of our immediate family with the families of my aunts and uncles was always close and cordial. It was much more so, however, with Mother's family than with Dad's family. With Mother's family we were almost like an extended family, certainly before Grandfather and Grandmother Campbell died and even so right down to the time when I became an adult and married.

Mother's oldest sister, Aunt Laura, was married to a man named Robert Lynn. They had two daughters, both of whom are still living: Helen, who is five years older than I, and Ruby, who is three years older. I remember Uncle Bob well because he died two years after my father. I was nineteen at the time, but even when I was young, he was sort of a mystery man. He never talked about his past. About all we knew was that he was a cook who spoke with a very decided southern accent. When I was a child he was cooking in a restaurant in Bingham. One day, either a snowslide or a landslide, I don't remember which, came down a Bingham Canyon tributary named Highland Boy. For a period of some twenty-four hours nobody knew who had survived in that slide and who had not. But Uncle Bob was one of those who did survive. Long after he died, I learned that when he came to Utah as a young man, he came as a fugitive. He had been following the mining camps in Colorado, got into a fight with a man, and believed he had killed him. He came to Utah and changed his name to Robert Lynn. I don't recall what his true name was, although

I've heard it. Later, he found that the man whom he believed he'd killed had not actually died, although Uncle Bob really was a fugitive because there were charges out on him for felonious assault. At any rate, he chose to live under his new name, and I don't know when my cousins or Aunt Laura found out that Lynn wasn't his true name or why he'd really come to Utah.

Mother's second sister, Florence, or Aunt Floss as we always called her, married Harold Roberts, a son of Brigham H. Roberts. Actually, although Brigham H. Roberts's first wife was a sister to my grandmother, Uncle Harold was a child of the second wife. So he and my father were not actually cousins, although they grew up in the same town and knew each other well. Aunt Floss and Uncle Harold had seven children: five boys and two girls. Mother's youngest sister, Aunt Nell, married Jefferson M. Haley. Uncle Jeff became a surrogate father to me after my own father died in 1931. They had no children.

The holidays generally would see the whole extended family together. On Christmas, after we had our own celebration at home, we would all go over to Aunt Floss and Uncle Harold's place, where my Grandfather and Grandmother Campbell had formerly lived. We would have a Christmas breakfast there, and later in the day would have our Christmas dinner either at our house or Aunt Nell's.

We also went to Aunt Floss's on Thanksgiving. In my early teens Uncle Harold's father, Brigham H. Roberts, would come out to see us during the late afternoon of the Thanksgiving celebration. I can remember him riding the streetcar. He got off down at Ben Brown's store, which was two blocks west of the house, and walked east on Center Street, using a cane. He was by that time a very old man, but still handsome, with an erect bearing, a great shock of white hair, and a commanding presence. People would come out from their homes as he walked by to greet him. He was really a source of great community pride for Centerville, although people disapproved of the fact that he was a polygamist. I don't know whether I remember him best because of his personality, appearance, and bearing; because of his reputation as a great church leader; or because I was impressed that there I was seeing an honest-to-goodness polygamist.

Our relationship with the Rampton side, Dad's brothers and sisters, was not as close as it was with the Campbell side; however, I don't want to leave the impression that we were at all estranged. I got along very well, with few exceptions, with my cousins on Dad's side of the family. Uncle Jim was Dad's oldest brother, and he married Eugenia Hardy, a granddaughter of Brigham Young. They had six sons. He and Dad were in business together from the time I was born until Dad died. Uncle Jim was to me in my early years a forbidding and austere sort of man. I learned later to like him very much, although I was rather afraid of him while I was growing up. I don't know whether he changed or whether I did. At any rate, after Dad died and Uncle Jim and I were in business together for two years, we got along well. Later, when he got to be an old man, I came to care for him very much.

Aunt Gene lived into her early nineties. When I was governor, she used to want me to come out and talk to her about state affairs, which I did on occasion. Although Dad and Uncle Jim were in business together for a long while, there was always a sort of rivalry between Mother and Aunt Gene. While the families were congenial, they were not close.

Dad's sister Aunt Emmalyn had married Ernest R. Woolley, and they had two daughters, Helen and Emmalyn. Depending on how you want to describe him, Uncle Ernest was a financier, a promoter, or a con man. He was a millionaire, intermittently, and in between those periods was in financial hot water and at least once in jail. I didn't see him many times because Aunt Emmalyn had died in childbirth before I was born; but Uncle Ernest would turn up occasionally at Rampton family affairs. He was a big man, rather florid, and on a number of occasions that I saw him he had on a formal morning coat. He was a man of great charm, as one might expect. When I got into law school twenty years later, I was amazed and amused to find that in our contracts case books were several cases that were cited in which Uncle Ernest had been a party, usually a defendant. These cases were selected to show the narrow line between the legal and illegal in contracts and in business.

Dad's youngest sister, Irene, married Jess Porter, who was part owner and an officer of Porter-Walton Nursery. Uncle Jess and Aunt Irene lived in a beautiful house on Butler Avenue in Salt Lake near the University of Utah. They had one son, Robert, who was two or three years older than I.

Another family with whom we were close, both because of family relationship and because we were neighbors, was the Charles R. Mabey family. The Mabeys lived next door to Aunt Nell on the west. I used to wander in and out of their house as a child, almost as freely as I did in my own. They had four boys: Rendell, Charles, Bob, and Edward. During the time I was growing up, both Charles and Bob were my close friends. Mrs. Mabey, Aunt Afton, was my dad's cousin; and of course, Uncle Charley Mabey became the fifth governor of Utah. When I was a child, he was president of the Bountiful State Bank. I remember him as a pleasant, almost jolly man. Of course, I didn't know anything about his prominence in Utah politics, nor did I know anything about Utah politics at that age. I knew, however, that he had been a rather celebrated war hero during the Philippine expedition.

I have a vivid recollection of a day that fell within a day or two of my seventh birthday. That morning I noticed there was a great deal of activity down at the Mabey house. There were many cars out in front and many people were there. I went through the back lot to the Mabey house and into the back door without knocking, as always, and I found Bob in the kitchen and asked him to come out and play. He said he couldn't, that he wanted to see all the people. I asked him why so many people were there, and he said, "My father has just been elected governor." I asked, "What's a governor?" And Bob said, "He's the boss of the whole state." That was a statement I would later find was a great exaggeration.

The Mabeys continued to live in their house in Bountiful for about two years after Uncle Charley was elected, and then they moved into a house they had built at 1390 Yale Avenue in Salt Lake. Uncle Charley lost his bid for a second term, and so they lived in that house while he was governor for only about two years; but they lived in it for a long while afterwards. Aunt Afton died there around 1940.

I visited with the Mabeys almost every summer for several years at their home in Salt Lake. I'd generally go down and stay for a week, and at least one of those occasions was while Uncle Charles was still governor, because I recall they did a certain amount of entertaining at the house. One of their guests was the singer Ernestine Schumann-Heink, whom I remember well. I didn't hear her sing, but I was impressed by two things: her considerable bulk and her German accent.

I don't know exactly why Uncle Charles didn't get along well in the governorship. People that knew him say he became arrogant and haughty, but I never saw that side of him. He was challenged for a second term by a man of his own party named William H. Wattis, and he just narrowly defeated Wattis in the convention. That split the Republican party, and George Dern was able to win the governorship in 1924. I was about eleven years old then, and I remember the election very well. Although I even then considered myself a Democrat, largely through the influence of my Grandfather Campbell, I was a partisan of Uncle Charles. I was interested in the Democratic slogan that year: "We want a Dern good governor, and we don't mean Mabey." It was probably as catchy a slogan as there has ever been in a political campaign. I felt bad when Uncle Charles lost.

Aunt Afton made a splendid governor's wife. She was a charming woman. She and her two sisters, at least the two that I knew best—Aunts Alice and Elaine—were all very handsome women. After Uncle Charley lost he went into the finance business in Salt Lake and continued in that business up until his death. Sometime after Aunt Afton died, he sold the house in Salt Lake and built a house in Bountiful, on Orchard Drive.

Immediately west of the Mabeys lived the Holbrook family. Mark Holbrook was a furniture merchant in Bountiful and his wife, Aunt Sarah, was a much younger half-sister of my Grandfather Rampton. So although she was his half-sister, she was my father's contemporary, maybe two or three years older. The Holbrooks had four sons and two daughters. The sons I was closest to growing up were Dell and Mark. Mark was drowned on a Boy Scout outing at Mirror Lake when he was seventeen or eighteen. Dell still lives in Bountiful. He's the father of Steve Holbrook, who has been a member of the Utah legislature.

At the time I was growing up in Bountiful, it was a small town. Its population probably had not reached the fifteen hundred mark by the time I celebrated my tenth year. I knew almost everybody in town, as well as most of the people in West Bountiful, South Bountiful, and Centerville. It seems to me that the winters were longer and more snowy then than they are now. It may just have been that no effort was made to remove the snow from the roads because there weren't many automobiles. There were some, of course, as my dad went into the automobile business while I was still a child, but the majority of people still moved about in horse-drawn buggies and wagons. Each year, about November, the farmers would take the wheels off their wagons and put runners on them, and they became what we knew as bobsleds. The bobsled was not just for riding in during a party. It was very much a working vehicle. It's what farmers used in their fields, what they used to get around town, and sometimes it was what they used to take their produce to market in Salt Lake. There was snow on the ground from November to March, and it was possible to use those bobsleds all during that period.

One of our favorite sports as boys was ice skating. We had no skating rink in Bountiful, but the marshes on the east side of the Great Salt Lake, before the waters that feed them mix with the waters of the lake, are fairly fresh, and they freeze into thick ice. There would be a strip of ice as much as a hundred yards wide, running clear from Bountiful up to Farmington. It made a beautiful place to skate.

Another favorite sport was sleigh riding on small hand sleighs. There were three principal hills in Bountiful: Tuttle's Hill, which is now Fourth North; Stringham's Hill, which is now Center Street; and Moss's Hill, which is now Fifth South. Tuttle's Hill was the steepest of the three, but Moss's Hill was the longest, about two and one-half miles from the top down to Main Street, where we generally terminated a run when the snow was deep. When the surface was good on Moss's or Tuttle's hills, we used to get speeds on those small sleds of up to forty or forty-five miles an hour, which seems very fast when you're lying on your stomach on a sleigh and the snow is three or four inches below your nose. Surprisingly, there were not many accidents, although once or twice each year somebody would get hurt. I remember a couple of occasions when someone ran into an automobile, but generally the automobiles weren't numerous. It was well known that kids went sleigh riding on those hills, so automobile drivers were cautious to make sure that they got up and down while the kids were not there.

Mother dressed me in the most awful clothes when I was a child. I used to wear patent leather shoes, with little white socks halfway up my knees, and a sort of pink or yellow pongee shirt with ruffles up the front. And although I didn't like it at all, that's the way Mother dressed me for the first day at the Stoker School. A lot of the kids from my immediate neighborhood had seen me before, and my clothes didn't bother them very much. However, some of the kids from over across town who didn't know me very well got on to me right away. I got in a fight, got bloodied up, and went home. Dad was home when

I got there and wanted to know what was the matter, so I told him. He understood right away. He took me over to the J. C. Penney store on First South and Main and told Mr. Hess, the manager, what the problem was. I got fitted out with a blue work shirt, some jeans, and some shoes with hobnails. I felt pretty good about that. Mother felt terrible, however, and it took the combined efforts of Dad and myself to get her consent to my going to school looking like that. But it stopped the problems I'd had with the tougher kids at school.

The Stoker School, which I attended for five years, was located in the block east of Main Street, between Second and Third South. It was in the block adjoining the big white church. The principal of the school while I was there and for many years before and afterwards was David R. Tolman, whom the kids called Dubby. Just why they called him that I don't know. He was a very strict disciplinarian. He was also the first counselor in the bishopric of the First Ward during most of that time, and so had a dual responsibility.

Out in front of the church was a large lawn, and a natural route for kids who lived north and west of the school was to go diagonally across that lawn on their way to and from school. Of course, it wasn't long before the wear of many feet was beginning to show. It became a cardinal rule at the school that we could not walk across the meetinghouse lawn. Generally the fear of the wrath of Dubby was enough to keep us from doing it, but sometimes when we were late and figured he'd be tied up somewhere else, the temptation to go across the lawn just couldn't be resisted. On several occasions I was subject to discipline when I found that either Mr. Tolman had been watching, or somebody had reported me. When I say discipline, I don't mean a lecture, either. Mr. Tolman believed in corporal punishment. I was swatted many times over the knuckles with a yardstick and across the buttocks with a strap that he kept for that purpose.

As far back as I can remember, up until the early 1930s, a streetcar connected Bountiful with Salt Lake and with the Salt Lake street rail system. The tracks followed what is now Orchard Drive north from White's Hill between Bountiful and Salt Lake to Fourth East until it came to First South in Bountiful, where it turned west to Main Street and then followed Main Street north to Chase's Lane in north Centerville. It took about forty-five minutes to get from Centerville to Salt Lake. The fare was only ten cents. The streetcar at that time was well patronized because there weren't many automobiles, and a drive of ten miles from Bountiful to Salt Lake in a horse-drawn vehicle took a considerable amount of time.

The streetcar was always the victim of pranksters. Some of the pranks, as I look back, were not very funny. Among other things that were done—and I'll have to admit to participating from time to time—was the soaping or greasing of the rails at the foot of First South where the streetcar came down a slight incline by the Stoker School and made a ninety-degree right turn to go north on Main Street. Generally the motormen were on the lookout for trouble, and they would approach that turn very gingerly. One evening when the rails had been soaped or greased and the motorman apparently was in a hurry, the car did get out of control and derailed and tipped over, injuring some people. I don't remember if anybody after that engaged in soaping the rail. I really believe that we didn't realize the danger inherent in what we were doing.

Another prank that in retrospect doesn't seem appropriately boyish was to take hold of the rope that held the trolley arm, pull it down as far as you could, then cut the rope. The trolley arm would spring straight in the air, and in order to get it back on the overhead wire, the motorman would have to get up on top of the car and pull it down.

Of course we devised pranks that didn't have the same degree of malice, although I'm sure the victims didn't appreciate them. A substantial number of the homes at that time had outdoor toilets, and a favorite prank was to wait until somebody went in there, then run out, nail the door shut, and tip it over with the person inside. This was always something that we talked about for days.

In the fall of 1925 I entered seventh grade at Bountiful Junior High School, later known as South Davis Junior High School. I didn't go to the sixth grade. There were two of us in my class, Keith Stahle and myself, who were moved from the fifth grade into the seventh grade. Whether that was a good move, I don't know. It upset my social life, and my social ties remained closer all through high school with the kids I had gone through grade school with. But the three years I spent there were enjoyable years. I remember some of my teachers with great affection, especially J. A. Taylor, who was the principal of the school and taught classes. I took some English literature classes from him. He was a very fine man and a good teacher. He always took an interest in me because he was a close friend of Mother and Dad.

Another teacher I remember at that time was Blaine Winters. Blaine was not more than twenty-six or twenty-seven years old when he was teaching there. I've been friendly with Blaine ever since. About the time I became an assistant attorney general in 1940, Blaine left teaching and became a school administrator, working with the office of the state superintendent of public instruction. In 1964, when I was elected governor, Blaine was assistant state superintendent, and my association with him was close.

The years I spent in junior high school were good years for our family. After having some difficult times in their business, Dad and Uncle Jim were finally doing well, and we were among the more affluent families in town. Uncle Jim and Dad at that time each drew one hundred and fifty dollars a month from the Rampton Automobile Company. Later, in 1929, it was increased to two hundred dollars a month. They were both blacksmiths when I was born, but about 1917 or 1918 they took a Studebaker dealership for about a year, and then became Ford dealers. They worked into the Studebaker automobile dealership because they had handled Studebaker wagons in connection with their blacksmith shop. When Studebaker began to produce cars, they started selling them, and about 1918 or 1919 they changed to a Ford dealership. They built a new brick garage, substantially larger than the wooden one, where the blacksmith shop had stood. That brick building still stands.

They did have some trouble in 1922, however – some bad financial trouble. The Ford Motor Company made a tractor called the Fordson which they apparently had trouble selling. The Ford Company assigned to each of its dealers a quota of Fordsons, which they had to take if they were to continue as dealers. Dad and Uncle Jim were assigned as many as a dozen, and they had a difficult time selling them. They had borrowed money to purchase the tractors, and they carried them through a year or more before they were all sold. It meant a tight cash situation for awhile, so when a Chevrolet dealership for the Davis County area became available in 1923, they gave up the Ford franchise and began selling Chevrolets.

Our house had been built in 1918 and 1919, and this trouble they had in 1922 caused further problems because Mother and Dad had taken out a mortgage. The house had cost $10,000, which was a great deal to spend for a house at the time. It was a big house, about 2,500 square feet, and fine brick construction. They had about $2,000 saved up, and they took an $8,000 mortgage. It was very difficult to keep up the payments on that mortgage when their business went bad. They were unable to complete the house, and we didn't have a bathtub in the bathroom for some time. We had all the plumbing for the bathtub, including the water faucets, but not the bathtub itself, and we used to bathe in a big round galvanized washtub. It must have been for two years that we bathed in that tub. It was fine, overall, because we had the hot water running into it. The problem was in emptying it, which we did with a pan. Also at that time, when the house was first built, we had not finished the basement and were without central heat. We had a heater in the dining room which heated both that room and the living room. The kitchen was heated from the coal stove on which Mother did the cooking. It was not until 1924 that we got the house completely finished, with the plumbing fixtures and the bathtub in, and the basement finished with a new gas furnace.

The Chevrolet dealership proved to be much more profitable than the Ford dealership had been. Dad was the principal and, for a time, the only salesman the company had. Uncle Jim ran the business, the shop, the front end, and kept the books. He had one secretary, a woman named Ida Sessions, later Ida Given. Dad spent most of his time selling. A typical day for Dad would be to arrive at the garage about eight o'clock in the morning and go over the cars he was going to sell—either the new cars that had been brought in and needed conditioning, or used cars that we had taken in that needed reconditioning. Dad would work in the shop washing, cleaning, and doing minor repair work until about noon. Then he began his selling activity. He sold all over Davis County which at that time was the range of their franchise. Often he wouldn't be home for dinner because the afternoon and the early evening time was when the men were home from work, and he could talk the sale of automobiles to them. He was a hard-working salesman, and a good one. In 1929 he received a prize for selling the most Chevrolets of any salesman in the state of Utah: 132 new automobiles and about 250 used ones. He averaged right around an automobile a day that year.

About the time I entered junior high school, I and the other young boys with whom I played in the neighborhood began to work at various jobs. For several years I worked in the fields for farmers. Most every year I would work for Elmer Barlow, who owned a fairly large farm, perhaps a mile from where we lived. I also worked for John Bangerter, who had a farm down in that area.

During my fourteenth and fifteenth years, I worked in the can room at the Woods Cross Canning Company. The second year I was superintendent of the can room. I liked that job because I got more money than before. During the first year that I was there, I got twelve cents an hour; the second year, when I was foreman of the can room, I got twenty cents an hour.

We kept a supply of salt in the can room. We were isolated from the downstairs area, and every once in awhile somebody on the filling machine would say, "Send me down some salt in a can," or "Send me down yesterday's funny paper in a can." And so we used the cans that were going down the chute as transits for things that we had up in the can room that people wanted downstairs. The problem was that sometimes one of the cans wouldn't be observed coming down. I have often thought of somebody opening a can of fine Woods Cross tomatoes, only to find that it was two-thirds salt or held a *Salt Lake Tribune* comic strip.

Later I began to work in Dad's garage after school and on Saturdays and full time in the summer. At first my job was to sweep out the place, which I must have done a thousand times. We sprinkled sawdust on the floor to take up the excess oil that had spilled from cars being repaired. When I first began, it seemed the back door had about a five-foot drop to the ground. By the time I had finished sweeping three or four years later, there was no drop at all.

Gradually I worked into doing minor repair work. We had several good mechanics whom I remember well, such as Wright Fernley, who had the reputation of being the finest mechanic in Bountiful. And I learned to be a fairly good mechanic myself. Cars, of course, were simpler at that time. When I look under the hood of an automobile now, I'm appalled; I would hate to overhaul modern cars, with their complicated motors.

The task that I liked best when I was working at the garage at fifteen or sixteen years of age was going into Salt Lake City for parts or to have a part worked on. At that time you didn't need a driver's license, and although you were not supposed to drive until you were fifteen or sixteen, there was no statute that set a minimum age. I learned to drive an automobile when I was thirteen years old, and by the time I was fourteen, I was driving into Salt Lake City. It took thirty to forty minutes then, a little longer than now, to drive from Bountiful to Salt Lake. I liked to take a radiator or a starting motor or a flywheel on an emergency basis into town to have it worked on because that meant I had to wait in Salt Lake until it was finished. It generally took two or three hours to repair, so I parked my car on Motor Avenue, which was the location of Western Auto Radiator and various other repair shops. I then walked down State Street to where there were three theaters: the Gem, the Empire, and the Isis. I suppose I averaged two movies a week in the summertime while I was waiting for parts to be fixed. As I recall, the admission charge was fifteen cents at the Gem and ten cents at the Empire and the Isis.

I was driving fairly regularly by the time I was in the ninth grade, and that was the first time that Dad let me take a car out in the nighttime. Neither we nor Uncle Jim owned an automobile. We always had fifteen or twenty cars in our used car lot, which was adjacent to the garage, and each family would use two or three of them as they saw fit. If you used a car, you were expected to restore it to the same condition that it was in before when you took it back because those cars were there for sale. And if you did something to the car that made it unsalable, it was your responsibility to fix it.

When I got to junior high school I had a new group of friends, partly because I'd been advanced one year, and the people who were now my classmates were those who had been a year ahead of me all through the lower grades. I knew most of them, however. Also, the kids from the South Bountiful School and the West Bountiful School took their seventh and eighth grades at Bountiful Junior High School. The kids from Centerville School had eight grades in the old yellow schoolhouse, and then came to Bountiful for the ninth grade. This was when my friendship with Max Rich really began, although we had known each other for years. Evelyn, Max's mother, was my father's cousin and my mother's best friend.

Max was three months older than I was. We had known each other really from the time we were in the crib together. In fact, it was said that when I started to walk, Max, who had learned to walk earlier because he was three months older, wasn't very happy with this new kid walking, and he would push me down every time he got an opportunity. Max and I would play together frequently when I visited with my grandparents in Centerville, but because it was two miles from Bountiful to Centerville, our close friendship did not develop until the ninth grade. We continued to be close until Max died in 1980 at sixty-six years of age.

By the time I got to junior high school, the social relationships among the boys had changed considerably. The old fistfights by which you established your rank in the pecking order were pretty much a thing of the past. Also, the years in junior high marked a change in my attitude toward girls. As we went through the first to the fifth grades, boys and girls had stayed entirely in separate groups. They didn't play together and were kind of disdainful of each other. To the boys, the girls were there mostly to be teased. That began to change by the time I got to junior high school, and there was more social comradeship between the girls and the boys. I don't recall many of the girls in the seventh grade class because the girls I'd grown up with were a class behind me and still in elementary school. But by the time I got into the eighth grade and they were in the seventh, the social pattern reasserted itself, and I went around with the people my own age but a class behind me. Probably the first time I ever had a date as such—that is, where I went to a girl's home, picked her up, took her to a social function, and then took her back home—was in the ninth grade. However, during junior high school more and more school- and church-sponsored functions were attended by both boys and girls.

Although most of the boys of junior high school age worked in the fields or elsewhere during the summer, I don't want it to sound as if Bountiful were a child labor camp, because we had a great many fun times. During those early winters there was no restriction on cutting pine trees in the canyons above Bountiful, and there were few Christmas tree lots. So beginning when I was about fourteen and Byron about ten, one Saturday in early December of each year we would make an expedition into the mountains to cut Christmas trees. Generally, I would try to bring two down, and Byron would bring one. The best of the trees we'd keep for our own use, and we'd sell the other two for fifty cents apiece, which was considerably cheaper than the average price of a Christmas tree at the time.

A favorite place of the kids in our neighborhood when I was between twelve and fifteen years of age was called Durham's Hollow, which was about three blocks from my home. This was a canyon or gully in which there was a rather heavy growth of trees, and through which a stream ran the year round. It was the stream flowing from what we called Ward Canyon. We would camp out there, and we would have Boy Scout outings there. Occasionally, we'd catch a fish in the stream, although that wasn't often. We used to play Tarzan and swing through the trees.

We got a great idea one day when I was about thirteen. There was a tree that forked about a foot above the ground, so that it looked for all the world like a huge flipper handle. We decided that we would make a flipper out of it. We got an inner tube, cut it, and secured it carefully with wire, one end to each of the branches. We really had a major catapult, and we had two mishaps with it. The smallest boy in our group was Alton Call; Tiny Call was his nickname. We wanted to see if this catapult would work, and so we decided to catapult Alton. We really didn't pull it back very far, but we were quite unprepared for what happened: it actually threw him about twenty feet and broke his arm. But it was obvious it would work. So the next thing we did was to get a rock—I suppose it might have weighed ten or twelve pounds. We pulled it back and let go. It took off and must have gone two hundred yards before crashing through the roof of Jim Smedley's barn.

On my twelfth birthday I had taken my test to be a Tenderfoot Scout. For the next three years I was very active in scouting. We had a scoutmaster named Carter Lee who was a wonderful man, the kind of man who could make boys love him. I advanced up through the ranks and became a First Class Scout. I was thirteen when I started enthusiastically working on my merit badges. I got about forty of them, but I never became an Eagle Scout because of the requirement that you had to have a lifesaving merit badge. At that time we had no place to swim, and so I was unable to practice for my lifesaving merit badge. I stayed active in the scouts until I was about fifteen, when interest in girls replaced interest in the scouts.

It was during the closing time of my interest in the scouts that something happened which gave me a considerable interest in public speaking. There was a Boy Scout public speaking contest sponsored by the Great Salt Lake Council. I entered it, as did several other boys from Troop 107 in Bountiful. I won the contest in Troop 107, and then we had an interstake contest. Max had won the contest in his troop in Centerville, and we were competing in a group of about ten who had to give five-minute orations. The judges decided that Max and I were tied, and although this wasn't supposed to happen, we both went to the regional finals in Salt Lake City. He got into the semifinals, and I got into the finals. I lost the finals to a fellow named Charles Romney, who was a boy a couple of years older than I was. He was a younger brother of George Romney, who later became the governor of Michigan.

When I began at Davis High School I rode the Bamberger Electric Railroad, which ran between Salt Lake and Ogden, to Kaysville. As a matter of fact, it was a link in a chain of three roads that ran all the way from Provo to Logan, but the one through Davis County was called the Bamberger. The students from the south end of the county rode the Bamberger to Davis High School. The railroad ran along Second West in Bountiful, and I had only to walk two blocks west and two blocks north to where it stopped to take on passengers, in order to catch the train. It was a special school train. We did not, except in cases of emergency, ride the regular commuter trains. It would generally have four or five cars, and between the three grades probably hauled around two hundred to two hundred and fifty students from Woods Cross, West Bountiful, Bountiful, Centerville, and Farmington. The train would stop right in front of the high school and let the students out. Then, in the evening, this train would pull up again, and we would load on and reverse the process.

The ride on the railroad (nicknamed "The Dummy") from Bountiful to Kaysville took thirty to thirty-five minutes. And, as you might appreciate, two hundred to two hundred fifty young people, varying in age from fourteen to seventeen, having thirty-five minutes on their hands, just did not sit and watch the scenery go by. A favorite trick was to pull the emergency cord while the train was moving. Usually we had sense enough not to pull it while the train was moving at full speed because it brought the train to a sudden halt and threw the students around, and that was looked on with great disfavor by those students. However, it was acceptable, if not approved, conduct among students to pull the cord when we were at a speed of ten to fifteen miles an hour; that would stop the train and jostle people about, but not badly. One day I decided I was going to pull the cord as we were leaving the Centerville station. I waited until I thought I wasn't being observed and pulled the cord, and sure enough the train stopped. I got a book out, and I started studying, feigning innocence. The conductor came right up to me and grabbed me, and said, "Don't you ever do that again." I said, "What made you think I did it?" He said,

"Look." And I looked above my head, and this cord, which had quite a lot of slack in it, had a dip pointing at me like an accusing finger.

The cars that made up the school train were old and decrepit. The seats were wooden, and on more than one cold day seats were broken up to make a fire inside the train to warm up the students. That, of course, wasn't approved by the Bamberger Railroad Company either. In fact, Julian Bamberger, who was the president of the company, and Hugh Balser, the secretary, would periodically take rides on the train themselves to observe what was going on. When they were on the train, I think there was more vandalism that at any other time because the students would just try to get away with it.

I came in later years to know both Julian and Hugh very well. In fact I saw Hugh just recently, an old, old man now. Julian's been dead a number of years. I used to reminisce with them, and even in their later years, they would get red in the face when they talked about the high school train and what was done. One of the times that Julian got most angry was during my junior or senior year. We had been told that if we tied a wire to the rail and threw it over the trolley, it would make a big flash of light, and so we decided one night that we were going to try this. We had an old Ford coil, and we took the heavier wire out of it. We had maybe fifty yards of wire, and we tied this to the railroad track and threw it over the trolley, and it made a fine big spark. Then somebody conceived the idea of throwing it over the high-tension line which paralleled the track and fed the boosters that were at various points along the track. We did that and there was a spectacular show of fireworks. The problem was that it knocked out all of the booster stations between Salt Lake and Ogden, and the Bamberger was nonoperational for a few hours.

Many years later, when I was a lawyer for the Public Service Commission, I cross-examined Julian on the witness stand when he had a matter involving his bus line. I had been roughing him up just a little bit, although we were good friends, but he was kind of irked at me. I said, "Julian, do you remember when some kids threw a wire over your high-tension line and blew out the booster stations?" He blew up, "Oh, I do. I do." I said, "Well, I did it." And he said, "You s.o.b., you've been giving me trouble for the last thirty years."

But all wasn't fun and games at Davis High School. We were expected to do our lessons, and indeed we did. I was a good student, and I also engaged in school activities. I had some fine teachers. The one that probably made the greatest impact on my life was Frank B. Muir, who taught civics, was the debate coach, and was also the principal advisor of the Boys' Association. Frank was an avid Democrat. In fact, for a long time he was chairman of the Democratic party in Davis County. Although my maternal grandfather already had me pretty well steered toward being a Democrat long before I got to high school, if there was any doubt about it, Frank Muir put the finishing touches on it. I regarded him not only as a teacher but also as a good friend.

When I was a sophomore, Frank, while coaching debate said, "Now look, you're doing fine on your material, but your delivery is not good at all. You're not very impressive. You don't look at your audience. Now, I want you to look at me while you make this debate talk." Well, I'd look at him at the start, and then I'd look away. Finally, he said, "I'll tell you what I'm going to do. I'm going to take some pieces of chalk back here, and every time you look away from me, I'm going to flip one of these right between your eyes." It didn't take long until he had my attention. I continued to debate during my three years at Davis, and in my senior year I was paired with a classmate, Allan Rice from Farmington, and we won the state championship.

Another activity at Davis High School was the Martha E. Barnes Oratorical Contest. Martha E. Barnes had been a student at Davis. She had died as a student or shortly after she got through there, and her father, John Barnes, made an endowment. Each year there was to be an oratorical contest among the students at Davis, and the winner would get a prize. Each winning contestant had his or her name engraved on a cup, and in addition to that won a gold medal set with two small diamonds and a "D" in the center. It was an attractive medal. Mother had mine for a long time, and Lucybeth tells me she has it on her charm bracelet now.

By the time I got there, the contest had been conducted for ten or fifteen years, and it carried a certain amount of prestige. Also, more and more of the students wanted to compete, and so they excluded sophomores from entering. I, therefore, couldn't try out the first year. In my second year, when I was a junior, there were about fifty or sixty contestants originally, and they divided them into groups, the winners of which went into the finals. The final speeches were limited to ten minutes, and were given before a student assembly. The contest was always judged by a relative of the donor, Salt Lake attorney Claude

E. Barnes, whom I was to meet in the U.S. Supreme Court on opposite sides of a case many years later. Max was among the finalists, but I won the Barnes medal my senior year.

During my junior year at Davis, a good friend of mine was a young man named Louis Clark, who was the son of Amasa Clark, the banker in Farmington. Louis was a senior that year, and he was the business manager of the *D-Book*, the high school yearbook. He asked me to be his assistant business manager, and I accepted. Principally, I was an advertising salesman. I went the length of Davis County selling ads in the yearbook to various businesses. As I recall, a full page ran twenty-five dollars; a half page, fifteen dollars; and a quarter page, ten dollars. I had a quota to sell, something over a thousand dollars worth of ads. In my senior year I inherited the job and was business manager of the yearbook. Max was business manager of the high school newspaper called the *Davis Dart*, so we were competing for ads at that time.

Strangely, I never did get interested in campus politics. I didn't run for an office until my senior year when I was secretary of the senior class. But in the spring of our junior year, Max decided that he wanted to run for student body president, and I agreed to be his campaign manager. Max was elected. A year or so later, he returned the favor and managed my campaign when I ran for the freshman presidency at the University of Utah. I lost. I kept telling Max it was because he had a much better campaign manager than I did. He said, no, it was because I had better material to work with than he did. We never did settle that argument.

During our senior year at Davis, Max and I were big men on campus, and we knew it. I think we were insufferable. We both fancied ourselves as singers. Max and I and Jack Thornley, who didn't sing any better than Max did and not much better than I did, decided to form a male trio. We never got any engagements, but one day we decided we'd rehearse in the student body room during school hours. Jack got the idea of singing up the ventilator shaft, which had the same effect as a public address system. And so here these three raucous male voices singing "Heartaches" rang out through the entire school. It was not long before there was determined rapping on the door and Mr. Morgan, the principal, wanting to know what was going on.

I remember my high school years and particularly my senior year as a very happy time. Whether that was influenced by the background of the dark year that was to follow, I really don't know. I remember the last two or three weeks of my senior year with particular nostalgia. In my senior year I narrowly missed being valedictorian of my class. I lost to Vern Pickering, who was an excellent student and who generally seemed to place above me in most academic categories.

I was valedictorian of my seminary class. I don't know why. Maybe Vern didn't take seminary. But at any rate, I can well remember the Sunday that we had our graduation exercise from the John R. Barnes LDS Seminary. It was held in Centerville at the old Centerville church. Just before I was to begin my address, Max sent a note up to me saying, "Hurry it up," because he borrowed his father's car and had it outside, and he had dates for both of us for that afternoon. I really had no steady girl. I dated a number of girls, mostly in the class behind me, and mostly from Kaysville and Layton. By then Dad let me drive a car whenever I wanted, and I really couldn't see any point in dating a girl to whose house you could walk. Of course we had regular dances at the high school, probably a dozen a year. In addition, the Lagoon resort in Farmington had dances on Monday nights during the summer months. The unwritten rule was that you came alone without a date, and made arrangements to take a girl home afterwards. Those were much more innocent times than now. I never was aware of the use of drugs or narcotics among the high school and young college people who went to these social functions. The use of liquor was also very restricted.

I worked in Dad's garage the summer of 1931 as a full-fledged mechanic. By the time fall approached, I had experience in doing about everything that could be done on automobiles, principally the Chevrolet and the Model T Ford. I ground valves; I even rebuilt motors, regrinding cylinders and fitting new pistons. So, although I wasn't drawing the salary of a full mechanic, and shouldn't have because I wasn't able to do the work as fast as a better-trained man, I developed into an excellent mechanic.

Freshman registration at the University of Utah was held about a week before the regular registration. It was the seventeenth or eighteenth of September that I went down and registered for the fall quarter. I signed up for a full course, including speech, English, math, and other classes that I thought would lead to a legal career. I was all set to begin school on the twenty-eighth or twenty-ninth, some ten or twelve days after registration.

On Saturday night, the day after registration, I was out very late on a date. Dad and I had planned to go down on Sunday morning to put the boat in the water for the duck hunting season, which was going to begin about the first of October. Dad, Uncle Jim, Uncle Jeff, and one or two others owned a section of land west of Bountiful that was tucked into a corner of the new State Gun Club. The duck hunting at our club was always very good. We had to hunt from a boat. We'd take the boat out over the shallow water into a blind where there were rushes and from which we could shoot the ducks. Dad and I had brought the boat up a week or so earlier because it had been lying out on the bank dry since the preceding winter, and we had caulked the places where the wood had shrunk away. Because I had been out late Dad apparently decided that he wouldn't awaken me but would go down and put the boat in the water himself. When I awakened late in the morning he'd already gone. Mother told me that he would put it in himself and that he would be back for dinner, which we planned for about 3:00 P.M.

Three o'clock came and Dad didn't get home, so we went ahead and ate dinner. By the time it was five or five-thirty and he still hadn't returned, Mother and I were worried. I decided I'd better go down and see if he was having trouble with the truck on which the boat was loaded, and so I drove down near the duck club. It was nearly sunset when I got there. I could see Dad's truck over in the middle of the section, about three-fourths of a mile away, and I could also see the tracks that went out there. It was obvious that the mud was very slippery. I assumed that Dad had got stuck, although I could not from that distance see any activity around the truck.

I decided that I would not attempt to drive the passenger car which I had brought across that slippery clay surface, so I left it on the road and walked over to Dad's truck. There were no signs of life as I approached it. I began to get a feeling almost of panic. I came up on the right side of the truck; the door was open, and I could see Dad's legs sticking out. I ran over and felt him. I knew the moment that I touched him that he was dead and had been for several hours, because rigor mortis was already setting in. He was cold and stiff. He was lying down on the seat with his head under the steering wheel and his legs out the door. I tried to sit him up in the seat, but I couldn't. He was much heavier than I, and I couldn't move him at all. This is a funny thing to remember at such a time—but I remember when I touched his face that he had a growth of beard on it; I knew that Dad always shaved closely every morning, and I wondered how a person's beard could keep on growing after he died.

It was almost dark by now, and I was over the panic but still in a state of shock. I walked back to the automobile and then up that road about half a mile to the home of a man named Anson Hatch, where I called my Uncle Jim and told him what had happened. He said he would be right out. I then returned to the truck and sat with Dad's body. I don't know how long it was, probably not more than half an hour, until Uncle Jim came with another truck and two men. They had put chains on that truck and were able to drive right out to where Dad's truck was. We went up into Bountiful and drove directly to the mortuary.

Mother still didn't know what had happened, but I knew she would be frantic at my long absence and Dad's failure to return. Uncle Jim said he would go tell her, and I said no, that I wanted to tell her, and I didn't want anyone else there when I did. I went home. By now I suppose it was eight at night. I remember Mother was standing in the living room when I came in, with an anxious look on her face. She took one look at me and knew what had happened, and she started to cry. And then I got Byron—I think he was down at the Holbrooks' playing. I was seventeen at the time, Byron was fourteen, and Virginia was just six. Of course, Virginia cried—mostly, I think, because Mother was crying. She really didn't seem to comprehend what was happening.

Reconstructing what probably happened at the gun club, I believe that Dad had unloaded the boat and then moved his truck two or three hundred yards from where he unloaded it. That area down there is composed of a very flat and slippery clay. Sometimes there's water on the surface and sometimes there isn't, but it's hard to get any traction to move a car across it. I think that Dad started out with his truck and was unable to get traction, and the wheels were spinning. He evidently thought that if he left the car in gear and kept it running he could get out and push, and that what pushing he could do while the wheels were turning would enable the car to move.

I don't know if Dad ever had high blood pressure, although it was a tendency present in his family, as my Grandmother Rampton and various other ancestors had had strokes. But whether or not he had high blood pressure, the strain of pushing the truck had caused a very bad cerebral hemorrhage. It did not result in his death immediately, because he climbed back into the truck, turned off the motor, and lighted his pipe. He lay down on the seat to smoke. I think that's so because the pipe was on the floor of the car with the stem turned crosswise, which made me think that he was holding it in his mouth. Whether he was just too dazed to realize what was happening, I don't know, but obviously the cerebral hemorrhage became worse and worse, and he died not too long (the doctor said probably not more than twenty minutes) after the blood vessel burst in his head.

Dad's funeral was held in the white church in Bountiful. I don't remember all about the funeral. I remember that the speaker was a man who had been Dad's best friend when he was a boy, a man named John Adams, who had lived right next to Dad in Centerville. It was a fine funeral sermon. Mother wasn't able to go to the cemetery; she was at the funeral, but for most of her life Mother was subject to bad migraine headaches. The day of the funeral she had one of those headaches and was scarcely able to walk. After the funeral we insisted that she go back home.

A day or two following the funeral, when Mother was somewhat recovered from her migraine, she and I and Aunt Nell and Uncle Jeff had a talk about what we should do, financially, in view of the fact that Mother had never worked. Although Dad had had a $10,000 insurance policy, it was going to take $2,000 of that to pay off the balance of the mortgage on the house, and although $8,000 was a much more substantial sum then than it is now, it certainly was not enough to keep a family of four going for very long. Mother said we could get by for awhile, and she wanted me to go to school which was to begin the following Monday. I told her I didn't want to do that, that I wanted to quit school and get a job, but she wouldn't hear of it. Aunt Nell and Uncle Jeff suggested that they close their house and move in with us for a period of time in order to reduce expenses, because although Dad's business had been doing well, there was no question that the depression was hitting the community. From that time until about eight or nine months later we all lived together. We had three bedrooms, so there was a bedroom for Aunt Nell and Uncle Jeff, one for Mother and Virginia, and one for Byron and me.

During that period we economized on food. I never ate so many beans in my life. Shortly after Dad's death Mother bought a gunnysack full of Mexican brown beans, and I don't know how many meals they made—hundreds, I guess. Every other night we seemed to alternate between beans and another dish Mother used to cook, which she called four-in-one. Four-in-one was a macaroni, tomato, beef, and cheese concoction that was quite good. We did the best we could that winter to conserve and not to cut into Dad's insurance money any more than was necessary.

Mother decided that she was going to work, and she did. She took a training course as a saleswoman in cosmetics. It wasn't for Avon, but for a similar company. The training course took only about six weeks, and she immediately started out selling. Mother was soon making over one hundred dollars a month on her commissions on these cosmetics. I'm sure that the ladies in Bountiful who knew Mother probably were more free in giving her orders than they would otherwise have been, but she was quite a good saleswoman anyway. Her sales pitch consisted of giving demonstration facials. Generally, a customer would have friends in; Mother would give a series of facials to them, and then they would give orders for cosmetics.

Meanwhile, I had enrolled in the university carrying a full load. I drove into school each day with a group of people from Bountiful. The people in the riding pool would pay the gas, and my cousin Dick and I would furnish an automobile from the garage. The autumn quarter went well; my marks were quite good. I also worked evenings and Saturdays as a mechanic in the garage, where I received an hourly salary. I don't remember how much it was per hour, but I earned forty or fifty dollars a month. Then, at the beginning of the winter quarter, I got another job at the university as janitor in the M Building, for which I received twenty-five dollars a month. This only took me an hour a day. I had only one floor to clean, and I was paid by the NYA, the National Youth Administration. I'd generally start about three and by four o'clock or four-thirty I was through cleaning up. Then I'd gather together the students who were riding with me, and we'd go home. I'd work from about five till seven o'clock or seven-thirty at the garage, after which I would go home, have dinner, and study.

The automobile that we drove to school belonged to the garage, and both my cousin Dick and I used it. It was a well-known car about campus. It was a 1928 Chevrolet, and we painted the radiator red, with a big white U in the middle. It had a very, very loud Klaxon horn. I used to park it in the lot behind the Park Building, where the Student Services Building now is. Because I was the one whose schedule was most uncertain, everybody would study in the library or around the campus until I got through and was ready to go home, and then I'd go out and honk the horn. You could hear it all over the campus. That went on for about two weeks, when one day I was told by one of the student body officers that President George Thomas of the University of Utah wanted to see me in his office.

I had an idea what it was about. I went into his office in the Park Building and told his secretary I was there. She told me to go in. I walked in and stood before President Thomas's desk. He was reading, and he ignored me for a few minutes. Finally he looked up from his book and over his glasses and said, "Are you the young man with the horn?" I said, "Yes, sir." He said, "It will not be honked on this campus again." And he went on reading his book. That's all that was said about it, and it wasn't honked again.

I told that story many times in later years when I was governor and when we were having all of the troubles on the campuses, contrasting confrontation in my days with confrontation between administrators and students thirty years later.

At the end of the winter quarter I registered for the spring quarter, but I took a lighter class load–about 12 hours–because I wanted to play on the freshman tennis team if I could make it, and I still intended to keep my NYA job and my job at the garage. About two or three days into the spring quarter, I played tennis very hard. It was on March 13, and it was fairly warm. We played on the outdoor courts; they're not there anymore, but they were west of the old gymnasium. Although I was perspiring heavily, because of the press of time I didn't take a shower. I went over and cleaned up the M Building. After that was finished, I got the people who were riding with me together and we drove home. Then I went over to the garage to work on a car that I had been repairing. I began taking a violent chill and wasn't able to stay with the job, so I went home. Mother had me take a hot bath and go to bed, and by morning I felt a little bit better. I went to school, but about ten o'clock, during my second class, I began to feel terrible. My third-period class was a speech class, which was downstairs in Kingsbury Hall. I went to the class, but just wasn't able to stay. I told the teacher—I think it was LaVern Bain—that I didn't feel well, and that I'd have to be excused. He told me I didn't look well, that I'd better go somewhere and lie down. I did. I went to the Student Union Building, which is now the Music Hall immediately west of Kingsbury Hall. I lay down on a sofa for some time, but I began to feel worse and worse, and decided I'd better find somebody and let him know what was going on.

I knew that my cousin Dick would be in the library on the third floor of the Park Building at that time, so I walked out of the Union Building and up towards the Park Building. The day had turned bad. There was a cold March wind blowing. It was difficult just to put one foot in front of the other, but I finally made it up there, got to the third floor, and told Dick that I was really sick. He said, "What do you want to do?" I said, "Well, let's go out to the car, and you drive me over to Aunt Irene's place. She'll know what to do." When we got there nobody was home, but I knew where the key was kept, so I got it and opened the door. Dick had a class, and he left. We thought that Aunt Irene would be home right away. I don't know how long it was before she did get home because I lay down on the sofa in her front room, feeling as sick as I have ever felt in my life, and that's the last I remember until I regained consciousness in a room in the LDS Hospital.

The next few days are a haze to me. I understand that my temperature reached 105 degrees, and I was semidelirious most of the time. That, of course, was before the days of sulfa drugs, and about all they could do for pneumonia was to keep you warm and give you some oxygen if your breathing became too difficult. I was in the hospital for about fifteen days. My doctor was J. Edward Day, whom we had always called Uncle Ed. He was married to Alice Rampton, a cousin of Dad's, and the families had always been close. From the time that Dad died until I got out of school, Uncle Ed took care of all the medical matters for our family and never permitted us to pay him anything at all.

After I got to feeling better and was able to get up and around, I went home to Bountiful. Uncle Ed told me that I had to stay in bed for about three weeks more—through most of April. By then the spring quarter was so far gone that there was no point in trying to get back in. I decided, against Mother's wishes, that I wasn't going back to school for two or three years. I had to get my health back, and I had to get us in a financial position where I could afford to go back to school. I talked to Uncle Jim, and we decided that I would work full time at the garage as office manager and bookkeeper. I had had a high school course in bookkeeping, and I also took an extension course. General Motors had a fine double-entry bookkeeping system which it mandated that all its dealers use. Actually, I think it wasn't General Motors itself, but General Motors Acceptance Corporation, the finance company, that demanded dealers keep their books on the uniform accounting system. GMAC bought the automobile contracts from the dealers more on the basis of the dealer's guarantee than on the credit standing of the purchaser of the car, so they had to know all the time that the dealership was sound. I got help from the General Motors people, and by midsummer I was getting along pretty well and was able to handle the bookkeeping.

Then during the first part of July, another minor crisis hit us. I had to have an emergency appendectomy. Fortunately the thing was caught soon enough so that the appendix wasn't ruptured; but once again, an appendectomy was something more than it is nowadays. Now they get you up on your feet after a couple of days, but at that time I was in bed while at the hospital, and remained in bed for another two weeks at home. Finally, I was able to resume my work as bookkeeper and office manager at the Rampton Automobile Company. As the inheritors of Dad's share, we were half owners, and Uncle Jim gave me the same amount out of the company that he took out for himself. It was down somewhat from the two hundred dollars a month that he and Dad had drawn because now we were full scale into the depression years.

The fall of 1932 saw my first entry into real political activity. I always had a considerable interest in politics, first because of my Grandfather Campbell and later because of Frank Muir. I remember as a child, when we had only radio, the long Democratic convention where McAdoo and Smith deadlocked and John W. Davis was nominated; and I also remember the 1928 convention, when Al Smith was nominated by the Democrats. I never was much of an admirer of Smith, although I don't know why. But as the 1932 elections approached and Franklin Roosevelt emerged as one of the front-runners for the Democratic nomination I, like many other people in the country, was caught up by the personality of the man.

I decided I wanted to become active, even though I was not yet nineteen years old and the voting age was still twenty-one. I told

Frank Muir that I wanted to be active in the campaign, and he said, "Well, I'm the chairman of the Davis County Central Committee. I suppose to be secretary officially you'd have to be twenty-one years old, but you can be assistant secretary." So I became assistant secretary of the Davis County party. That fall the Young Democrats—we used to call them the Junior Democratic Club of Utah—decided to organize in Davis County. I recall the evening we had the first meeting, which was followed by a dance. I was elected president of the club at this meeting. That night I also met two men who were to have a great deal of influence on my life over the years. They were John Boyden and Allan Crockett, who were officials in the state organization. They had come out to organize the Davis County club. I remember John had Orpha Sweeten with him. They weren't yet married, although they eventually would be. Later, I practiced law with John for a period of time, and, of course, Allan Crockett was a justice of the Utah Supreme Court for many years and chief justice a great deal of the time I was governor.

I was caught up in the campaign, and I campaigned hard. I passed out handbills, and I made speeches for Mr. Roosevelt and for the Democratic candidate for governor, Henry Blood. Henry Blood came from Kaysville. He had been a successful businessman, a banker, and an owner of a flour mill in Kaysville. Later, he had been appointed chairman of the State Road Commission. From this position, he had secured the Democratic nomination for governor. He was the father of Evelyn Blood, who was Max Rich's steady girlfriend during this time. Over the preceding two or three years, I had spent many a Sunday afternoon and evening in the Blood parlor in Kaysville. I came to know the governor-to-be very well, and I think he liked me. He always went out of his way to talk to me about politics and explain things to me, and we got along well. The 1932 election, of course, was a Democratic sweep in Utah, and needless to say, I was elated.

I continued to be office manager at the garage through the winter of 1932-33 and all through the summer of 1933, but now I wanted to get back to school. I decided to take a six-year combination degree law course that was available. Under this program you took the first three years of regular undergraduate work, so that at the end of your first year of law school—your fourth year of college—you got your undergraduate degree, and then at the expiration of the next two years, you got your LL.B. I had saved up some money, and Mother was still selling. At some point she had changed from selling cosmetics to selling corsets for the Spirella Company, but I don't remember just when the transition was.

I talked to Uncle Jim about school, and he said, "I'll tell you what I'll do. I'm not particularly eager to go on in this business either. I think I can get appointed postmaster of Bountiful with the Democrats coming in, if I want to. I'll divide the property up into two parts and then give you your choice of which one you want to take." He did that, and we took an automobile and some items that were readily convertible to cash. We took all the accounts receivable. From the proceeds that we got out of our division of the garage, we raised about $10,000, and we still had about $6,000 left from Dad's insurance money. I therefore started back to the university in the fall of 1933, carrying a full course. I couldn't play tennis. I'd been told that the pneumonia had injured my heart, and I shouldn't play for some years. I did get a job with the NYA once again—I think this time at thirty or thirty-five dollars a month—doing various jobs. For example, I dug the concrete footings for Carlson Hall. Another one of my projects, and I did this all alone over a period of about four months, was to plant all the sumac trees on the stadium slopes. Those big sumac trees that are there now were put in as little saplings all those years ago in 1933.

We also decided at that time to use the money from Dad's insurance and from the sale of the garage to build a motel in Salt Lake. We had located a piece of land on Second West and North Temple that was well situated and up for sale. Uncle Jeff said he would take care of building it for us, and that we would be able to build it with the $16,000 we had. In fact our contract on the building was only about $11,000; the rest of it was for furnishings. We built a twelve-unit motel, which we called the Temple Tourist Court. Several years later an apartment building next door known as the Fenton Apartments became available for purchase. We bought that, too, and made the apartments over into motel rooms; we now had eighteen units and had to hire janitorial help. Mother still kept our home in Bountiful, and she drove in every day to run the motel during the daytime while Max and I lived in the office at night. We would get up in the middle of the night, if necessary, to rent a room.

Shortly before we built the motel, Byron and I leased first one service station, and later another, in Salt Lake City. The first station was on the corner of South Temple and First West. It was a Parco station, later to become Sinclair. It wasn't a very good one. It was also in a poor location because it was right next to the Claude-Anne Apartments, a rather large west-side house of prostitution. The patrons of the house continually parked their cars in our driveway. The lady who owned the house (I don't think she was the madam, but just rented it) was named Edna Brennan. She took a liking to us and helped us police the thing, but it was still difficult.

The station didn't have a great deal of volume. After we had been running it for about three months, a much better service station belonging to Texaco became available one block to the west, and we decided to lease it. The Parco people wouldn't let us out of our lease, however, and for five or six months we ran both stations, which was rather difficult because we were both in school. Byron was a senior in high school, and I was doing my second year of college.

The Texaco station was a very successful one in the summertime. It was on a well-traveled tourist route, and we would pump up to 30,000 gallons of gasoline a month. But in the wintertime that would drop down to about 5,000 gallons, and it just barely paid its way. Between the two stations we had about five or six employees.

Immediately north of our Texaco station was the Number 2 Fire Station of Salt Lake City. It was manned all the time. As I recall, there were two twenty-four-hour shifts, and there were six or eight people on each shift. Of course someone was always awake at night there. There was a rash of service station robberies at that time, and the firemen got a rifle and put it in the upstairs window. Word must have gotten around because although the service stations on all the other corners from us were robbed, after the firemen took us under their wing we never had any trouble with robbers at our station.

We ran the Texaco station for about two years. Meantime, I completed my necessary three years of undergraduate work. I'd been carrying a rather heavy load, and with the two quarters I took before I got sick, I had accumulated enough credit hours to enroll in law school in the fall of 1935. I stayed in law school during the 1935-36 school year and the autumn quarter of 1936.

I remember fondly some of my professors at the Utah law school. I had a particular affection for Dean William H. Leary who, in addition to being dean of the law school, taught a number of classes, including torts. He was a colorful teacher and a good teacher. I also remember a professor by the name of Pomeroy, who taught contracts, as well as Willis Ritter, who taught trusts. Willis was a very good teacher, and he and I got along well. I was his reader for a period of time, once again under some kind of government-student program. I would read and grade the papers from all the trust classes he taught.

Between the jobs of running the service station and building and running the motel, I was very busy, and for the first year I didn't do as well at law school as I should have done. At one point, Dean Leary called me in and told me that while my marks were above the average, I was not doing as well as I should if I were to make an effort. He said, in effect, that law school is for those who really want to try, and either I drop some of my work and concentrate on law school or I should get out. I told him that I would try to do so, but it was necessary that I have a fair income. Although Mother was still selling either face cream or corsets—I don't remember which at that time—and was also working daytime in the motel, our income wasn't particularly good. Virginia, of course, was still just a little girl of around ten years. Byron helped in the service station, but his earning capacity wasn't very great. Law school or not, I had to remain the principal wage earner in my family.

The future governor of Utah assessing the situation on the home front.

Lewellyn S. Rampton, Calvin Rampton's father on the right.
Photo taken at a mine near Cardston, Alberta, Canada.

Calvin Rampton's Stoker School classmates and teacher in 1921.
Rampton is fourth from left on front row.

Rampton's father Lewellyn S. Rampton is on the right.
He was the first president of the Utah Fish and Game Association,
which is now the Utah Sportmen's Association.

Left to right is an uncle, Jeff Haley; Haley's mother; Lucille Haley;
Calvin L. Rampton's mother, Janet Campbell Rampton; and Calvin.
The child on the right is Calvin's sister, Virginia.

*A typical Rampton family outing, about 1925. The Rampton
family with the car on the left. Calvin Rampton is leaning against the
storage box. The automobile is a circa-1922 Hupmobile.
The photograph was taken at Smith's Fork near Lyman, Wyoming.*

*The Davis High School Tennis Team, 1931(?).
Left to right, Harold Wilcox, Keith Smith, Calvin Rampton, Jack Thornley,
David Steed, and Ralph Tanner. Rampton was a senior that year.*

Photo of the Texaco station leased by Calvin Rampton while he was in law school. His younger brother, Byron, worked there as well. The station was at the northwest corner of South Temple and 300 West streets.

CHAPTER TWO

TO THE WARS: CAMPUS AND CAMPAIGNS

In the spring of 1936 something happened that made a great change for me as far as both work and school were concerned. Frank Muir, who was still the Democratic chairman of Davis County, told me that Will Robinson, the congressman from the Second Congressional District of Utah, was going to hire a new secretary. That was the top spot in the office—later to be called administrative assistant. Frank said that if I wanted to apply for the job, the Davis County organization would back me up. I sent a letter and a resumé to Mr. Robinson in Washington and received a letter back from him saying that he would be home in early June and had several applicants. He said he would like to interview me along with the others.

The date for my interview was while I was attending summer camp with the National Guard at Camp Williams, near the Point of the Mountain between Salt Lake and Provo. I went down to Provo for an interview with Mr. Robinson in my army uniform. I didn't wear the uniform to make an impression, but because that was all the clothes I had at the camp. The interview went very well, and about the first of July Mr. Robinson told me that I could have the job. The first thing I had to do was act as his campaign manager for the 1936 campaign, which was just beginning. Mr. Robinson was then running for his third two-year term. I immediately quit all my other employment because the new job with the congressman was very time consuming. I think we closed up the service station shortly before that, and now I cut down my hours at the motel.

The first thing he told me to do was to take a full month and visit every district officer in the Second Congressional District. That totaled almost a thousand people. I didn't visit them all, but I saw most of them, and that gave me an acquaintance with the basic political structure in Utah that put me in good stead after I myself became a candidate. One such acquaintance was Sunday Anderson, who lived at 122 Concord Street in the second ward. I knocked on the door, and this tall, rather severe-looking woman came to the door and asked me what I wanted. I told her, and she proceeded to give me quite a lecture because she had backed somebody else for the job with Mr. Robinson and was unhappy about my appointment. She unloaded on me, but I sat and listened. After she had talked herself out, she said, "Now, what do you want to know?" And we had another long talk. After that she was one of my most consistent political supporters, right up until her recent death.

Other people I got to know down in the second ward were Nellie Jack, Mrs. Mayne, and Walter Anderson and in the third ward, Nick Jouflas, a deputy county sheriff who was really the boss of the third ward. My friend Edna Brennan, from the Claude-Anne Apartments, was a political power in the third ward there, too. These were people who, while they seldom held elective offices themselves, were generally patronage employees and really the backbone of the party at that time.

The 1936 election was the last time that we had the convention system in Utah for the selection of party candidates. By 1938 we had gone to the double-primary system, which lasted only a few years, and then we went to the present combination convention and primary system. At any rate, Will Robinson's only opponent for the Democratic nomination in 1936 was a fellow I had known in college, even though he was several years older than I, named Warwick Lamoreaux. Although Warwick was an energetic and articulate young man, there was a feeling that this wouldn't be a particularly difficult convention, and it proved not to be. Mr. Robinson won with at least 70 percent of the votes at the convention.

But the big contest that year was for the governor's nomination. Henry Blood was running for reelection after serving one term. His opponent for the nomination was Herbert B. Maw, who had been a speech teacher and dean of men at the University of Utah, and also president of the state senate. The Democratic party in Utah at that time was quite liberal in its inclinations, as was the national Democratic party. Herbert Maw was a liberal state senator, and fairly young at that time — about forty-one. He was an excellent public speaker, an impressive looking man, and had succeeded in getting many liberal measures through the Utah legislature. On the other hand Henry Blood, although he was a fine man and a good governor, was shy and retiring. The Maw followers were determined they were going to get enough votes at the convention to dump Henry Blood. The convention that year was held in a place known as McCullough's arena, on State Street and Ninth South. It was a big arena built by a lawyer, Vern McCullough, where they held wrestling and boxing matches.

The congressional meetings had been held the night before the opening of the Democratic convention, so the congressional nomination was already behind us when the state convention was called to order. Because Will Robinson and Henry Blood were close friends, and also because of my own earlier association with the Bloods and my regard for the governor, I decided to do all I could for him by working with delegates that evening and the next day. This was a close race, and there were things done on each side that probably were improper. There were stories about some of the Blood leaders getting the more gullible delegates drunk and keeping them away from the convention. But the next day at the voting, Blood had a majority, though not a great one—probably 53 or 54 percent of the vote. The Maw people took it rather hard, and some of them didn't support Blood in the election. Once again, however, that wasn't a worry at the time because Franklin Roosevelt was coming up for his second term. His opponent was Alf Landon, the governor of Kansas, who didn't prove to be a very formidable opponent. As I recall, Ray Dillman of Roosevelt, Utah, was the Republican nominee for governor, running against Governor Blood.

The year 1936 was the last time the LDS Church took an official position concerning candidates in an election. They took no position on the Utah governorship, but they ran a front-page editorial in the *Deseret News* endorsing Alf Landon for election as president of the United States over Franklin Roosevelt. I remember the national committeeman of the Democratic party at that time, A. S. Brown—a non-Mormon, although not an anti Mormon—saying, "If the *Deseret News* and the Mormon church can carry the state of Utah for Alf Landon, I'll join the church because I'll have seen a miracle." However, Utah went at least 60 percent for Roosevelt, so Brown was never put to the test.

Mr. Robinson was not going to return to Washington after the election until the first of the year because they had no short session of Congress between the election and the new year. He told me it was all right if I enrolled in law school at the University of Utah in the fall of 1936. I did enroll for the quarter, and by the time 1937 came around I had completed four quarters of law.

A few days after Christmas 1936, I left for Washington by train. A friend of mine from college named Howard Anderson went with me, and we arrived on New Year's Eve. I had never been to Washington before, and upon coming out of the Union Station and seeing the Capitol I was deeply impressed. We were tired from the trip and immediately began looking for a hotel. There were at that time, and still are, some hotels in the area around the railroad station. We found two rooms that night in one of the cheaper ones, called the Phillips Hotel. It's no longer there, but was torn down when the American Legion monument was built around twenty years ago. We just stayed in that night, and the next day we went looking for a place to live. Somebody had told us that a family by the name of Hales, who were from Spanish Fork, Utah, took in boarders, and we were given their address at 1437 Taylor Street in the northwest part of Washington. Howard and I went out there in the early afternoon, met the Hales family, and ended up renting rooms from them. I lived there, when I was in Washington, for the next two years.

George Washington University was on a semester basis rather than the quarter system I was used to at the University of Utah, and the second semester at George Washington did not begin until near the end of January or the first part of February. Therefore, I had a period of time in which to orient myself to my new job before I had to enroll in school. I found Mr. Robinson a very easy person to work for. He expected you to do your job, and he wanted it done right, but he didn't hang over you all the time to see that you were doing it. He didn't like to write, so one of my jobs was to write speeches for him. He seemed to like my writing, and many of the speeches I wrote for him at that time he either read on the floor of the Congress or, as is sometimes the case, they were merely inserted in the *Congressional Record.*

Besides myself, there were two other employees in the office. One was a woman named Melba Bachman, who I think had been Mr. Robinson's secretary when he was a lawyer in Provo. I had a difficult time with Melba at first because she felt I was replacing her, and also because I got a little higher salary than she did. The other person in the office was a woman named Marcia Osmond, who was about my age, and who became my fast friend and remained my friend until she died about thirty years ago in childbirth.

Mr. Robinson was by now one of the senior members of the Public Roads Committee, so in addition to the regular constituent work with Utah, I worked closely with the committee staff in preparing legislation. Our office at that time was in the old House office building—the Cannon Building—although the new Longworth Building was there, having been occupied in 1935 or 1936.

During my first year on Capitol Hill I didn't get well acquainted with the people in the various offices. I did have one or two friends, although they were mostly people like me who were working in congressional offices and going to school at night. We were expected to be at work from nine until five, and classes at George Washington started at five-thirty and went to eight. I'd generally not get home until close to nine, and then I'd get dinner and spend two hours studying. When you do that six days a week—and I did it six days a week for a period because I had some Saturday classes—it doesn't leave you much time for socializing.

But I did have one friend who worked next door whom I remember very well, partly because I have another friend now with the same name. His name was Fred Ball, and he worked for a congressman from Ohio. Fred was a practical joker. One afternoon we were sitting in his office which, like ours, was on the inside of a court, and from which we could see across the courtyard into the lighted offices on the other side. We could look right into the office of a congressman from Texas named Maury Maverick. We knew Maury's secretary. She was a flirty, young, good-looking girl, and apparently Maury was having some domestic difficulties—maybe over this girl, I don't know. Anyway, he neglected to pull the blind, and we could see this girl on Maury's lap; he was making advances and she was making half-hearted resistance. Fred said, "I'll fix that s.o.b." He called Maury's number and apparently there was no one in the outer office because Maury let go of the girl with one hand, picked up the telephone, and said, "Yes, yes, who is this?" Fred said, "This is your conscience." Fred hung up the phone, and Maury dropped the girl.

My marks that first semester at George Washington were satisfactory—not spectacular—but I did well. I don't remember much about my professors at George Washington. I was on the campus only a few hours each day, so it was just a matter of going to school and then leaving again. I remember Dean Van Vleck, however, a good teacher who taught me a couple of courses. There was also a man by the name of Davidson, who was an expert on federal procedure. He had written and continued to write books about it, and even today Davidson's are considered almost Horn books on the subject.

Davidson had a biting tongue. Among other things that he taught was admiralty law. Apparently he didn't like to teach admiralty, but somebody had to teach it, and since he had an open period, the class was assigned to him. I had to have a course that same semester, and I also had an open period when his class was being taught, so I took admiralty. I didn't like to be in there any more than he liked to teach it. About the third day, he looked down his nose at me and he said, "Rampton, Rampton, admiralty. You're from Salt Lake City?" And I said, "That's right, sir." And he said, "You're aware that the law of admiralty doesn't apply to prairie schooners." That was typical of Davidson's comments, so I remember him, but not kindly.

Congress recessed in the spring of 1937 about the same time that school let out. Mr. Robinson was returning to Salt Lake and wanted me to come back also and spend my time working again with the political people. When I moved to Washington that first year, I was entirely without "wheels." I had to go everywhere by public transportation. In February or March I bought an old secondhand automobile, used it for the rest of the school year, and then sold it. I then took a train to Detroit where I bought a new automobile and drove it home to Salt Lake.

I enjoyed being home during the summer of 1937. It seemed a relief to get out from under the heavy load of the job and law school. I opened an office for the congressman in the old Federal Building on Fourth South and Main. I worked there about half the day answering mail, and spent the other half of the day contacting the various political figures in the state.It became evident that Will Robinson was going to have stiff opposition for renomination on the Democratic ticket the following year. The Maw forces, in spite of their reluctance to support Governor Blood after he won, utilized the state patronage system to build up their forces. They not only wanted to have Maw run for the governorship in 1940, but they also desired to take over the other places on the ticket. For some reason, they felt that Mr. Robinson was too conservative for them. Among the Maw people were Ed Watson, who had been state engineer, and Hugh Woodward, who was a professor of political science at Brigham Young University. To defeat these contenders and to get ready for the 1938 campaign, it was therefore necessary that I work reasonably hard during that summer in mending political fences.

During the last year I was at the University of Utah, I became acquainted with a girl from Ogden named Elma Skelton. She had been a member of the debate team at Weber College. At that time Weber was only a two-year college, and when Elma finished her two years, she came down to the university, where we were on the debate team together. I began taking her out, and by autumn quarter 1936 we had sort of an informal engagement, or an engagement to become engaged. I never actually gave her a ring, but it was pretty well understood that sometime we would get married. And so when I came out again in the summer of 1937 to stay from June until George Washington University's law school started the first of October, I kept going with Elma. I would drive to Ogden on the weekend and maybe one other day during the week to see her.

I don't recall when Congress started in the fall of 1937, but I had to get back to Washington for the beginning of the school year. I rode with Abe Murdock and Mr. Robinson in Mr. Robinson's big black sedan. When we arrived, I moved back to the Haleses' house and started school. Although I saw Elma when I was in Salt Lake, I had not been out on many dates during the preceding several months I was in Washington, as I knew very few people there at the time. Then there came a Halloween party sponsored by the Utah State Society. The Haleses' oldest daughter, a girl named Beth who was about seventeen or eighteen at the time, asked, "Have you got a date for the Utah State Halloween party?" I replied, "I don't know anybody to take." She said, "Well, I know a girl who's engaged to a man at Harvard, and she doesn't have anybody here, either. I'm going to arrange a blind date for you." It was to be a masquerade party. I got a khaki uniform and dressed up like Adolf Hitler, who at that time was becoming a frightening figure in Europe. Beth had arranged my date with a girl named Lucybeth Cardon, whose parents lived a mile and a half or two miles from the Haleses on a little street called Argonne Place, near the Sixteenth Street Mormon church. I called for Lucybeth that night. I was a little worried because I'd never seen her and Beth had told me many times what a bright girl she was, so I didn't know what to expect as I went to the Cardon house and knocked on the door.

Lucybeth had dressed up as a Russian peasant girl, and after rather stilted introductions, we went to the party.

I don't remember much about the party that night except that we did go, and I think I had a good time, though I'm not sure Lucybeth did. I think she felt a little guilty about going out on a date when she was engaged to a student who was away. I took Lucybeth out occasionally for the rest of the 1937–38 school year. It would generally be a matter of picking her up on Sunday evening and going to church, and then maybe going up to the Hot Shoppe for a thick malt afterwards; or, sometimes, if I didn't have to study, we'd go to a movie. I don't know how frequently we went out during that year, but we probably had these after-church dates a dozen to fifteen times during the seven or eight months before I came home in June 1938.

Things at the office were not much changed. We still had the three employees there, but we moved our office from the Cannon Building over to the Longworth Building. It was a more modern office and much more convenient.

I began to get better acquainted with my associates on the Hill. There was an organization at that time called the Little Congress, which was made up of the administrative assistants and other clerical workers of the congressmen and senators. I had joined the Little Congress during the short period I was there in 1937 and had gone to the meetings, but my acquaintanceship wasn't broad. They always had their meetings over on the House side, and the House members dominated the organization. I think most of the Senate administrative assistants and senior staff people felt it was beneath their dignity to attend, although some Senate people did come.

Lyndon B. Johnson, who in 1937 was a freshman congressman, had been the speaker of the Little Congress in the spring of 1935. After Lyndon was elected to Congress, a fellow from Mississippi with whom I became good friends, Jim Coleman, was elected speaker of the Little Congress. The term of the speaker was only for three months, and in the fall of 1937, the elected speaker was a Texan named Gore Hinsey. He was the speaker through the fall of 1937 and into the spring of 1938.

The Texans, who were very active members, were determined to elect another Texan as speaker, and they had selected as their candidate Lyndon Johnson's brother, Sam Houston Johnson. Some of the other members thought that we'd had enough Texans for awhile and urged me to run for the speakership. I did run, and it was quite a hot campaign. Jim Coleman was my campaign manager, and Capitol Hill was broken up into two warring factions. There were campaign posters put up, but I think what really won me the election was the overconfidence of the Texans. Several days before the election, Gore Hinsey, the outgoing speaker from Texas, had gone downtown to a photographer with Sam Johnson, and they had a picture taken of Gore Hinsey handing Sam the gavel. Jim Coleman found out about this and got a negative of the picture and blew it up to great size. As he was giving my nominating speech, he displayed this picture to the four or five hundred people who were gathered in the caucus room. It engendered some resentment among the others that the Texans would have been so overconfident, and so I won the speakership. Jim Coleman later became governor of Mississippi and is now the retired chief judge of the Fifth Circuit Court of Appeals.

Within a week or ten days after the election we had a banquet at which I was installed as speaker. Lucybeth went with me to the dinner. The dinner speaker that evening was Congressman Lyndon Johnson, and that was the first time that I met him and Lady Bird.

I enjoyed being the speaker of the Little Congress. We would meet one evening a week for about three hours and debate the bill or bills that we thought were going to be the most controversial on the floor of the House and Senate the following week. Our meetings were generally well covered by the press under the theory that the administrative assistant, who was a member of the Little Congress, would probably vote on that bill in the Little Congress the same way his boss would vote on it in the House or Senate. So we received good press coverage, and it was a job that gave me some visibility on the Hill. It especially gave me social contacts that I hadn't previously had.

The Little Congress took a weekend trip to New York every year, and, as speaker, I was in charge of arrangements. I had to go to New York for a weekend, two or three weeks preceding the trip, to complete all arrangements, and I asked Lucybeth if she would go with me. I think she was intrigued but also sort of aghast at the idea of being unchaperoned with me. I told the problem to Marcy Osmond, my friend in the office, and Marcy said, "I'll go with you, too. The three of us will go up." So we all three went to New York and spent a good weekend there. One night we went to see the show at Billy Rose's Casa Mañana. This wasn't the first time I had been to New York, but it was the first time I'd been out to a nightclub. That night Lucybeth ordered a sloe gin fizz, which was probably the first alcoholic drink she'd ever had. I think she had a good time up there, but I believe it also bothered her conscience a little because after that she started cutting down on the frequency of our Sunday night dates.

I left Washington immediately after the end of the 1938 school year because I had to get back to Utah for the campaign. It was really getting heavy. I told Lucybeth good-bye and said I would be back next year. Robert Mabey, a girl named Venice Redd, and I drove to Salt Lake in forty-eight hours without stopping. I was very tired when I got there, but I immediately launched into the 1938 campaign. I was still working for Congressman Robinson and was more or less in charge of the details of his campaign, although we did have a fairly sizable campaign committee.

The day after I arrived in Utah I drove to Ogden to see Elma. I felt somewhat guilty because I knew my interest in Lucybeth was much more than casual. Elma and I had been together only a few minutes when she said, "This is not going to work, is it?" I agreed. She said she had to attend the wedding of a friend the next day and needed an escort. I went to the wedding with her and that was our last date. A year or two later she married and moved to New York, so I have seen her only a few times over the last fifty years. She is still an attractive and charming woman.

Soon after that Frank Muir and the man who succeeded him as Davis County Democratic chairman, Charles Gardner, suggested that I consider running for county attorney of Davis County. The current county attorney, Orlando Bowman, had decided not to run for another term. An announcement had been made by Thornley Swan that he would seek the Republican nomination, but so far no one had indicated a desire to run on the Democratic ticket. I had not yet taken the bar examination and I still had about a year to go before I would complete law school, but at that time the law did not require that one be a member of the bar in order to be county attorney. It didn't take very much talking on their part to convince me that I should seek the Democratic nomination. This gave me a double job: I had to work with the congressman's campaign during the daytime and for myself at night.

In that year we still had the double-primary system rather than the convention-primary system which we have now. If two high-scoring candidates emerged from the first primary and neither one of them had a majority of the votes (assuming there were more than two candidates), then they would engage in a runoff primary which would select the eventual winner to run in the November election. Not long before the final filing date, William King who was a relative of U.S. Senator William King and who resided in Layton where he had been practicing law for some time, decided to run for the Democratic nomination for county attorney. I was thus faced with primary opposition. Whether I would have declared for the position had I known there would be opposition, I'm not certain. At any rate, there he was, and so I did what I had to do. Taking time out from Mr. Robinson's campaign, I was able to get a fair majority in the first primary. By and large, Bill King carried the north end of the county, and I carried the larger south end, so I won. Then I had to face Thornley Swan in the general election. Swan had the Republican nomination, although I don't recall whether he had primary opposition.

Once again, Mr. Robinson also had opposition in the Democratic primary. In 1938 his opponent was Ray VanCott, Sr., who had sometime in the past been district attorney of the Third Judicial District. He was the father of Ray VanCott, Jr., who served for a long time on the district bench. During the 1938 campaign Ray VanCott, Sr., was seventy years old and was not a vigorous campaigner, so Mr. Robinson won fairly easily. That year we were not faced with the same problem of two years before when the Maw organization backed an opposing candidate.

After the primary was over and the fall election came around, it appeared that it was still a Democratically inclined country and that Utah, even though it was less so than the average state, would probably vote Democratic. In Utah and Davis counties that proved to be true. Mr. Robinson won reelection that year by a comfortable majority, and I was elected county attorney by a reasonable margin. The campaign had not been bitter. Thornley Swan and I had been friends in high school, and we still are.

A day or two after the election I caught the train for Washington in order to finish up at the office. With my election as county attorney, Mr. Robinson had employed another man to take my place, and I had to go back to arrange things to turn over to him. Also, I'm sure that was a rationale for getting back there so I could see Lucybeth again because I couldn't quite accept the fact that she was going to marry this fellow from Harvard. I was determined to see what I could do about it.

As quickly as I got to Washington, I called her at the office of Ernest L. Wilkinson, whose legal secretary she had become. She seemed glad to hear from me, and we had lunch. For the next month I saw her occasionally, but I didn't appear to be making much progress. When I left to take my new job in Utah, I thought I was never going to see her again. I picked her up near her home one morning, drove her down to work and let her out in front of the Earle Building on Thirteenth Street. We said good-bye, and I was very sad.

I came on home, getting there a little before Christmas. I had to do many things between Christmas and shortly after the first of the year. I had to get ready to assume my duties as county attorney, and I had to get my credits transferred from George Washington University so I could finish the winter and spring quarters at the University of Utah, at the end of which time I hoped to get my degree. Also, as Mother by this time had sold the house in Bountiful and moved to Salt Lake, it was necessary for me to set up a residence in Davis County in order to maintain my eligibility to serve as county attorney. I therefore moved into Aunt Nell's basement. I got a bed, some lamps, and some other bedroom furniture and fixed the basement up, and I lived there from the time I took over as county attorney until March 1940.

The position of Davis County attorney at that time was a part-time job. It paid only seventy-five dollars a month, the supposition being that the attorney who held it would carry on a private practice as well as his public office. But during the early part of 1939 I was not eligible to practice law privately. Mr. Robinson, fortunately, having had his allowance for staff increased, asked me if I would work part time for him in Utah. The staff allowance had been increased to permit a representative to stay in the congressman's home district and take care of matters there for him, and I was pleased to do so. For a period of time I worked from 7:00 or 8:00 A.M. until noon at the county attorney's job in Farmington. After, I would go to school in Salt Lake for about three hours, and then down to the Federal Building at about 4:00, where I would work until 7:00 or 8:00 taking care of the branch office the congressman had established there. I tried to spend most of the day Saturday at Farmington catching up on whatever I needed to do in the county attorney's job. This regular daily routine was inter-rupted two days a month when the county commission had their meet-ings, for which I had to be present. It was a very busy time.

There suddenly came a letter from Lucybeth's mother dur-ing the spring of 1939. It was a short letter saying, in effect, "I don't think you should stop writing to Lucybeth because I'm not sure that there isn't some promise for you and her, and as her mother I want to see her happy." I didn't need a great deal of encouragement, and so I did write. They were rather platonic letters I'm afraid, describing my daily routine, but she usually answered them, and we continued to correspond through the spring months. When the summer of 1939 arrived I had more time, as my schooling was completed and I received my LL.B. degree from the university in June. I immediately set about cramming for the bar examination, which was given in the early fall. This gave me a great deal more latitude in scheduling my activities than when I had to make classes at a certain time of day. The exami-nation results, as I recall, were not announced until October, and so it wasn't until sometime after that that I was admitted and sworn in as a lawyer.

About the time I was taking the bar examination I received a letter from Lucybeth saying that she and her fiancé had decided they would not get married, and that she and her sister, Margaret, were going to take a trip to Europe. They were leaving right away; by the time I received that letter they'd probably already gone. At any rate, she wrote me a couple of postcards from various places in Europe, and they got out just a few days before war broke out there. In fact, the sinking of the *Athenia*, which really took the Britons a long way toward war, occurred while Margaret and Lucybeth were at sea on their way home.

I continued to write, and I think the letters got a little more affectionate and less pedantic. I decided in the fall that I had had enough encouragement, and that I'd go back to Washington. Virginia, Mother, and I caught the train and went to Detroit, and I picked up a new Oldsmobile and drove to Washington where we stayed with the Haleses. I called Lucybeth immediately. We had a couple of dates, and then on the evening of Armistice Day we went to a dance at the Shoreham Hotel. The entertainment was Ted Lewis and his band. I asked her that evening if she'd marry me. She said she would, and so we left the Shoreham and drove home to tell her folks. That night, as I was leaving, I kissed her for the first time. Our romance certainly wasn't a torrid one up to that point. Mother, Virginia, and I stayed in Washington for three or four more days, and the Cardons had us over to dinner, where we laid more definite plans and decided that we'd get married in the spring. In the middle of this conversation, there was a great crash out in front. We ran outside to find that either Miss Summy or Miss Walker, the two ladies who lived across the street from Lucybeth's parents, had backed out of the driveway and crushed in the side of my brand new Oldsmobile coupe.

Shortly after the three of us returned home, and having been admitted to the bar, I decided to give up the congressman's office at the Federal Building and to continue my work for him out of a new law office. I was able to rent one in a four-office suite on the eleventh floor of the Continental Bank Building. The other three lawyers in the office (I was not in the firm) were Courtney Draper, Delbert Draper, Sr., and John Boyden. John I have mentioned before. Courtney was the son of Delbert Draper, Sr., and was a year or two older than I. We had a fine relationship there, and I learned a good deal, particularly from Mr. Draper, Sr., who was a good lawyer and, more than that, a very wise and tolerant man. He taught me a great deal about the practical aspects of the law, helped me to learn some of the techniques that you don't learn in law school but which come through on-the-job training.

My law practice was slow in picking up. My first client was the Union Furniture Company in Bountiful, which turned over to me a substantial number of delinquent bills for collection. Meanwhile, Lucybeth and I decided to have our wedding in Washington on March 10, 1940. A few days before that date my friends threw a big bachelor party for me. I then got on the train once again for Detroit, picked up a Chevrolet for Mother, and drove that on to Washington, arriving a couple of days before the tenth. I stayed with the Haleses, and on the day of the tenth we had the wedding ceremony in Lucybeth's house. We stood in front of a wall mirror on a small oriental rug that had been given to Lucybeth by Hy Westover, a family friend. We were married by Wallace Hales, Pa Hales as I had come to call him, with whose family I had lived intermittently for the preceding four years. After the wedding we had a big reception. The weather was quite warm. They opened the house, and I stood in a line for hours and heard people tell me what a fine girl I was getting. Nobody came through to say a word for me.

After the reception was over, we left and spent our wedding night at the Shoreham Hotel, where we had become engaged some three months before. The next day we started for Salt Lake in Mother's two-door Chevrolet. I believe they called them coaches then. It was a bigger car than a coupe, with two seats but only one set of doors. We piled that car full of wedding gifts, of which there were many. What we needed was a Conestoga, rather than a two-door Chevrolet, to get all those gifts across the country. When we got home we found two or three places where gifts in boxes had rubbed through the upholstery, it was so tightly packed.

It took about five days to drive west, and as we approached Salt Lake City, I could see Lucybeth was getting more and more apprehensive. Although she knew Salt Lake and Logan, I'm not sure what idea she had of Bountiful. It was undoubtedly her feeling that Bountiful was sort of a backwater town. She has reminded me recently that I was partially responsible for the dim view she took of Bountiful because between the time we became engaged and the date of the marriage, I sent her some photographs which I told her were of Bountiful. Actually, they were photographs I'd taken sometime or another in a little town in the Midwest, showing a very dry place and a city park with a broken-down bandstand. I still don't know whether she really believed they were of Bountiful.

At any rate we arrived in Utah, and then we had to look for a place to live. The first day or two we stayed at the Temple Tourist Court which we still owned. In the morning I commuted to Farmington to take care of my duties, and in the afternoon Lucybeth and I went house hunting. We finally located a small over-and-under duplex on East First North in Bountiful, since I still had to maintain my residence in Davis County as county attorney. It was about one block east and across the road from Aunt Nell's place, immediately adjacent to a lumberyard. The ripsaw was right outside our bedroom window. The house belonged to Vern McCullough, a Salt Lake lawyer with whom I had dealings, and whom I have mentioned before. Vern was not a generous landlord. He did not keep the place up. It had one bedroom, a bath, a kitchen, and a little combination L-shaped dining room and living room. But it was comfortable, and we liked it. It was nice having a home of our own, and we lived there through the balance of 1940.

With the coming of early fall in 1940, there was another election upon us. The county attorney's term at that time was only two years, so my term was coming to an end, and Mr. Robinson once again had to run for reelection as congressman. Because I was getting quite a lot of work in private practice, during the summer I gave up the work that I had been doing for the congressman and devoted my time to my job as county attorney and to my law practice. I told the congressman I'd help him with his campaign as much as possible, but that I no longer had time to be a staff person. I also had my own situation to think about, and decided in the early fall not to run for reelection as county attorney. I didn't want the job again, and besides that I had been asked by one of the candidates for attorney general on the Democratic ticket, Grover Giles, to be one of his assistants if he won. I decided to run for state senator, and if elected, I would forego the assistant attorney general's position.

By that time it was obvious that we were veering back toward the Republican party in Davis County. In 1936 the Republicans had elected a state senator from Davis County, Lloyd Riley, despite the fact that that was a heavy year for Democratic victories. But Lloyd Riley's term was expiring, and since he decided not to run again, I decided I would run.

I don't remember who were the candidates on the Republican side in 1940, but the eventual winner of their primary was William Dawson, who had been county attorney of Davis County several years before me, and who was currently practicing law in Layton. Two other men and I filed for the Democratic nomination. One of them was Ed Muir, who had been a county commissioner several years earlier, and had continued to be active in Democratic party circles. The other candidate was Joseph Sill, who was the justice of the peace in Layton.

Joseph Sill at that time was in his mid-seventies. He was the father of Sterling Sill, who became one of the general authorities of the LDS Church. He'd only been justice of the peace about two years, having been elected at the same time I was elected county attorney. One of the first cases that I had was a severe traffic violation. I tried the case before Justice Sill without a jury. The defense attorney was Vern McCullough. Not only was this the first case of any substance that I had tried, but I think it was the first case of any substance that Mr. Sill had tried. Obviously Justice Sill was impressed with Mr. McCullough, who was a big-city lawyer with a considerable reputation, and he was not at all impressed by the young county attorney who wasn't even a member of the bar. It was obvious that I wasn't making much of an impression on him as I presented my evidence. When I completed questioning my last witness and said, "The prosecution rests," Vern McCullough said, "Your honor, I move for a dismissal." The justice of the peace responded, "Second the motion."

In any case, Mr. Sill didn't get many votes for state senate, and I won. I received about two-thirds of the votes in the first primary and didn't have to run in the second primary. I believed that I was a political power and felt that it was unnecessary to do much campaigning for the general election.

I knew Bill Dawson and respected him but, I thought, he'd been a long time out of the public eye. About ten days before the election, the state chairman asked me if I would go in a caravan through southern Utah with Abe Murdock, who was switching from the House to the Senate, and Walter Granger, who was running for Abe's vacated seat in the House. I told him I would, because I didn't think I had any problem in Davis County. That summer I had been elected president of the Young Democratic Clubs of Utah, and so I felt that I should certainly do something for the party. I spent the last eight or nine days of the campaign in southern Utah and was greatly shocked on the night of the election when I lost to Bill Dawson by less than two dozen votes. Actually, I had more relatives than that who didn't bother to go to the polls. Thus I was effectively out of office after completing my final two months as county attorney. I knew, however, that I was going to become assistant attorney general on inauguration day, the first Monday in January, so from the time of the election to the end of my term was just a transition period.

In the late fall, an embarrassing thing happened to me. I had convicted a fellow of drunken driving, and he had been put in the county jail at Farmington. He behaved so erratically there that he had to undergo a psychiatric examination, and was then committed to the forensic medicine ward at the state hospital. He hadn't been there more than about two weeks when he escaped, but before he did he made some dire threats as to what he was going to do to me when he got out. He was going to shoot me, he said, and I believed him fully capable of it. I had inherited a pistol from Dad, but it was a big western-type six-shooter, and I didn't think that was the sort of thing for a county attorney to be carrying around in his car.

I therefore went to a pawn shop in Salt Lake and bought a .32 automatic, which I carried on my person. I had never fired it. One day I had the pistol in my bedroom and thought I'd better get used to the trigger squeeze on it. Sitting on the edge of the bed I pulled out the cartridge slide, took deliberate aim at my image in the mirror, and squeezed the trigger. What I had not known was that this .32 automatic, unlike the .45 with which I was familiar, kept one round in the chamber. To pull out the slide didn't disarm it. It went off and the bullet went through both the mirror and the wall, put a big dent in a teapot in the next room, and embedded itself in the big green chair we'd bought from the Union Furniture Company. Lucybeth was standing by a window not more than eight or ten feet from that chair. She came running into the bedroom where I was sitting on the bed, holding the smoking pistol in my hand. She said my face showed a combination of fright and embarrassment, and the first thing I said was, "Don't tell Max or By."

During the summer of 1940, I was elected president of the Young Democratic Clubs of Utah. The clubs were much larger and more active than they are now, with five thousand active members in the state. My opponent at that time was Clyde Miller who, although he was a couple of years older than I, had been at the university while I was, and would be secretary of state during the twelve years that I was governor. Clyde and I carried on quite a vigorous campaign, albeit a good-humored one. We had our election at a huge downtown dance hall called the Rainbow Rendezvous. There was a large group of delegates there, and it was very close, as I beat Clyde by only twenty-five or thirty votes out of five hundred cast. I served in that position for two years.

Immediately after the first Monday in January, I was sworn in as assistant attorney general under Attorney General Grover Giles. The attorney general's office now has some forty assistant attorneys general, but at that time we had six. Besides myself there were Zar

Hayes, with whom I was later to be associated in the practice of law, Art Miner, John Brennen, Durham Huffaker, and Herbert Smart. We were not departmentalized, but took opinion requests and cases, whatever they were, as they were assigned to us. I had an opportunity to get a considerable amount of experience in appellate work because at that time the attorney general's office handled all appeals in criminal cases, even though the cases were tried by the district attorney in the district court. I tried many cases for the state and got a substantial amount of experience in trial work both in court and before commissions. I often represented the state before the Public Service Commission. I also worked closely during this period with Governor Maw because Grover had me handle matters that came out of the governor's office. I would be in Governor Maw's office two or three times a day talking to him about some problem or another. This was a pleasant experience. I enjoyed the people I was working with and liked Grover very much.

During the summer of 1941 we decided to move into Salt Lake. Shortly after Lucybeth and I were married, we sold the motel and also another smaller apartment house that we had purchased to supplement our income from the motel. We used the funds to purchase the Federal Heights Apartments, which are located on the corner of South Temple and Virginia Street. In late summer, we moved from our little house in Bountiful into one of the apartments.

Meantime, Lucybeth became pregnant. The baby was to come in the fall, close to my birthday. We grew more and more excited with expectations of the new baby and were making preparations for the birth. Then one Saturday afternoon we had tickets for a football game at the University of Utah, and Lucybeth started having labor pains. I called our physician in Bountiful, Dr. Trowbridge, and gave him a description of the pains. He said, "I don't believe that the baby's going to come very soon. I wouldn't take her to the hospital yet." I told him we would just wait, and then asked where he would be that afternoon. He replied that he would be at the football game, and that we should go, too, and enjoy ourselves. So we went to the football game and the labor pains subsided, but a day or two after that they started again in earnest. I took Lucybeth up to the LDS Hospital and Meg was born on November 4, 1941, two days before my birthday.

Meg was a beautiful child. Even then, her hair was red and her features were very delicate. We were proud of her. Immediately after she was born, and while Lucybeth was still in the hospital, I was told that there was a murder trial in Junction, Piute County. The district attorney, who was Zar Hayes's brother, was ill and the case had to go to trial. Something had to be done about it, and I was assigned to go down and try the case while Lucybeth stayed in the hospital.

It was a colorful case. A man named Walter Neilsen was accused of shooting his nephew to death on a ditch bank in a quarrel over water. He claimed self-defense, asserting that his nephew, Chad, had attacked him with a shovel. It was a jury trial. The defense attorneys were D. A. Skeene and Sam Thurman, Jr., the father of Sam Thurman III, who became dean of the law school at the University of Utah, and the son of the Sam Thurman, who was once in the Utah Supreme Court. The trial lasted almost a week. People came in from all over Piute County because nothing like this had happened down there in a long time. There was standing room only in the courthouse, and the people had divided up into cheering sections. Every time I would make a point, a murmur of approval would go up from one side of the courtroom, and every time Sam Thurman or D. A. Skeene made a point, a murmur of approval would go up from the other side.

One day while we were involved in a tense part of the case, the whole building suddenly shuddered; this was followed by a loud bang and the floor tipped to one side. There was a hush, and Judge Bronson, who had come down from Salt Lake to try the case, looked over and said, "I think a beam has broken. I don't know whether it's going on down. Now you people back near the door start filing out, very gently." We filed out gently and cleared the building, and nothing more happened. A beam had indeed broken, and the floor dropped almost two feet on one side and, fortunately, lodged there. We finished the case in the meetinghouse. The jury brought in a compromise verdict of voluntary manslaughter; Mr. Neilsen was given probation and moved away from the state.

I returned to Salt Lake and took Lucybeth and our new baby home after they had been in the hospital ten days. We set about making the adjustments that are necessary with a new baby. Meanwhile, the clouds of war were gathering, and we were apprehensive about what was going to happen. We knew that if war did come it would cause a great change in our family life. On December 7, 1941, Lucybeth and I had taken Meg to church to have her blessed. She was then just a little over a month old. We came home from the church, and I had lain down to take a nap when Lucybeth came and shook me and told me that the radio had announced that the Japanese had attacked Pearl Harbor.

I first became involved with the military in the summer of 1932, just after I had partially recovered from pneumonia. Max and I decided we would join the Utah National Guard. There was a battery of field artillery headquartered at Bountiful—Battery B of the First Battalion of the 145th Field Artillery. I don't know if we were attracted to the organization more because military service was interesting or because we got a dollar per drill every week. The four dollars a month seemed quite attractive. We both signed up in May 1932 and after it was over told our mothers about it. They were dismayed because the National Guard just wasn't socially acceptable in Bountiful at that time. For the most part, the enlisted men were a fairly rough element, and our mothers saw us falling in with evil companions. Nonetheless, we'd already signed up.

I wondered if I would be able to get through the physical examination in my rather weakened condition, but that didn't really offer much of a problem. We went over to see Dr. J. C. Stocks, who did the physical examinations for the guard. As I recall, he simply asked how we felt, and we said fine. He filled out five detailed pages of documentation, signed it, and gave it to us; we took it back to the armory, took the oath, and were in.

At that time Battery B was horse drawn. We had a stable of about thirty horses at the armory. Most were draft animals for pulling the guns and caissons, while others were riding horses for the officers and the top noncoms. The armory in Bountiful was a converted lumberyard. It had a big hall on the ground floor. The headquarters where we dressed were not particularly good. We were issued World War I uniforms, including the canvas puttees and what was called a "campaign hat," which is a broad-brimmed hat like Smokey the Bear wears. Our unit was to go to Camp Williams in July, and we had about six weeks to train for the first encampment. Unfortunately, it was just two or three days before we were to leave that I was stricken with appendicitis, so I didn't make camp the first year. Max went, but I was out of drill for a month or six weeks. When I finally got back into it, we would go every week to drill. We learned the various duties, and would drill every Monday night from about seven until ten o'clock.

In the fall of 1934, as I was approaching my twenty-first birthday, I started work on some army correspondence courses, hoping that there would be a vacancy as a lieutenant and that I would be able to get it. At about that time my cousin Dick was transferred to another unit, thus leaving a vacancy, and I was commissioned a second lieutenant in the summer of 1935. When I went to Washington in 1937, I transferred my commission to the reserve corps.

I did no further work in regard to reserve service until I was called to active duty in World War II—except to finish the "twenty series" of the correspondence courses, which should have entitled me to a promotion to first lieutenant. However, I didn't do the summer encampments that were necessary for a promotion because most of the summers I was either commuting between Salt Lake and Washington or I was running political campaigns and didn't have time to take off for military duty. So I continued as a second lieutenant, just doing the minimum necessary to keep my commission active. That was the situation in which I found myself when Pearl Harbor was attacked.

As we had expected, when the United States declared war, my orders to active duty were not long in coming. I received them in mid-December and was told to report on January 19 to Camp Murray in Washington state. Lucybeth, Meg, and I were then living in the Federal Heights Apartments. As the day approached that I was to leave we were pretty emotional. We couldn't help being so because we didn't know what the future held for us. We decided that Lucybeth would stay, for a time at least, in the apartment.

I first reported to Fort Lewis and was assigned to some barracks there before I could join the Camp Murry unit to which I was actually assigned. There was a big celebration at Fort Lewis the day I got there. Lt. Colonel Dwight Eisenhower was being relieved of command and sent to some war games in the Louisiana area. The next day I was sent to Camp Murray. It was a terrible place, and there were no hardtop roads, as it had just been opened for emergency purposes. I was assigned to a field artillery unit of the North Dakota National Guard. During the month I was there I never saw Mt. Rainier, although it was only a few miles away, because it rained hard every day. We walked around in mud well over our ankles.

I had been at Camp Murray about a month when a most unexpected telegram arrived announcing that on rechecking the results of the physical examination I was given at Fort Douglas in mid-December, the doctors found that I had some problems. They said that the electrocardiogram test indicated heart problems and they relieved me from active duty. I went home very sheepishly because although I was glad to be back with Lucybeth and Meg, it was hard to face some of my friends after they'd given me farewell parties, a going-away watch, and all that sort of thing. I went to Fort Douglas to find out what was the matter. It appeared that somebody else's electrocardiogram might have become attached to my papers, so I immediately went to a doctor downtown and had an electrocardiogram taken, and my heart proved to be all right. I went back to Fort Douglas and the doctors said they would take a look at the new results.

Then began a long series of letter writing as I tried to get back into the service. I wrote dozens of letters and had several electrocardiograms taken and sent in, but all I could get out of the bureaucracy was: "Your physical examination shows you do not qualify." I tried every avenue I could think of, and finally it appeared that I might be able to get into a section of military government that was just being created and for which they were taking some older men and lawyers. I processed my papers to get into this quasi-military unit and was all ready to get a commission there. The minimal commission was captain, which made me very happy, needless to say, when here came another telegram saying, "Report back to duty as a second lieutenant of field artillery. Your papers have been cleared, and you're all right."

This process had taken about ten and a half months and, once again, I was to leave in January—this time in January 1943—and was to report to the field artillery training center at Camp Roberts near Paso Robles, California. I stayed at Camp Roberts from mid-January until the latter part of April. During the first thirty days I was there, I lived in barracks on the post; then we decided that I might be there for a while and that Lucybeth and Meg could come down and join me, which they did.

Although I was in the field artillery training center, I had very little field artillery work there. This was a training and replacement center. New recruits were going through quickly and, since many of them were getting into trouble, there were many courts-martial. As

I was a lawyer, they gave me a temporary assignment to the judge advocate's office, usually as a trial judge advocate, though sometimes as a defense counsel. One of the soldiers I was assigned to defend was a supply sergeant accused of stealing supplies. The principal evidence against him was the records of the supply room, which showed a great deal of missing property. The records, however, didn't prove what he had done with the property, or if he had received it. I therefore set about to prove that the general record keeping of the whole artillery training center was so fouled up that nobody could tell anything from the records, and that the prosecution's evidence was inadequate. My man was acquitted. General de Hoyle, the commander of the field artillery training center, was furious! I don't know why he should be furious with me because I'd uncovered the thing. I didn't foul up the records.

But at any rate General Lane, the camp commander, heard about it and called me in one day. He said, "Lieutenant, I don't think I want to send you back to the field artillery training center. I don't think you'll do very well there, but the judge advocate general is a friend of mine, and I think I could get you transferred if you would like." I said, "That's fine with me." He called Major General Myron Cramer, who said if I would come to Ann Arbor and take a twelve-week course, I would have my commission transferred from field artillery to judge advocate. I agreed, and I got the orders. Lucybeth and I packed Meg into the automobile and started from Paso Robles toward Ann Arbor, Michigan, by way of Washington, D.C., where I would leave my family for the duration.

The course at Ann Arbor was held in the Law Quadrangle, which is a large and beautiful complex. We were the twelfth officers' class of judge advocates. There were about a hundred and twenty officers in the group, ranging from second lieutenants to colonels. It was really a cram course and we worked hard. For six days a week we went to class from eight o'clock in the morning until six in the evening, with only a short time for lunch in the daytime. In the evening, from about seven-thirty to ten, we did supervised study in the hall.

About halfway through the course Meg and Lucybeth came up from Washington. While they were there, the annual spring music festival was on in the Michigan Union, which was adjacent to the Law Quadrangle. I was able to get a room at the union for that weekend, and Lucybeth, Meg, and I stayed there. The first night we were there, a man next door kept playing scales on a violin. I wanted to get to sleep because it was Saturday night and I had the next day off and wanted to go over to Detroit with Lucybeth and Meg. I called down to the desk and said, "Will you tell that guy next door to quit sawing on the fiddle?" The desk clerk said in a very shocked voice, "Sir, that is Fritz Kreisler." He kept on playing.

Lucybeth and Meg went back to Washington to stay with her parents while I finished my course at Ann Arbor. I finished third academically in the class, but they decided to do a sneak inspection of quarters a night or two before graduation. Although we were a judge advocate's outfit, we were required to observe military rules strictly. Everything had to be in apple-pie order: you had to have your shoes polished and the laces tied. Your shirts had to hang all in one direction and be buttoned. For every single thing that was wrong, the inspection team would write a little notation. For every notation, you got a demerit. The average number of demerits was about six. However, when the inspecting officer opened the door to my room, he quickly closed it and wrote on his sheet, "Room in general disorder." The girl doing the computing gave me one demerit, and that was enough to elevate me to top man in my graduating class.

Immediately after graduation from Ann Arbor in July 1943, I was promoted to first lieutenant and assigned to Washington as assistant trial attorney to the War Department Board of Contract Appeals. The job called for a captain's rank, so in January 1944, as quickly as I had done my six months in grade, I was promoted to captain. I continued as trial attorney until May 1944, when orders came stating that I was to be assigned to the foreign claims service and was to report immediately for a six-week training course at Lebanon, Tennessee, after which I would be shipped to Europe.

There was a lot of talk at that time about the second front and the invasion of Normandy. There was much speculation as to when it would take place. Those of us who wanted to see something of the war were rather eager to get overseas, if we were going to make it at all. So I went down to the claims course in Lebanon, which was held on the campus of Cumberland University. The buildings were old and not in very good condition, but it had quite a tradition as a law school. Cordell Hull was their prize graduate. As at Ann Arbor, I underwent a very rigorous course in army claims procedure.

My schedule included mandatory athletics. One day during a baseball game I hit a ball rather well and thought I could make a double of it if I could just get around first base quickly. But first base wasn't a bag; it was a piece of wood about a foot square, and I didn't realize that there was a hole in the ground under it. I hit that turn and suddenly my foot just gave way. The pain was excruciating. I couldn't stand on it. They took my shoe off, and it was already beginning to swell badly. The general consensus was that I had broken my foot. I wasn't sure that I had, but they called an ambulance and hauled me off to Thayer General Hospital in Nashville. I told the ambulance driver as he let me out, "Don't you move this ambulance out of this driveway because I'll be right out. I'm going back because our outfit's being shipped out." He said, "Yeah, yeah, I've heard that before." Actually it was six weeks before I came back through that doorway, so it was a good thing he didn't wait. X rays of my foot showed that I had a separation of all of my metatarsal bones which, while in some ways was not as bad as a fracture, actually took longer to heal.

I was finally discharged from the hospital in mid-July and given ten days' leave in Washington. My foot and leg up to my knee were in a cast, and I walked with a cane. In addition, our second daughter, Janet, was obviously well on her way. We were embarrassed when we went to a movie and stood in a long line. The ushers came for us and rushed this pregnant young woman and her "wounded" soldier husband up to the front of the line.

I was to join my unit at Camp Reynolds in Pennsylvania early in August. I was only at the camp for about a week, although I'd expected to be there longer. Our time there was spent mostly drawing equipment and taking weapons instruction and gas drills. Each day we would go through the gas chambers and learn to use our gas masks. We also had to qualify with both the carbine and the Colt .45. About the first of September 1944 we received orders to move to a port of embarkation at Fort Hamilton, New York.

Fort Hamilton is located just outside of New York City, at one end of the Narrows Bridge. During the daytime we were more or less on a holding pattern. We drew more equipment, received instructions on how to conduct ourselves on the ship, and so on. In the evenings they let us go over to New York, and they said, "Until you get your orders, you're free to call home if you want; but after you get your orders, you won't be able to call anymore. Your wife will know that you've gone by the fact that you've quit calling." I went over to New York on several evenings, and I called Lucybeth in Washington and sometimes Mother at home.

Finally, one morning the orders came saying we were moving out tomorrow. We weren't allowed any communication from that time on. My foot was still giving me a great deal of trouble, and we had packs to carry which weighed about eighty pounds. We had all of our equipment in the pack and a duffel bag that we carried over the other shoulder. As we marched out of Fort Hamilton down to the dock, I was in a great deal of pain, but I made it all right. They took us up the river in big flatboats to one of the piers, and we pulled in beside the *Ile de France*, which was to be our ship for the crossing. It was just getting dark when we got there, and we boarded her. I was still carrying my equipment and having considerable trouble with my foot. The *Ile de France* was greatly changed from when she had been a luxury liner. All of the wood paneling was covered with plywood and the carpets were all removed. We were in a stateroom which I suppose was designed for two people, but there were fourteen of us in it. We were in bunks piled three high. You had to have your gear in the bunk with you and it was quite crowded, but at least we weren't double bunking like some of the groups. Each of us had a bunk to himself.

Not long after daybreak the next morning the tugs moved us away from the wharf, and we got out in the middle of the Hudson River and started down. We went by the Statue of Liberty and on out past Sandy Hook, and by this time the ship was beginning to pitch and roll a little bit. The *Ile de France* was a fine ship and a fast ship. We traveled without a convoy because she could outrun any submarine, but there were certain things that we had to do because we didn't have a convoy: we had to take evasive action. It was impossible to tell just which way we were going, nor were we allowed to throw anything overboard that might give any clue to our general direction. We knew, of course, that we were going to stage in England, but we didn't have an idea of how we would arrive there, whether we would go around the north of Ireland, or around the south. It was a fast crossing, taking five days. The weather was a little rough but not too bad. It was a tense time because we would have lifeboat drills every day, and we seldom saw any other ships. On the fourth or fifth day some aircraft appeared, and we were greatly relieved to know we were under the protection of the U.S. Army Air Corps, as it was called then, which was stationed in Britain. Before long we saw land ahead of us, and they told us that we were skirting the south end of Ireland and were going up through the Irish Sea and into the Firth of Clyde, where we would dock.

We stayed in England at a place called Feesey Farms, near Birmingham. My stay there was exciting because I had never been in a foreign country before except on short one-day trips across the Mexican and Canadian borders. I was, however, homesick and very concerned about Lucybeth. I knew when the baby was expected in October, but that's about all. There was nothing I could do, and after ten days at Feesey Farms we received our orders to cross the channel.

We went by motor convoy from Birmingham. We skirted London then turned northeast to the channel and spent the night between Hastings and Eastbourne. We visited the site of the Battle of Hastings and also a small cottage which legend says was where Harold spent the night before the battle. Next morning we drove along the channel to Southaby where we boarded a liberty ship for the crossing of the channel. Our vehicles, which were going with us, were placed down in the hold, and we were told to just leave our blankets and gear in the vehicles because we'd only be on the channel for one day.

The only equipment we brought on the ships with us were three K-rations because we were probably going to have to eat three times during the crossing. We were very crowded on the ship. I don't know how many men were on it, but obviously many more than the ship was equipped to handle, as we expected to cross the Channel and disembark on Omaha Beach in the evening. We had plenty of air and naval protection as we crossed the Channel, but as we got near the French coast a heavy storm came up. I think it's the worst storm I've ever seen at sea. The ship pitched and rolled until the deck would almost ship water, so even though we could plainly see the French shore in the early evening (it was probably not more than three or four miles away), we just lay off the shore because there was no way to unload the boat. It stormed for five days as we continued to lie off the coast. Although it was not freezing cold, it was chilly at night without blankets.

Ours was not the only ship standing offshore: there must have been fifty or sixty ships, and several of them were strafed by German planes. The German planes were not numerous because of American and British air superiority at that point, but one ship a mile or two from us struck a mine and sank. It was quite a long time going down, though, and I'm sure the crew got off safely.

On the day before we landed, I hadn't eaten for three days and didn't want to eat most of the time because I was seasick. The crew of the ship had plenty to eat, of course, but there were five hundred men on the ship and only rations for twenty, and the crew had to conserve them. The senior army man aboard the ship was a major, and he ate with the crew. One day I thought, "I just can't stand this any longer." I went up to his room and said, "You've got to get me something to eat out of that galley." He said, "I'll go see what I can do." He came back and said, "I've looked all over and even the crew's supplies are running low. The only thing I can find are dried crusts of bread and some cold mashed potatoes." I told him to go back and make me a mashed potato sandwich. He did, and it was delicious.

On the afternoon of the fifth day the wind went down, and it was decided we would try to put ashore. We were off Omaha Beach. We couldn't go in close, so they put us on landing barges. These barges, or lighters—they were just flat floating platforms—were brought up beside the liberty ship, and there was a big rope net thrown over the side of the ship down which we had to climb to get into the lighter. That was not at all easy to do because the waves were still high and the vertical position of the lighter in relation to the side of the ship would shift ten to fifteen feet every two or three seconds. You had to climb down far enough so that the thing wouldn't come up and hit you, and yet when it came up, you had to take the chance and drop off on the lighter.

Once more I saw that perhaps I had made a mistake in leaving the hospital too early because my foot wouldn't hold me on that rope ladder. We had all our gear on our backs as we went over the side. Climbing down this rope ladder, I had one foot that I couldn't use at all, and had to draw myself up with my arms and move my good foot down. I really didn't know whether I was going to make it, but finally I was able to step off onto the lighter. The lighter took us in towards shore until it struck sand in water that was roughly shoulder deep. We stepped off into the water and went ashore where we were delighted to find that although they couldn't unload our trucks right then, there were other trucks available for us.

The beach was being shelled by German long-distance guns, but I think those guns were ten or fifteen miles inland, as this was ninety days beyond D-Day. We faced no hostile infantry fire. We left the beach immediately in the emergency trucks and drove to the little town of Bayeux, where the Bayeux Tapestry is located in a special building. The tapestry is not really one at all. It is a celebrated embroidered linen (231 feet long and 19½ inches wide) depicting the Norman Conquest of England. Dating from the eleventh century, it has seventy scenes and an accompanying legend in Latin. We had our first real meal in some five and a half days. Although our blankets and bedding were still on the trucks, we did have some personal things and were able to shave and wash. We were glad to be on French soil, and we spent the night near Bayeux.

We were told that our destination was a little town near Le Havre, but as no crossing of the Seine was possible downstream from Rouen, we had to leave Bayeux and go toward Rouen to cross. Our own trucks had been taken off at Bayeux, so we had all our equipment back and were traveling in our own trucks. The first town we came to after Bayeux – which for some reason had been left untouched, maybe because of the tapestry – was Caen, which had been almost destroyed. There was hardly a wall or house left intact. We drove on eastward along the south bank of the Seine. There we saw great quantities of German equipment that had been abandoned on either side of the road.

Major Tomkins, our commanding officer, had studied high school French, and he undertook to question the natives along the way as to how to get to Rouen. We'd pull up to a group, Major Tomkins would laboriously ask for directions, and the French people would stand there with puzzled looks on their faces until he got to the word Rouen, and then they'd light up and say, "Tout droit, tout droit, monsieur." This happened three or four times, and the major was beaming: "Oh, it's just wonderful how my French has come back." Then Captain Heffernan, the executive officer, said, "Let me try that, major." So when we came to the next group Heffernan leaned out the window and said, "Cadillac, walk back, Chevrolet coupe, Rouen," and he got exactly the same response that Tomkins had got: "Oh, Rouen, tout droit, monsieur." But we did get there, although it was slow going. I would say the distance from Bayeux to Rouen is not more than about seventy miles, but it took us all day to make it. That night we were assigned by the military government to a big abandoned house, where we just put our sleeping bags on the floor. There was a local unit with which we were able to eat.

Next morning we went on through Rouen and back west along the north bank of the river to Le Havre, but we didn't stop there. The city was too badly bombed, particularly the port area. Instead we traveled north along the coast for twenty or twenty-five miles to Etretat, which is a beautiful little resort town on a quiet harbor. It had been the home of two French writers: both de Maupassant and Flaubert had lived part of their lives at Etretat. On the beach there was an overturned rowboat, sort of a monument to de Maupassant. There was a statement of de Maupassant's on a plaque on the boat that said, "If I had a friend who'd never seen the sea, I would like to show it to him first at Etretat."

Our smaller group of claims officers joined up with a larger group under the command of a Colonel Parris at Etretat. We were quartered in a French hotel and got two or three days' rest. I was then assigned to take a detachment of four officers and an equal number of enlisted men and open a temporary claims office in Le Havre.

Army claims were considered on the following basis: we did not pay our allies for combat damage that we caused, but if damage or injury occurred for reasons other than combat, then we did pay compensation. We were processing claims not only against the United States but against England too. The Germans had occupied Le Havre for a long time under American and English bombardment. The Germans pulled out and went north, and the next day when the American bombers came over, the people of Le Havre flooded into the streets and waved greetings to the Americans. The Germans were gone; liberation was here. But the American bombers didn't know that the Germans had gone, and they unloaded on the city. Some people were saying that there were as many as ten thousand civilians killed in that bombing raid, and claims were thus being presented.

All of this was happening while I was becoming more and more concerned about what was happening at home, because I felt sure as we got into mid- and late October that the new baby would have arrived, but I wasn't getting any mail. As I later found out, Janet was born on October 20, 1944. The first letter that I received from home arrived on my birthday, November 6, announcing her birth. It had been since August that I had had any real communication with home, and I was delighted to get this letter. Lucybeth had sent me many letters and cablegrams about the baby's birth, but they never got through. However, for the rest of the time I was in Europe, except for a brief period when we moved quite a distance, the mail came through regularly.

In early December claims team number fourteen left Etretat as its principal base and moved to Rouen. I stayed in Le Havre for a few days and then was told to take my detachment on east of Rouen to Beauvais. Beauvais is forty or fifty miles north and slightly west of Paris, on a tributary of the Oise River. It has a large, old cathedral—not particularly beautiful outside, but marvelous inside. Again I arranged for a house and interpreters through the appropriate army authorities, and we commenced the processing of claims in Beauvais.

Driving from Beauvais one day investigating a claim, I passed by an army unit that was stopped and out of their motor vehicles. Suddenly, by the side of the road, I saw Max. This was his battalion, and they were moving up toward the Battle of the Bulge. I told him where I was in Beauvais as well as I could, and two or three days later he came back and spent an evening with me. We drank champagne, wrote letters home, sang old Davis High songs, and had a really good reunion until about two in the morning, when Max had to leave to rejoin his unit.

We were some distance from the actual fighting in Beauvais—about one hundred and seventy-five miles—on a direct line between the English and American airports and the Battle of the Bulge. As the Christmas season approached, the weather was very foggy, and this helped the Germans because it either grounded or made ineffective the American air attacks. I remember the first clear day: it was just a day or two before Christmas, and the American daylight bombers came over. That really spelled the effective end of the German push, because since the Americans and British had air supremacy, they were able to stop the German ground attack.

The day before Christmas I drove from Beauvais to Rouen and stayed there Christmas Eve. That night we went to a service in the old Rouen cathedral, which is large and bleak. It had been damaged by bombing earlier, so the windows were out. It was a cold night and the wind was blowing, but still it was a very moving service. A chorus of U.S. Army nurses sang that night, and I'll never forget how touched we were by it all.

About this time we had a rather scary experience. There was a small airfield near Beauvais, and as the Battle of the Bulge was winding down after Christmas the Germans, attempting to get the drive started again, bombed the airfield and also dropped a great number of parachutists around the area. Therefore, we all had to answer with passwords when we were stopped at the various checkpoints. I was with a group that did capture one of the parachutists. He was a very young man, and it didn't require any particular aggressiveness to capture him; he was pretty well ready to give up.

I think the most danger I was in during that alert was from an American army sentry. He stopped me at a checkpoint and asked me for the password, but I couldn't remember it. He brought his gun up and said, "What's Blondie's husband's name?" I thought for a minute and I drew a blank. I said, "I can't remember, but he eats those big sandwiches." The sentry laughed and said, "Okay, you'll do," and allowed me to pass.

At the end of January both our Beauvais office and the Rouen office were ordered closed. The whole claims team was being moved north to Holland, and as we went eastward through Belgium and Holland, we got into an area of intense combat damage. In particular Louvain, a Belgian town that I am sure had once been very pretty, had sustained heavy combat damage. I recalled from World War I history that Louvain had been badly damaged and fought over then, so those people had had it twice in a little more than a generation.

As we moved eastward, we came closer and closer to the combat zone. We were headed for Eindhoven, which is thirty or forty miles from the Rhine, where the principal fighting was going on. The Germans, of course, were attempting to harass the Allied forces by air and other means. They couldn't do much about it because of Allied air superiority, but they were strafing and we had to leave our automobiles a number of times. The roads were bad. Most of them had been brick surfaced, and they didn't have much of a base beneath them. The heavy tanks going over them had mixed the mud and the bricks up so the roads looked like fudge with nuts being beaten in a bowl. Although we did not get strafed, we did have a close call. Just about evening we heard a German V-1 bomb coming. V-1s were the first missile bombs. They ran almost like airplanes, with wings and little jet motors, and they made a putt-putt sound. As soon as we heard it we stopped the cars because we wanted to be able to get out if it was aimed near us. As it got about over us, we heard the motor start missing and then cut out entirely. Suddenly the thing dived through the overcast, and it appeared to be headed right at us. We barely had time to get under the vehicles. That may not have been a good idea had it been a direct hit, but fortunately it hit about one hundred yards away from where we were.

We were able to get on into Eindhoven, where the military had arranged quarters for us. We had our meals in a hotel downtown, and the officers of our group were scattered around in various homes. I was in the home of a Dutch citizen named Hart, a much younger half-brother of William S. Hart, the cowboy movie star who had come to the United States many years previously.

Eindhoven was an Allied command post. Canadians, English, and Americans all had units there. While I was there Eisenhower, Churchill, and Montgomery visited the area, checking on the progress of the attempts being made to cross the Rhine near Nijmegen. One evening we were in a small room in the hotel that served as an officers' club. It was very noisy; the officers were drinking and singing. Eisenhower and Montgomery came in. Immediately the English officers came to attention and ceased whatever they were doing, but the Americans kept right on with their singing and drinking. They were not nearly as impressed with Eisenhower's presence as the English appeared to be with Montgomery's.

The following day at noon, Montgomery's pilot had lunch with us. He was American and had been a pilot for Montgomery for a long period of time. We talked to him about the Allied military leaders with whom he had had an opportunity to get acquainted. It was evident that he didn't like Montgomery a great deal. He indicated that in his opinion the African campaign had been planned and executed principally by Alexander and Tedder, rather than Montgomery. He did like Eisenhower, and he knew and liked Bradley very much.

I was next told to take my detachment of four or five officers and enlisted men up near the front to Veghel, a town of ten or twelve thousand. It was the town where the 101st Airborne had landed. Paratroopers don't take very much with them when they drop, and they have to live mostly off the land. Upon landing in Veghel, they had gone out and taken what they needed. This informal requisitioning came within the purview of our claims service. We opened our office in a room in the school. It seemed strange to me that school would still be going when that town had been fought over only three or four weeks before, but nonetheless school was in session.

The claims in Veghel were settled fairly quickly because they all fell into much the same pattern. We knew what kinds of things the soldiers would have taken. We were not as restrictive in our demands for evidence as we ordinarily would be because we were sure that the claims there were substantial and valid. The fighting was heavy in the nearby towns of 's Hertogenbosch, Grave, and Nijmegen. During the three or four weeks we were in Veghel, it was about ten or fifteen miles from us, and we could hear the big guns clearly. I was always a bit worried because we had no liaison with the British there, and we wouldn't know about a German advance until it overran the town. Fortunately, that didn't happen.

The town was bombed almost nightly, not with big bombs, but with little stick bombs. The family with whom I lived would go into the bomb shelter every night because they had had a very difficult experience when the Germans pulled out three or four weeks before. A German soldier had taken refuge in their cellar. The woman's husband was away in the army, and she was there with the children and had tried to conceal his presence; but either she told an English officer that the German was there or the English officer surmised it, and he started down the stairway. The German and the Englishman had a gun battle on the basement steps, and the German was shot and killed. Of course the children were there and saw it, and they were pretty well shaken up.

Our time in Veghel coincided with the real turning point in the war. The Germans had been turned back a month previously in the Battle of the Bulge. The bridge at Remagen had been captured intact, and the German effort was winding down. Near the end of March I received orders to close the Veghel office. Our whole claims unit was ordered to move southward into the Limburg Province, with the main headquarters to be set up at the town of Maastricht.

After a few days there I was told to take the detachment to Heerlen, which is a town only about five miles from the German border and ten or fifteen miles from Aachen. Aachen had held out against the Allied advance for a considerable period of time. We went over there a day or two after I got set up in Heerlen, and from a distance the town looked like it was not damaged at all because it had not been bombarded from the air. Rather, the Allied artillery, with guns of up to 105 mm, stayed outside the town and went up one street and down the other putting artillery shells into these buildings. They'd been gutted but not blown down. When I got there the Germans had been gone from the city for about three days. The streets were deserted, and we wondered if everybody had been killed. We were the first American troops to come in after the combat troops had moved through and left sort of a vacuum. We had to go over there almost every day, and pretty soon the people started coming out of the basements. It was evident that the surviving population was living underground. While I'm sure there were many civilian casualties, the entire population was by no means destroyed. Years later, in 1985, we took a bus tour of the Balkans. Horst, our tour leader, said he was from Aachen. When I told him this story about the shelled city, he said, "I was one of the children who came out of the basements."

By now the Allies had crossed the Rhine at several points, and it was evident that within a few weeks the war was going to be over. There were troops that had been in constant contact with the enemy for ninety days or more, and so various places were set up back of the combat lines for rest and recreation. One of these was a hotel in Heerlen where we ate at the officers' mess. We had rented a house nearby for quarters and offices. Many American officers came back to the hotel for a few days' rest. While there I saw quite a number of people that I'd known from Utah, including Dick Woolslayer and Morris Guss, and one day who should show up but Max. He stayed there for about four days.

The time we spent in Heerlen was enjoyable because the war pressures were off. Our claims load wasn't big, and we figured we would get out of there before long. We therefore decided just to take it easy, and it was almost like rest and recreation for us. About a week after I got to Heerlen, word came through that I'd been promoted to major. I had been down for an interview with a General Jacobs sometime before that, but I didn't know whether I was going to get promoted. First, Jacobs didn't seem very enthusiastic about me, and second, there was a rumor going about that because of the imminent end of hostilities, all ranks were to be frozen. My promotion to major did come through, however, and two or three days afterwards they decided to have a big party in the hotel at Maastricht with the whole claims team. Colonel Parris, the commandant of the claims service of Europe, came up and it was quite a wild evening.

Another memorable incident occurred there in Maastricht after the south of Holland had been liberated for a few weeks. During the occupation these Dutch people had had almost nothing to eat. They ate tulip bulbs and things like that, and even after the liberation of the south, those around Maastricht didn't have much food. At that time the only military units in the area were our claims unit, which consisted of thirty or forty people, and the 29th Attack Aviation Group, which had over a thousand. The aviation group moved out suddenly, but apparently the quartermaster down at Rheims didn't get the word, and rations kept coming through for one thousand people. Of course we called immediately and told them to stop and asked what we should do with the extra rations we had. They said, "Ship the staples back and the perishables you'll have to use as you see fit." I wasn't sure whether a frozen side of beef was a staple or a perishable, but we interpreted it as a perishable. We had six or eight frozen halves of beef, which we put in a big locker at the hotel. We decided to have a celebration and told the burgomeister that if he could get enough flour to make bread, we would have a barbecue with this beef. The burgomeister found the flour, and we served around ten thousand sandwiches. It was really quite a sight to see those people. I think some of those ten- or twelve-year-old children could not remember eating meat before.

We were shocked shortly after this celebration to hear the news of President Roosevelt's death. Although our spirits had been high because we knew we were winning the war, this almost seemed like losing a battle. But as bad as the American soldiers felt, the Dutch people seemed to feel worse. They would come up to American soldiers on the street and tell them how sorry they were, with tears in their eyes, as if the person who was dead had been a member of the American's family. Naturally our claims office was well known in the town as an American military office, and the Dutch people brought in bouquets of flowers because they did not see how the war was going to go on without Roosevelt. They thought that this might make a great change in the course of things. As far as the soldiers went, Truman was pretty much an unknown, but we had confidence in the continuity of our government which the Dutch people didn't have.

Then came V-E Day: the Germans surrendered. The Dutch had been on an orgy of celebration because of their liberation, followed by a period of mourning for Roosevelt's death, and they started in on a second round of celebration for the end of the war. I thought they had brought every bottle of schnapps out from every haystack in the area when they celebrated the liberation of Holland, but they found more for V-E Day, and it was a great celebration.

Around the first of June 1945, I was informed that because I had been promoted to major, I had too high a rank for the command of the small detachment. There was no spot for me to fill in the claims team headquarters, so I was told that I was being transferred from the administrative to the judicial side of the claims service, and was being sent down to Rheims as a member of a three-man claims commission.

When I got to Rheims I found that there was a big backlog of cases, and the other two men who were to be assigned to this particular claims team hadn't yet arrived. I started in on the claims and had quite a lot of them analyzed by the time the other men got there, fortunately, because neither of them stayed long. During the month and a half that I was at Rheims we almost needed a revolving door for the number of officers that came and went. While in Rheims I was officed for a time in a chateau that had been the property of the Baron Mumms, the producer of Mumms champagne. Baron Mumms, although a French citizen, was of German descent, and after the Allies liberated Paris he was arrested as a collaborator, which left his chateau vacant.

The thing I enjoyed most about my two months in Rheims was that most of the time Max was at the redeployment camp at Troyes. His unit was waiting to be shipped back to the United States. The thing we talked about most was that after we got back to the United States we were going to have to go on to Japan and fight the war there. Then one night while Max and I were at a restaurant in Paris, the news came of the dropping of the atomic bomb. We were skeptical about the bomb because much more was claimed for it than we could believe was true. But when the dropping of the two bombs forced

Japan out of the war within just a few days, we knew that the power of the bomb had been understated rather than overstated.

About the first of September, I received orders to go to Nancy to be a claims commissioner with a claims team that was still operating. I was in Nancy for a little less than a month. Near the end of September came orders for me to leave Nancy and go to Paris to be a member of the senior claims commission, which considered claims between $2,500 and $5,000. The commission also made recommendations to the Congress concerning claims that couldn't be settled under the $5,000 level.

When I arrived in Paris around the first of October, the entire claims group was located in Versailles, at 9 rue Reservoir. It was a suitable office building just outside the front gate of the palace. As I understand, it had been quarters and offices for the palace retainers. The palace was just to the west of us, and to the east were the big stables. I was quartered in a large and elegant house that had been built by the Rothschild family between the two world wars. When the Pétain government was in power, it had been the presidential palace. Then Eisenhower had used it as his headquarters for a period of time, and now that Eisenhower was gone, it was used for officers' quarters.

The Senior Claims Commission was made up of myself, Scrubby Reeves, whom I had known at officers' school at Ann Arbor, and a full colonel named Hart, who was on leave as chief clerk to the court of claims. The workload was very heavy. For a long time, this three-man commission had consisted of Colonel Hart, Colonel Reeves, and a General Max Traurig. It had little to do because the larger claims had taken a while to work their way up through channels. Now, however, the work at the lower commissions was beginning to fall off, and the claims of which the larger commission had jurisdiction were just hitting their peak. In one month we processed about one hundred and twenty claims. When you got up to this level, you had to write an opinion on each claim. The opinions followed a standard form, but you had to be as careful in your research and judgment as you would be if you were writing a decision for an appellate court.

Many interesting claims came to me. I've even kept a book of the decisions we wrote. Some of the claims took me to interesting places outside of Paris to investigate. One was a multimillion-dollar damage claim from the crystal factories at Baccarat. Fairly late in the war, probably in January 1945, American troops had come up through Baccarat; they went into the crystal factories and walked along with their bayonets, deliberately pushing priceless crystal onto the floor and breaking it. This left a bad taste in people's mouths because the Germans had been there for a long period and nothing like this had happened. Why it happened, I don't know, but it did happen because I personally interviewed a substantial number of witnesses. The claim was for about $2.5 million. Obviously it was far beyond the jurisdiction of our commission, but we had to make a recommendation to Congress, and I wanted to substantiate the claim. I went down with the concurrence of my two fellow commissioners and got supplemental statements from witnesses. We decided they probably were overvaluing the claim, but still there was no question that the damage was done by American soldiers.

Sometime in November we moved our offices from Versailles into the old Majestic Hotel in Paris. It was on Avenue Klebert, maybe two hundred yards from the Arc de Triomphe. By this time all officers and men who could get home were going home. Those who had been there longest got home first. We had a point system. You got so many points depending on how long you'd been there, and so many points for each dependent you had, and after you reached a certain number of points you could be rotated home. The work continued to be quite heavy, but it was work that I enjoyed. All considered it was quite a good time.

However, even though the Paris life was all right, by Christmas 1945 I was ready to go home, and I began pushing—my point total was getting up to a level where I was eligible. The government didn't want me to go until I finished all the claims, but it was obvious that the work would go on for three or four months. I did get an offer from the army to send me home for a month and then bring me back. I mentioned that in a letter to Lucybeth, and she didn't react at all favorably, so I continued to push just as hard as I could to be sent back to the United States permanently. Finally, about January 20, I received orders to report to a redeployment camp called Lucky Strike near Le Havre.

I took a train out of the Gare du Nord and went up to the camp. Some of us got there a little too soon and were around the camp for about five days before our boat came for us. The boat was called the *Andrew W. Soule*. It was a liberty ship converted to a troopship. This ship had one problem: it had been rammed by a destroyer a little while before in the Mediterranean, and all they'd done in dry dock was to put a big cement block in the rather sizable hole in the bow. It had not given any particular trouble up to that time, but it was to cause us considerable trouble on the way home. We boarded this ship around February 1 in Le Havre.

We had been at sea only two or three days when the weather turned bad. We ran into terrific storms that had the ship pitching and rolling so badly that the bow would go under with each pitch. The captain of the ship came to me, as the senior army officer aboard, and said, "We've got a problem. I don't want this to get around, but come with me and I will show you the situation." The cement block filling the gash in the bow had split. The split was no wider than a pencil lead, but every time the bow went under a wall of water would squirt through that crack. The problem facing the captain and me was to decide whether to turn back to a British port or to see if some kind of an escort could be put together from among other ships then on the Atlantic. The pumps on our ship were able to handle twice the amount of water coming through the crack at that time; what concerned us was the likelihood of the split widening if the storm continued.

We chose to pass the word to other ships to keep in touch with us. We were slower than the regular troopships, which passed and mothered us all the rest of the way. The storm died out, and the last three days of our crossing were in good weather.

After nine days we approached the American coastline. I'm not sure just how we came in because we were told that the first thing we could see was Long Island. We came south for some distance until we could see Sandy Hook. Then we came up the Hudson into New York harbor, and all of us were on deck waiting eagerly to see the Statue of Liberty. It was a thrill to be home again. I'd been gone almost a year and a half, and some of the men on the ship had been gone much longer. We pulled into one of the berths on the Hudson—I think around Forty-fifth Street. We disembarked and walked down the gangplank. The Gray Ladies were there to give us what we wanted in the way of coffee, lemonade, and so on, but almost everyone asked for milk. We hadn't had any fresh milk for a year and a half. We'd had the powdered milk that you could whip up, but it was not very good.

It took three or four days before I was free to go to Washington because they had told me that they were going to send me to

Fort Douglas in Salt Lake City to be discharged. I told them I didn't want that because Lucybeth was in Washington. It's awfully hard to break up army routine, but finally they agreed that I could be debriefed and discharged from Fort Meyer, Virginia. I took a train down to Fort Meyer and the discharge took only a day. I then caught a taxi, and Lucybeth was waiting for me with Meg and the new baby, Janet, at 1730 Crestwood Drive. That day in February 1946 was the first time we'd seen each other since August 1944.

Although I had been discharged from the army, I had a fair amount of terminal leave. I didn't have to get right back to work, but I really wanted to. We decided that we wouldn't drive our car out west at that time, although Lucybeth still had the Pontiac we'd bought just before the war. We took the train to Salt Lake, and I went back later and got the car. The train ride gave me a chance to get to know the children. I think Meg resented me a little at first; this new member of the family was doing a considerable amount to dilute her position. Janet, of course, wasn't old enough to feel that way, and we got along very well.

When we got back to Salt Lake I took a few more days off, and then told Grover Giles that I would like to come back into the attorney general's office. He said that he had been holding a job for me. A man named George Ross, who had taken the job while I was away, knew it was a temporary job, and so I moved back into the office and took up where I'd left off three years before.

Billie Rich, wife of Max Rich, with Calvin and Lucybeth
at the Ramptons' first residence in Bountiful.

At the Federal Heights Apartments on South Temple Street. Left to right,
Jeff Haley, Nell Haley, Irene Callister, Ruth Rampton, Calvin's
mother, Calvin holding daughter Meg, Virginia in front, and Lucybeth.

The graduates from the University of Utah Law School.
Rampton is fifth from the right.

Calvin L. Rampton as an Army officer in World War II. His principal service was in the Judge Advocate General's Corps.

CHAPTER THREE

PRACTICING: LAW, FAMILY, AND COMMUNITY

I t wasn't simple picking up the threads of civilian life again. When you are in the army, you lead a very disciplined life: food and clothing are furnished for you; you have specific tasks to do; and you get used to living alone, outside of the family environment. I, along with most other soldiers who returned, underwent a period of adjustment. This was a hard time for Lucybeth as well because she sensed I was having trouble readjusting. Fortunately, this period didn't go on long. By the end of three or four months I was pretty well acclimated to civilian life again.

Immediately after returning to Salt Lake we had to have a place to stay, but there was no available housing in the whole city. In the summer of 1946, we saw an advertisement for houses that had been built by the government in Dragerton (now East Carbon City), Utah, to house coal miners. The war ended before they were used, and the government was offering them for sale with the provision that they had to be hauled away. We took a trip out to Dragerton and saw the houses. They were little square frame places, but we decided that one would do for a while. We looked around Salt Lake for a lot on which we could put a house, and we found what we were looking for on University Street, a little half street between Sixth and Seventh South across from Mt. Olivet Cemetery.

We bought this lot and dug a basement for the house. We had to cut the house in two pieces to bring it in from Dragerton. It wouldn't go through Price Canyon because of a highway tunnel, so we had to take it up Indian Canyon to Duchesne, and then bring it down to Salt Lake. But we finally got it into town and put it on the foundation, repaired it, and built another room onto the front so that we had a living room, a dining room, a kitchen, two bedrooms, a bath, and, of course, the basement. All told, including the lot, we had invested around $5,000 in the place. While we were living in that house, Tony was born, Meg started school, and we enjoyed a pleasant existence.

At the same time, midsummer 1946, I went into a law partnership with Zar Hayes and Harry Pugsley, both of whom had worked in the attorney general's office. This partnership would continue until 1964, when I was elected governor. We opened up offices on the seventh floor of the Continental Bank Building and, at first, the practice was slow in building. Although Harry and Zar had remained in Salt Lake during the war years and their legal work went uninterrupted, we had few clients. However, it wasn't long before we knew we'd make it all right, as a variety of cases came in. Zar and I were still in the attorney general's office, but both of us were able to spend a part of each day at our downtown office as well. I continued to be an assistant attorney general until mid-1948, when I resigned to devote full time to the law practice. As I recall, Zar stayed in the attorney general's office about the same length of time that I did, while Harry worked full time at the law office from the beginning.

I retained an active interest in politics and ran for the state senate in Salt Lake County on two separate occasions – in 1948 and 1952. On both occasions I won the Democratic nomination but lost in the election. Although I spent substantial time on politics, I was never elected to a political office during the years between coming out of the army and 1964.

After living in the little Dragerton house for about two years, we decided that we needed more room. There were now three children, and we needed separate bedrooms for the two girls and for Tony, so we started looking for a lot where we could build a house that would meet our needs. We eventually purchased one just west of the Salt Lake Country Club and built on it.

The law practice continued to develop and to do well. During the time I was in the attorney general's office after the war, I was assigned to work with the Public Service Commission. In this position I became acquainted with the factors affecting utilities law. There weren't many attorneys in the state at that time, except those who were employed directly by utilities companies, who had any great familiarity with utilities law; so when I left the attorney general's office in 1948, I was approached by a group of Salt Lake businessmen who called themselves the Utah Citizens Rate Association. A man named

Harold Ellsworth, who until his recent death remained a good friend over all the years, was the executive officer.

The chairman of the group was Morris Rosenblatt, who was also to be a real friend and who helped my practice grow. I had an experience with Morris like none I've had with anybody else. About 1949 I took a case for the Rosenblatts against Utah Power and Light, which was trying to raise the rates on its electric furnace at American Foundry and Machinery Company. I was successful in holding down the raise to a reasonable figure, and so I felt I had done a good job. I wasn't quite sure how I should bill for this job, though, because it was a bigger case than I had generally handled. Initially, I thought I'd bill them a hundred dollars a day, but on reconsideration I felt that wasn't enough because I did a good job for them. Therefore, while one hundred dollars a day was pretty standard for Salt Lake at that time, I billed them one hundred and fifty dollars a day—$1500 for the ten days I'd worked on the case. The unique part of the experience came shortly after, however, when I received a check from Morris for $2500 and a note saying that I had to revalue my services—that I should not sell them too cheaply. I think that's the only time such a thing has happened to me during my practice.

Through my relationship with the Utah Citizens Rate Association also came many cases involving railroad rates. The members of the association were from businesses in the Salt Lake area that shipped extensively by railroad, and my job generally was to appear before the Utah Public Service Commission or the Interstate Commerce Commission and try to hold down the rates as much as I could. One of these cases was a famous railroad rate case called *Ex parte 175*, which stretched over several months and required my being in Washington intermittently for a week or more at a time.

These cases of the Utah Citizens Rate Association attracted public attention and resulted in my being offered positions in some of the large law firms in Salt Lake City. Around 1950, I received an offer from Marr VanCott to go into his firm. Although I liked Mr. VanCott, I thought he would be something of a martinet, so I discussed the matter over lunch with Dennis McCarthy, one of Marr's junior partners and a friend of mine. Dennis admitted that Marr was a little hard to work with, and I decided I did not want that. I was more tempted when Will Ray offered me an opportunity to come into his firm. This was the firm I was ultimately to join after leaving the governorship, but at the time I decided against that move as well. Nor did I want to become attorney for the Union Pacific Railroad in Salt Lake, an offer which I received at about the same time. In the end I decided that I had done well with my two associates and that I should stay with them. We brought in a young lawyer at about this time named David Watkiss, moved our offices from the Continental Bank Building to the El Paso Building, and after two or three years added his name to the firm title of Pugsley, Hayes, and Rampton.

During the years immediately after the war, while I was still in the attorney general's office, I had a series of encounters with a person who would be involved with me in various matters over a long period of time—who still is, as a matter of fact. I refer to J. Bracken Lee, one of the most colorful political figures in Utah history.

I had not known Mr. Lee prior to the war, although I knew that he was the mayor of Price, a town that had a considerable amount of illegal activity, especially in liquor and gambling. These activities were prohibited by state law, but were countenanced by the administration in Price even though bitterly opposed by some of its citizens. By the time I returned from army service, Mayor Lee was becoming a figure on the state political scene. During the war he had made two unsuccessful runs for higher office. He secured the Republican nomination for congressman from the First District and lost narrowly to Walter Granger, probably in 1942. Then in 1944, he won the Republican nomination for governor. Governor Maw was running for his second term that year, and it was a bitterly fought campaign with charges being thrown on both sides, some of them libelous. One of the turning points in the campaign came with the circulation of a pamphlet called *Morals and the Mayor*, which was written by Francis Kirkham. Although I was not in Salt Lake for that campaign, I have studied it since and read copies of the brochures. *Morals and the Mayor* charged that Mayor Lee was running Price in an open fashion in defiance of the law and, although charging no dishonesty, it made broad hints of corruption in government. Whether this was the decisive factor in the campaign I do not know, but Governor Maw won a second term over Mayor Lee by a margin of two or three thousand votes.

There then ensued a sort of running feud between the administration of Mayor Lee in Price and the state administration in

Salt Lake. Liquor control officers raided a private club in Price and took possession of some premises in which Mayor Lee's brother had an ownership interest. While the state liquor control officers were in the club the Price city police, under the direction of Mayor Lee, demanded entrance and charged the state liquor enforcement officers with illegal entry. One of the state liquor enforcement officers was a man named Chester Dowse, whom I'd known for many years. Chester was a very emotional sort of guy, and he told them to get out of there. There followed a physical fight between the Price officers and the state liquor control officers, and it resulted in the state officers being arrested by the Price city police. Chester Dowse was beaten about the head. This happened when I was still in the service, but almost immediately after I got back a group of citizens from Price who didn't like the way things were going there, particularly in regard to gambling, called on Attorney General Grover Giles and demanded that he intervene in Price and prosecute all violators of the gambling and liquor laws.

It was well known that many of the businesses in Price had slot machines. These were not only in bars but in grocery stores and other businesses as well. The ire of the local citizens was principally directed against these slot machines, so Grover told his assistants, Zar Hayes, Art Miner, and me, to go out to Price and seize them. Knowing from what had happened previously that we could not expect much help from the Price city police or the Carbon County sheriff, we determined where the slot machines were located, and then went to District Judge Fred Keller for search warrants. Fred Keller, a fine judge and a man I loved and admired, was philosophical about it. He said, "Well, I guess it's against the law. I have to issue the search warrants. You're going to have trouble serving them, but I wish you well. Come back here when it's over and tell me about it."

We got the search warrants and then called in all the highway patrolmen in that part of the state. The warrants were served quickly. There were twenty or twenty-five violators served, and we hauled the slot machines out of their places and onto the sidewalk near the curb while we waited for our truck to come by and pick them up. Standing on the main street of Price, you could look the full length of the street, and it was lined with slot machines on both sides. We then placed the machines in the sheriff's evidence storeroom. The machines almost entirely filled a room about twenty feet square.

We finished this work during the morning, and then Zar and I went to a place in Price to get something to eat. They refused to serve us. We thought we'd better report back to Judge Keller to tell him what happened. He was amused at the whole incident and particularly at the fact that this restaurant had refused to serve us. He said, "I don't know that you're going to do any better in any of the other restaurants, so I better call my wife and tell her I'm bringing you fellows home to lunch."

One mistake we had made in storing the machines was to not use our own padlock on the door to the sheriff's evidence room. It just had the sheriff's lock on it and it was his key. When we went back two or three weeks later to get an order from the court to break up these slot machines, all of them were still there, but there was not a penny in any of them. They had all been opened and the money removed. We did get the order from Judge Keller to destroy the machines, though, as I recall, the old ones were destroyed while some of the better ones were sold in the state of Nevada.

This didn't end the feud, however. It wasn't more than just a few months later when a highway patrol trooper named Joe Arnold was taking the victim of an automobile accident from the scene of the accident to the Price hospital. He wasn't a critically injured victim, but he was bleeding and needed emergency attention. Arnold was observed going through the streets of Price in excess of the speed limit by Mayor Lee himself, and Lee had the Price city police arrest Arnold for speeding. He was charged with this offense in the city court in Price, and Grover told me that I had to go out and defend the officer.

I was a little concerned about the venue of the case. The Price city judge was a man named Sweetring. He had been appointed by Mayor Lee, and while he had a good reputation as an attorney, I wasn't quite sure how well I'd fare in his courtroom. I did give some thought to seeking a change of venue, but in view of the fact that it was a Price city ordinance and not a state law that Arnold was accused of violating, I decided that I would probably not get the change of venue and would only further alienate Judge Sweetring—if I could get a fair trial before him in the first place.

We went to trial before the judge, and the principal witness for the prosecution was Mayor Lee himself. He took the stand and testified that he had observed trooper Arnold driving his car through the streets of Price at a speed substantially in excess of that allowed by city ordinance. I undertook to cross-examine Mayor Lee, and it was a vigorous cross-examination, a thing to which Mayor Lee didn't take kindly. It went on for an hour or more, with both of us getting a little intemperate in our statements. We were constantly warned by Judge Sweetring that we had to get this personal vendetta out of the case and get down to the facts.

After the city rested its case, I moved for a dismissal, which Judge Sweetring granted. That infuriated the mayor. As soon as court was out, he accosted me in the hallway of the city building, and we came very near to blows. He first said he wanted to go out behind and whip me. I was younger than Lee and somewhat larger, but he looked pretty tough. I wasn't really enthusiastic about the thing, but I couldn't see what else I could do, so I said, "All right, let's go." And then his dignity reasserted itself, and we got along without a physical encounter. He has a remarkable facility, however, for forgetting quickly and working with people. Although we've discussed that occasion and laughed about it over the subsequent years, I don't think it colored our relationship.

The 1946 election year brought with it a sad situation as far as I was concerned. Will Robinson had been in the Congress since 1932. He had been elected to seven terms, which is longer than any congressman from Utah had ever served before or has served since. He was challenged many times for the Democratic nomination, but these were the New Deal and the post-New Deal years, and Democrats everywhere had done well.

I don't recall whether Mr. Robinson had primary opposition in 1946, but I'm inclined to think he did not. The Republican nominee that year was William A. Dawson, who had once defeated me in an election for the state senate, and Mr. Robinson was a heavy favorite to win reelection. Abe Murdock was also favored to win his reelection bid for the Senate. Abe left the House in 1940, had been elected to the Senate, and was now coming up for a second term. Abe's opponent for the Senate spot was a little-known state district judge from Utah County named Arthur V. Watkins. Finally, Walter Granger, who had succeeded Murdock in the House for the First District, was being challenged for the seat by a man named Douglas Stringfellow. It appeared to all of us—and I think justifiably so—that this was going to be another Democratic year. But we misjudged the rumblings across the country. Whether we could have improved matters by harder campaigning, I really don't know; but early in the afternoon of the election, as we began to get reports from eastern states, it was obvious that there was a strong trend away from the Democrats. By late afternoon, before our polls were even closed, I was very worried about what was going to happen to Will Robinson, Abe Murdock, and Walter Granger.

The fears that I felt that afternoon were justified because when the votes started coming in from Utah shortly after the polls were closed, it was evident that there was a definite swing to the conservative side—the Republican side—not only across the country, but in the state of Utah as well. Granger, Murdock, and Robinson were all defeated. A Republican Congress was elected for the first time in many years. This was the famous, or infamous, Eightieth Congress, Harry Truman's whipping boy which he labeled the "do nothing Congress" when he ran for election in 1948.

By the time the 1948 election came along, the Maw administration was also in poor standing. The leaders of the Democratic party could see that Governor Maw was going to have a difficult time being elected to a third term, and a number of people filed for the Democratic nomination for governor that year. Of course Governor Maw himself filed, as did my boss, Attorney General Grover Giles. Another candidate was John Boyden, my friend of long standing with whom I had been associated in law practice before I entered the service. Other candidates were David Trevithick, who at that time was a teacher well known in the Democratic party and who would later become postmaster of Salt Lake City, and Rulon White of Ogden, who was the speaker of the house of representatives.

This primary election forced me to make a difficult decision. I really wanted to support Boyden because I felt that he was better qualified than Grover to be governor. However, Grover had employed me for a number of years, and although I was no longer working for him when the campaign came along, I felt that I had an obligation to him and should support him for the position. This resulted in an estrangement between John and me which lasted for eight years. In any event, Governor Maw did win the Democratic nomination, but even though Harry Truman carried Utah against Dewey by a small margin, Mayor Lee defeated Herbert Maw for the governorship.

After I left the attorney general's office in 1948 and began working in my law partnership full time, my practice grew both in terms of quantity and quality. I was getting more work from which I could command a sufficient fee, so we were doing reasonably well financially. Also, the family was growing. Tony had been born in the little Dragerton house in 1947, and five years later, after we moved into the house where we now live on Twenty-third East, our last child, Vince, was born. His birth was on April 29, 1952. I remember the night particularly well because that was when the big flood occurred in Salt Lake. I had taken Lucybeth to the hospital because she was having labor pains. When I got there the doctor told me the baby would certainly come that night, but not for several hours, and I should get out of there in the meantime. About eleven o'clock I drove down to Thirteenth South, where the whole street had been sandbagged off on both sides to the height of about three feet. Thirteenth South from about Thirteenth East to the Jordan River was a torrent of water.

I kept an active interest in politics, and sometime prior to 1952 I ran for the position of state chairman of the Democratic party and was defeated. In 1952 I ran for the position of national committeeman and was defeated again. However, I was the chairman of the Utah delegation to the Democratic National Convention that year, and I had the delightful experience of getting to know Averell Harriman. Harriman was then and continued to be one of my favorite people in the world. He came out to visit the Utah delegation, and most of us immediately took to him. We had visits that year from quite a number of other prospective presidential candidates, too. Richard Russell, the senator from Georgia, came out and met with us, as did Estes Kefauver, although Kefauver really was not expected to do well that year. In the early going, Adlai Stevenson had not been mentioned at all. In fact, he came on the scene just before the Chicago convention and, with the help of the Chicago newspapers, was able to stampede the convention – something I didn't like at that time, although Stevenson turned out to be a fine man. But almost all of the Utah delegation were for Averell Harriman, and I decided that, in addition to being the chairman of the Utah delegation, I would be the Utah chairman for Harriman.

One experience Lucybeth and I love to recall is of the time Harriman came out to visit us, and we wanted to take him to a function where there would be a great many people present. This was in the fall of 1951, and because it was deer hunting season it was hard to assemble a crowd anywhere. However, an annual celebration called the Uintah Basin Industrial Convention was going on in Vernal, and we decided Averell could get more exposure riding in the parade there than by going anywhere else.

Averell even then had a hearing problem, although he heard a great deal more than you thought he was hearing. As we were waiting for the parade to start, two of the local fellows were debating how Averell was to ride in the parade. One of them said, "Shall we put him in a carriage or shall we put him on a horse?" The other said, "No, he'd fall off a horse." And Averell turned around and fixed those two men with an icy stare and said, "How many ten-goal polo men do you have in Vernal?" Averell, of course, had been a member of the U.S. Olympic Polo Team when he was young and was a most accomplished horseman.

I also took a fairly active part in the gubernatorial campaign in 1952. The two contestants for the Democratic nomination for governor were Heber Bennion, who was the Utah secretary of state, and Earl J. Glade, who was the mayor of Salt Lake City. I was supporting Mr. Bennion and did all I could for him. Unfortunately, he lost in the primary to Mayor Glade, and then Mayor Glade lost in the election to Bracken Lee when Lee was elected for his second term. That was not a noticeably spirited election. Many of us had a feeling that Lee was going to be reelected, and also that Eisenhower was going to win the presidency; and so we were not at all surprised on election night when both feelings proved true.

By the time the 1956 election was approaching, however, the magic of Bracken Lee's unorthodox personality was beginning to wear thin, and the feeling generally was that he was vulnerable. Of course the Republicans could see that too, and they were casting around for someone to run against Lee in the Republican primary to make sure they didn't have to back him in a general election. The contest that year in the Republican primary was, therefore, between Bracken Lee and George Dewey Clyde. George Clyde was an engineer who had been dean of the engineering school at Utah State University for many years, in the thirties and forties. He was an authority on water and was so recognized by people throughout the West, and near the end of the war he moved to Washington, D.C., to work for the federal government in the Soil Conservation Service.

Sometime before 1956 Clyde had become a close friend of Senator Watkins, who was at that time the senior senator from Utah.

Senator Watkins made Clyde his protégé and Clyde was hired to come back to Utah to head up the water and power board in the state government. This was a time when water was a very dramatic issue in Utah, and the Eisenhower administration was trying to cut down on the number of water projects financed by the federal government. Eisenhower had announced the policy of no new starts. In other words, they wouldn't leave a reclamation project just standing on which substantial investments had been made; they would finish the project, but no new starts would be made.

The problem we had in Utah was with the Central Utah Project, a transmountain diversion project that would ultimately bring Uintah Basin water into the Great Salt Lake Valley. It had gone through the feasibility stage, and a lot of engineering work had been done on it, but we were concerned about whether it was far enough along in the expenditure stage so that it would not be cut off by the no new starts policy.

It was in order to combat a possible cutoff of funding that George Clyde, who had been a member of the Eisenhower administration, was brought out to head up the water and power board. He and other people associated with him organized bipartisan state support. To back the Utah position in an attempt to get the Central Utah Project funded, groups called "Aqualantes" were organized throughout the state. I joined the Aqualantes and did a great deal of work with them at that time.

The fact that water was such a dramatic issue in the 1956 elections had forced Clyde to the front in this election, even though he did not have a very striking personality. With the backing of the old-line Republicans who were either tired or afraid of Lee, Clyde managed to come out of the Republican convention on an equal footing with him. I am not sure who won more delegate votes in the convention, but it was close, and they both went on the primary ballot.

On the Democratic side there were several candidates for the governorship, but two stood out: L. C. Romney, who had been a Salt Lake City commissioner for several years, and who was a very charming fellow; and John Boyden who, as I mentioned, had run for the Democratic nomination for governor eight years earlier but had lost to Governor Maw. Fortunately, John and I had resolved our differences in the interim, and I supported him in the 1956 election.

This was one election where cross-voting in the primary elections—that is, people crossing from one party to the other to vote in the primaries—had an effect on the outcome. Under Utah law a person could vote in either primary. When a voter went into the polling booth, he was given a joint primary ballot which contained tickets for both parties. He took it into a booth, marked the ballot of his choice, tore it down the perforation in the middle and then put the ballot of the party for which he had voted into a counting can and the other into a discard can. No one else knew in which party primary a person had voted, although he could not vote in both because he had to put one ballot in the discard can.

The Utah Education Association was bitterly opposed to Lee's reelection. There had been constant fighting and friction between the school people and the governor during almost all the time he was in office, and so the UEA members were determined to get rid of him if they could. They didn't particularly back Clyde. Although he had been a college professor, there was little empathy between college professors and public schoolteachers, but he was acceptable to them. On the other hand John Boyden had been the attorney for the UEA for a long time, and he was very much their favorite. They wanted him badly. However, the primary proved that hate can be stronger than love. Large numbers of schoolteachers who were normally Democrats voted in the Republican primary for Clyde and against Lee to get rid of Lee, and thus couldn't vote for Boyden in the Democratic primary. The result was that they defeated Lee, but they also left Boyden without full teacher support. Thus the victors in the primary election, determined by this rather ill-advised action on the part of the UEA, were Clyde and Romney. In the election in 1956, Clyde defeated Romney.

During the first years after we were married, Lucybeth's father had worked his way to very high positions in the U.S. Department of Agriculture. He became assistant director and then director of the Agricultural Research Administration. Then, in 1954, he was elected director general of the Food and Agricultural Organization which was an adjunct organization of the United Nations. The FAO office was in Rome, and Lucybeth's mother and father, Vince and Leah, took up residence there. He was to hold this job only for about two years, however, when poor health forced his retirement.

Lucybeth and I had planned a trip to Rome to see her parents. We were to go over in April 1956, and we had the tickets bought and everything ready when, in February, we learned that Vince had to come home. We decided we would take the trip anyway. We flew Icelandic Airways, stopping first in Reykjavik and then in Luxembourg, where we rented a car. We visited the scenes of World War II that I had witnessed ten years before as we drove south into Rome, wandered along the Riviera, and then returned to Paris where we stayed for a while. We rented my former suite at the Prince des Galles, though one night was all that we could afford. Finally, we returned to Luxembourg and home. It had been a delightful and memorable trip for us both.

In the spring of 1958, the American Field Service was seeking families that would accept high school students from various foreign countries for one year. We talked about it as a family and decided we would like to have a student from some other country live with us and attend Highland High School, where Meg was going to be a senior. We contacted the American Field Service and told them we would like a girl approximately Meg's age so that they could attend the senior class together.

In midsummer we were informed that the student who was to live with us for the next year was a girl from Frankfurt, Germany. Her name was Bärbel Feller. The whole family was at the airport to meet the plane on the evening it arrived from New York. I don't recall whether we had a picture of Bärbel or just a description of her, but even though there were some twenty foreign students coming to the Salt Lake area on that flight, we knew who she was as soon as she got off. And she knew who we were, too—I guess because we were looking at her so intently. Bärbel lived in our home from August 1958 until June 1959, when she graduated along with Meg from Highland High School.

Nineteen fifty-eight had been an interesting election year in Utah. Senator Watkins ran for his third term. He'd first been elected in 1946 and then reelected in 1952. In 1958, he ran for yet a third term. Bracken Lee, of course, had been defeated for the governorship in 1956, and in 1958 he decided he would try for the Senate. He filed against Senator Watkins. On the Democratic side the contestants were Frank E. Moss, who was the Salt Lake County attorney, and Brigham

E. Roberts, a well-known Salt Lake lawyer. This was quite a close contest. Moss won the Democratic nomination in the primary, and Senator Watkins defeated ex-governor Lee for the Republican nomination.

At that time a person could file as an independent candidate by getting a sufficient number of signatures on a petition, and he didn't have to file the petition until some time after the partisan primary. Believing that he had been done in by Republican politicians in the primary but that he still had clout with the people in the party, Lee took advantage of this statute and filed as an independent.

There was a three-way race, then, with Moss the Democrat, Watkins the Republican, and Lee the Independent. Lee did very well. The vote was surprisingly evenly split among the three men. Moss won the election because he was the high vote getter of the three, but his total only came to about 36 percent of the vote. Watkins was second with around 33 percent, and Lee had about 31 percent.

Just after Christmas 1959 my family had a traumatic experience. We had all been skiing and had returned home on a Saturday evening. We went to bed, and sometime around twelve-thirty I awoke. I don't know what woke me, whether just a feeling of uneasiness or whether I could smell smoke, but I went into the front room, looked out the window, and noticed that the snow seemed brightly lighted. Suddenly I realized there was a fire. I ran and looked in our garage, and indeed, both the garage and the station wagon were engulfed in flames. Our other car, a Ford convertible, was in the driveway safe from the fire. The fire had started in a box of fireplace ashes stored in the garage, which a strong wind had revived.

I immediately shouted to Lucybeth, and as I was running back and forth, the girls in their bedrooms downstairs heard me and awakened the boys. The boys' bedroom was on the north side of the house, adjacent to the garage where the fire was, and we had them out of there but a very short time before the pine paneling in their room and in the recreation room ignited, almost spontaneously, from the heat. I tried to get the station wagon out, but it was just too hot for me to touch. Meantime, Tony had got a hose out and was attempting to get the water on, but he got himself all wet and it was so cold that his pajamas froze on him right there.

We got everybody out. I don't know whether any of us had coats on. Some of us had slippers on our feet, but mostly we were just in our night clothes. I backed the Ford convertible away and put it in front of the house, and everybody, including our two dogs, climbed in. Somebody had already called the fire department because we could hear the fire trucks coming. By now the whole roof was engulfed in flames. The bitter cold that night was augmented by the wind, blowing from the north at forty to fifty miles per hour. The flames from the roof were driven almost horizontally forty to fifty feet out over the canyon beyond our house.

The firemen arrived, and about thirty minutes later the fire was under control. The house, however, was badly damaged. The roof was gone, the basement was gutted, and the kitchen looked as though it had been bombed. The damage would have been far greater if the house had not for the most part been built of stone. Many of our neighbors brought clothes for us because they saw we had nothing except our night clothes. I was given many shirts and sweaters, several pairs of boots, and some underwear, but nobody brought me trousers; so there was I with this great secondhand wardrobe but without trousers to put on.

We restored the home and moved back in early in April, and of course everything was shiny and painted, and the furniture and appliances were all new. The smell of the smoke still permeated the house, however, even though it had been closed up for a period of time and fumigated. Three decades later, in the closets under the stairs where the fire was the worst, the smell of smoke from that fire is still noticeable.

Although I continued to be an active party member, my interest waned somewhat after the 1956 campaign, not returning until the 1960 election came along. Governor Clyde was preparing to run for a second term. Although I thought Governor Clyde was a fine man, I regarded him as rather a lackluster leader and felt that we would be better off with a change. There had emerged as a prominent figure in the Democratic party a young man from southern Utah named William Barlocker, and many of us felt he would make a fine candidate for governor. Barlocker had made a substantial amount of money in St. George. He was in the turkey business, had bought a bank, and had done very well financially, although I was later to learn that his enterprises were not sufficiently well based. He was to have financial troubles and ultimately lose everything he had. But at this time he was riding high. He had been elected mayor of St. George, an almost unheard-of thing for a Democrat. Also, in 1959, he was elected president of the Utah Municipal League, so he had excellent contacts with municipal officers throughout the state.

Barlocker was an unusual character. He was a large man, quite crude, aggressive, bright in some ways, but without good judgment. He was personable, colorful, and caught the public imagination. His principal opponent on the Democratic side was Ira Huggins, a lawyer from Ogden who had been president of the Utah state senate. Ira was an able lawyer and a fine man, but he was slow and deliberate and he had gray hair, and his mannerisms and his hair made him look much older than he was. I'm sure that Ira at that time had not even reached sixty, but to look at him and hear him, you would believe he was a man of seventy-five.

It was obvious to everyone that Barlocker, with his force and power of personality in contrast to the aged appearance of Ira Huggins, was going to win in the primary and indeed he did. On the Republican side, Governor Clyde didn't have an easy row. He was opposed by LaMont Gunderson, who was a commissioner of Salt Lake County, and by Cleon Skousen. This was before Skousen was chief of police, so he probably was still a professor of religion at Brigham Young University, where he had become an acknowledged leader of the ultra-conservative faction of the Republican party. However, he lost in the convention, and Gunderson and Clyde went into the primary where Clyde ultimately won. Thus Clyde and Barlocker faced each other for the governorship in 1960.

This was one of the bitterest campaigns that I can recall. Barlocker had been divorced, and that was played upon. While he was forceful in his public appearances, his grammar was poor, and he was ridiculed. Still, a poll taken shortly after the primary showed that he was leading Clyde by a considerable amount, and it appeared that Barlocker would be the next governor. However, a combination of factors—lack of good judgment, ill-advised actions, and obvious crudeness—began to erode Barlocker's strength and, once again, the Republicans won the governorship.

It was also around this time that Lucybeth first experienced an episode of the depression that would recur in 1974 in chronic form. I recall that during the summer of 1960, shortly after the school year had ended, we decided that we'd take a trip to Albuquerque to attend the Western States Democratic Conference. I was still active in Democratic affairs, and it was my intention in the 1960 election to support, once again, Stuart Symington for the presidential nomination. I, along with Harry Truman and a congresswoman named Lenore Sullivan, had seconded the nomination of Stuart in 1956, and I was still very much in favor of the senator for the nomination in this election. We knew that Symington would be at the Western States Democratic Conference, as would Lyndon Johnson and John Kennedy. The western states were a great prize, and this was an opportunity for them to meet the prospective delegates in those states.

At this conference Lucybeth was severely depressed. As a result of my concern for her, I don't remember too much about the conference. I recall that the various candidates were there and addressed the delegates, and we got to see each one of them up close. I knew Symington and Johnson, of course, but this was the first opportunity I'd had to get well acquainted with John F. Kennedy. I had only met him at the 1956 convention, where he gave the keynote talk and was a contestant for the vice-presidency.

We came home from the conference in Albuquerque, and at the Democratic state convention in early July I was elected as one of the delegates from Utah to the national convention in Los Angeles. We decided to make a family vacation of the convention. Lucybeth was feeling better, and I thought it would be a good diversion. Through an agency we rented a house on Santa Monica Beach, which was a fair distance from the downtown Los Angeles convention center, but not so far that I couldn't commute.

During the first day or two of the convention, it began to appear that Kennedy had the nomination fairly well locked up. I was not a Kennedy fan by any means because I was for Symington; but on the third day, the roll call was taken and Kennedy was selected. Then came the jockeying for the vice-presidency. Stan Fike, who was Senator Symington's administrative assistant and a good friend of mine, called me to see what I felt about having Symington seek the nod of the new presidential nominee for the vice-presidency. I was not at all in favor of it. I felt that Kennedy probably couldn't win, and I preferred that Symington hold back until some future time.

There was talk about Johnson being the vice-presidential nominee, but I just couldn't believe that. On Thursday morning I got several calls from Stan keeping me informed of the selection process. Finally, he called me and said that Kennedy had chosen Johnson and that Johnson had accepted. I didn't like it at all. It seemed the height of cynicism to me at the time. Kennedy did not like Johnson and chose him only to help carry the South. But, that's the way it was.

On Thursday the children, Lucybeth, and I piled into the car and went to the convention. I had my delegate pass to the floor, and passes for my family in the gallery. We got down there in time to hear Johnson nominated for the vice-presidency and to hear Kennedy's masterful acceptance speech, the famous "New Frontier" speech, and after I heard it I felt better. Following the acceptance speeches I brought the children down on the floor. Tony and Vince got to meet both Bobby and Teddy Kennedy. Teddy was in his mid-twenties at that time. Everyone had a good time, and we came on home feeling all right about the Democratic ticket.

Nixon, of course, won the Republican nomination that year in spite of the fact that Eisenhower was lukewarm about him, and he seemed to be leading in the early stages of the presidential campaign. That all changed with the famous debates between Kennedy and Nixon. Without question, those debates were what gave Kennedy the rather narrow edge that he had over Nixon. Nixon did manage to carry Utah in 1960, however, and George Clyde along with him.

Beginning in 1960 I became involved in one of the most important legal battles in which I have ever been engaged. Two large railroads, Southern Pacific and Santa Fe, wanted to take over the Western Pacific Railroad, which ran from San Francisco to Salt Lake City. Generally, the people in Utah did not want Western Pacific to be taken over by either one of these large railroad companies because we felt we'd be better served by an independent railroad. We would rather have seen Western taken over by Union Pacific, if anybody, but certainly not by Southern Pacific or Santa Fe, neither of which had any close ties to Utah.

Joe Rosenblatt had become a member of the board of directors of Western Pacific Railroad, and I had represented the Rosenblatt interests for a long time in transportation matters. When Joe and a number of the other minority directors of Western Pacific decided to resist the efforts of Western Pacific management to sell out to Santa Fe, I was employed as the attorney for the dissident group of directors to fight this takeover.

The contest was a hotly fought one. The Southern Pacific pulled back somewhat, so it became an effort of the Santa Fe to take over Western while the dissident directors fought to keep it independent. Union Pacific Railroad was involved in the case, and they were nominally supporting the takeover bid of either Santa Fe or Southern Pacific. However, I knew very well that Union Pacific would rather have Western stay independent, although because of their interfreight ties with these other large railroads they were in a bind and had to give at least lip service to the Santa Fe proposal.

We held the final hearings before an ICC examiner named Paul Albus in San Francisco. The hearings went on for several weeks. A witness for Union Pacific was the chairman of their executive committee, Robert Lovett, who had for a short time early in the Kennedy administration been secretary of the treasury. He was a distinguished lawyer, and he was to go on the witness stand just to give a perfunctory endorsement to the Santa Fe bid. I knew that he didn't really want the takeover to succeed, so I was eager to cross-examine him.

I called Francis Malia, the Union Pacific attorney, the night before Lovett was to go on the stand and said, "Is there any way I could see Mr. Lovett before he goes on that stand to find out exactly what his attitude is? I know what yours is, you're just giving lip service; and if Lovett is too, maybe on cross-examination I can really negate the endorsement." Malia said, "I'm sure if he were asked the right questions he would probably on cross-examination say, in effect, 'I think it would be better for the country as a whole if Western stayed independent.'" So I asked again if he'd let me see Lovett, and Malia replied, "All right, I'll arrange for you to see him this evening."

I went up to Mr. Lovett's room. He was a frail man and not well. He had some sort of a skin rash, and couldn't wear a collar. He had a silk scarf around his neck. I said, "Mr. Lovett, I really don't believe that you personally would like to see Western Pacific swallowed up." He said he wouldn't, and I continued that I'd like to ask him some questions in court that might reveal his point of view. This was a fine idea with Mr. Lovett, so I said, "I'll tell you what the questions will be and then I'll suggest some answers." He said, "No, young man. I'll tell you what the questions *shall* be, and I'll tell you what answers I'll make." I followed his suggestion.

His cross-examination did negate the endorsement. Western Pacific stayed independent for a number of years, although eventually it was taken over by Union Pacific. My total fee for that case, which stretched across three years, was about $250,000. If I were billing today on that case, the fee would probably be $1.5 million.

Nineteen sixty-two was yet another election year. In the early spring the polls showed that Wallace Bennett, who was running for his third term as senator, was vulnerable. I felt that there was a good chance for someone to beat him, and as I had received a lot of public exposure through the Western Pacific case, I decided that I'd like to run for the U.S. Senate. The only problem was that David King, who was an incumbent congressman, having completed two terms, decided that he wanted to run as well.

David had a more liberal image in the state than I did. I've always been regarded as rather a conservative Democrat, although I feel I have been a fiscal conservative and a social liberal. At any rate, this was the public's perception of us. I felt that if I could get the nomination I could beat Bennett, but I knew I would have a hard time getting the nomination because the Democratic party in the state at that time was (and still is) inclined to be liberal and therefore likely to nominate liberal candidates in spite of the fact that, pragmatically, we should recognize that liberals have less chance of winning.

David and I had been good friends for many years. One day, early in the spring, I asked him to have lunch with me at the Ambassador Club, and we sat there talking and trying to jockey each other out of position. I told him that I was going to run, and he said he hadn't made up his mind whether he would. I told him I would run whether or not he did, hoping that would convince him not to run. Finally, however, we both filed for the Democratic nomination. There was a third candidate as well, a man named Joe Weston, so we had to have a contest at the convention.

David and I both came out of the convention. I got about 40 percent of the convention vote, Dave about 56 percent, and Joe Weston about 4 percent. It really wasn't a spirited primary because neither David nor I was willing to attack the other, but it was an interesting election. Bracken Lee had filed against Bennett for the Republican nomination, and so we had primaries in both parties, with Lee and Bennett running on the Republican side, and King and I on the Democratic side.

I tried to get Dave to debate me publicly, but he wouldn't do it, and I don't blame him. Then Lee and I got together and made arrangements for a debate between us because neither was getting very much attention. Finally, though, just before the debate was to come off, he called me and said, "I don't think I'm going to do that. I think

I'm much better known than you are, and if I should beat Bennett and you should beat King, we'll debate then, but not now." The Democrats in the state seemed to regard Dave as an incumbent, and he was of course an incumbent congressman. He beat me better than two to one in the primary election. Bennett beat Lee in the Republican primaries, and in the election of November 1962, Bennett defeated King to win his third term in the Senate.

An interesting anecdote from the campaign: about a week before the primary, I got a call from a man who said he was an Indian named Frank Takes Gun, and that he was the head of the Native American Church, which I believe was true. He asked me to meet him at a downtown motel, which I did, and he told me that if I would give him some money he would campaign for me among the Utes. I think he wanted a thousand dollars. Finally, I paid him two hundred and fifty dollars, but there weren't fifty Utes who turned out to vote. I was with Dave King one day after the election was over, and I said to him, "Did you ever hear of an Indian named Frank Takes Gun?" Dave turned very red and said, "Yes. How much did he get from you?" I answered, "Oh, I don't know—about two hundred and fifty dollars." He said, "I gave him five hundred." Later, after I was governor and Bracken Lee and I were at a head dinner table one night, I said to him, "Brack, do you remember an Indian named Frank Takes Gun?" Brack almost choked on his coffee and said, "Oh, that son-of-a-bitch. How much did he take from you?" I told him two hundred and fifty dollars, and he replied: "I gave him two thousand dollars."

After the 1962 elections I thought that a political career was not for me. I was doing fine in law, and the practice kept growing. Lucybeth had recovered now, and our family was getting on well. Everything seemed to be going well, and yet I have to admit that every time there was a political campaign, whether municipal or any other, I tended to get involved and I enjoyed it all. I enjoyed the electioneering; I enjoyed meeting the people. And so I suppose it wasn't strange that two years later—in spite of the protests of my law partners—I became a candidate for governor of the state of Utah.

CHAPTER FOUR

TO THE
POLITICAL WARS

Thu thought of running for governor had never greatly appealed to me until the spring of 1964. I'd always wanted to join the U.S. Senate. I suppose the fact that I had been exposed to Congress during the years I worked for Mr. Robinson had a great deal to do with this. It's rather strange because Ted Moss, as he was coming up through the political ranks, had wanted to be governor. But in 1964, the Democrats had no obvious candidate for the governorship. There were a number of names being mentioned: Bill Barlocker, who had lost to Governor Clyde in 1960, still had gubernatorial ambitions and let it be known that he was probably going to run. A Salt Lake County commissioner named Clarence A. Brady had a wide state following due to the fact that he had been not only a commissioner, but early on had been a sheriff's deputy and was just completing a term as the chairman of the County Officials' Association. Another man frequently talked about was Milton Weilenmann, who had recently returned from the presidency of the Alaskan Mission of the LDS Church to his business of running some restaurants in Salt Lake City. Milt had a good political background. He'd been state chairman before he left—in fact, he beat me for that office at one time—and now he wanted to run for governor. Another potential candidate who was often mentioned was Herbert Smart, a Salt Lake City commissioner who had been with me in the attorney general's office many years previously. Finally, there was Ernest Dean of Utah County, who had been in the state legislature for many years and had been the speaker of the house of the Utah legislature. Ernest wanted to run, and eventually did so as my primary opponent.

In the early spring of 1964, Wally Sandack and Don Holbrook came to see me in my office in the El Paso Building with the suggestion that I run for governor. They felt that although the results of my senatorial campaign two years earlier were disastrous, the exposure I had received might serve to help me out in the gubernatorial campaign. At first I didn't take to the idea, but after I had been urged by them and a substantial number of other people (I'm sure at Don's and Wally's urging), the idea seemed better.

I talked it over with Lucybeth and the family, and while I can't say they were enthusiastic about the proposal, they were not opposed. I also discussed it with Zar Hayes and Harry Pugsley. Zar thought it was a good idea; Harry didn't like it at all. I had taken a considerable amount of time off from work during the Senate race, and it really was a burden on the other partners. I told Harry that if I decided to run I would expect to have my share of the partnership proceeds reduced, commensurate with the time I had to take off for campaigning.

Within a few weeks I had pretty well made up my mind that I would enter the campaign and I put together a group of advisors that Lucybeth came to call the "backyard mafia." Besides Don Holbrook and Wally Sandack, it included George Hatch, John Klas, and Wally Bennett from the University of Utah Law School. Others who met with us on occasion were Paul Geerlings, a lawyer in Salt Lake, and Sid Baucom, who had earlier been a law associate of Don Holbrook and Frank Wilkins.

The "backyard mafia" formed an ad hoc campaign committee. We looked at the issues and at the probable opposition to see whom we would be running against both in the primary and in the final election. Governor Clyde had indicated that he would not run again, but there were a great many people in the Republican party who had half announced themselves. The Republicans over the previous several years had fairly well controlled the state legislature, and there were a number of senior state legislators who were considering the prospect.

The problem we faced was one of timing. We didn't want to come out too soon and make the campaign any longer than it had to be; on the other hand, we felt it wise for me to be the first one to announce on the Democratic side. About the first of April it appeared that Ernest Dean was going to run and would probably announce very soon, so I put together an announcement statement and got into the fray.

In view of the fact that the Republicans had held the governorship for sixteen years, and also because there were so many potential candidates on the Republican side at this early date, there wasn't much I could do in the early campaign but center my fire on the Clyde administration. The Clyde administration had been entirely free of corruption, so there was nothing that could be done on that basis. On the other hand, it had been an unimaginative administration. Governor Clyde had been a caretaker governor and not very innovative. For example, even though everyone could see the great number of war babies rolling through the elementary schools toward college, Governor Clyde had made no effort to meet the obviously imminent need for new buildings on the campuses of our universities. Thus, one of my planks was that I would seek a bond for the construction of buildings at the universities and colleges. Furthermore, the public schools had been in a rather desperate condition as the Clyde administration and the Lee administration before that had held down appropriations for schools. The Utah Education Association, under the leadership of John Evans, was at loggerheads with the state school board and the local boards of education throughout the state. I therefore adopted as an additional plank an adequate public school financing program.

Utah, after having had an unemployment rate lower than the national average through most of the fifties, had changed positions coming into the sixties. Our unemployment rate had increased so that it was now substantially higher than the national average. Our young people were leaving the state in great numbers to find jobs. Out-migration was greater than in-migration, so even though we had a high birthrate, our population growth rate was slow. Also, Utah's wages were lower than the national average; lower, even, than the average of the surrounding states.

There had been an industrial promotion activity inaugurated by Governor Maw while he was governor, but immediately upon assuming the governorship in 1948, Governor Lee shut off all funds and the organization died. Then, sometime during the Lee or Clyde administrations, the industrial promotion department was deleted from the state statutes altogether. Therefore, as another major plank, I decided to resurrect the industrial promotion department in order to stimulate growth and the development of new jobs.

Also during the years of Lee and Maw there had been some tourist promotion activity in the state, but it wasn't funded well enough to realize a high return. I determined that could probably give us the biggest initial impetus toward economic recovery, and so yet another plank I decided to focus on was to greatly increase appropriations for the promotion of tourism.

Immediately after I announced my candidacy for the governorship I called Milt Weilenmann and Herb Smart and asked them if they would come in to see me. They knew of course that I was running, and I think they both resented my jumping the gun without talking to them, since they were considering the possibility of running themselves. This was a very delicate issue for me to handle because I liked them both very much and they were both good friends. Furthermore, I knew that I wanted the two of them in my administration if I were elected, and yet I didn't want to promise a job to anybody during the campaign period. I wanted to establish rapport with these men so they would help me and so that immediately upon my election, if I were elected, I could get them to start working with me. I wanted Milt to head up industrial and tourist promotions, and I wanted Herb for finance management. They were a little cold at first, but soon warmed up, and each took a major part in my campaign. Both men started with me near the beginning of my first term. In fact, Herb started before I became governor – in the transition stage – and Milt came on board a few months after my inauguration. And they both stayed with me the full twelve years of my governorship.

Five Republicans filed for the governorship. One was Mitchell Melich, a lawyer from Moab who had made a substantial amount of money as attorney for Charlie Steen, the developer of the rich Mi Vida uranium mine. Mitch had been a state senator from Grand County. He had also been a member of the Republican National Committee and was well known in party circles. A second candidate was James Cannon, who had been a Salt Lake businessman, and for several years Governor Clyde's director of tourism. Bracken Lee, who was then mayor of Salt Lake, also filed for the Republican nomination for governor, as did Lamont Toronto, who had been Utah's secretary of state for twelve years. The fifth candidate was a state legislator from Tremonton named Cleon Kerr.

For a period following the filing deadline there was little overt activity on the part of any of the seven candidates, although I suppose the others, like myself, were making plans. I continued to meet with the "backyard mafia" once or twice a week around the swimming pool in our backyard.

The first thing that we had to do after announcing my candidacy was adopt a campaign budget. After a great deal of discussion we settled on a budget of $150,000. This seemed like a great deal to me and I didn't see how we could possibly raise it, but most of the others felt that we could. Two years previously the Senate campaign left me ten or twelve thousand dollars in debt, and I didn't want that to happen in another campaign, so I told my advisors that we weren't going to spend any money before we had it. It was all right to set a budget for that amount, but I didn't want to go ahead and spend merely on the expectation of getting the money at some later time.

The Democratic state convention was in July 1964, but neither Ernest Dean nor I expended much of our funds on the convention. We both felt that we'd get through the convention all right. At that time, in order to eliminate your opponent when there were only two candidates running, you had to get 80 percent of the vote (it was later lowered to 70 percent), and neither Dean nor I felt that we could get the 80 percent. Each of us, of course, hoped to be the high man coming out of the convention. We used direct-mailing tactics on the delegates, but we thought the use of media resources at this point would have been a waste of money. I personally set about trying to see all of the delegates that I could, as working with them was pretty much a candidate's responsibility. Seeing them all was a hopeless task, however, as there were about twelve hundred delegates statewide, but I did get to see nearly three hundred and fifty of them.

I came out of the convention with more than half of the votes, although the margin between Ernest Dean and me was not great. Dean was quite popular among the people he'd served with in the legislature. These Democratic legislators from all over the state formed the nucleus of the Dean organization. Heading up his campaign in Weber County was Gunn McKay, who was later to become my administrative assistant, but who was working very hard for Dean at that time. Dean had an excellent organization, probably better than mine was in terms of contacts with the Democratic grassroots out in the counties.

The Republican convention, on the other hand, was a hard-fought affair because they had five candidates, only two of whom could come through. It generally had been supposed that Bracken Lee, because of his name, his exposure, and his contacts with some of the older leaders of the Republican party would be one of those who came through the convention, with the other winner being either Mitchell Melich or Jim Cannon. Nobody gave Senator Kerr a chance, nor was Lamont Toronto very seriously regarded. At the convention, however, Mayor Lee did not have the popular support people supposed he had. He finished third, and Mitchell Melich and Jim Cannon qualified to go into the Republican primary election.

Immediately after the conventions the primary campaigns got into full swing. We proposed to spend about fifty thousand dollars in the primary campaign, reserving a hundred thousand dollars for the election. We got out the standard bumper stickers and lawn signs and began a series of meetings around the state.

I beat Ernest Dean in the primary election with around a three-to-two margin—about 55,000 votes to his 37,000. The Republican race was very close, with Melich winning about 55,000 votes to 50,000 for Cannon, so there were more people who voted in the Republican primary than voted in the Democratic primary. This, of course, gave us some concern for the general election.

In the meantime, the school situation in Utah had reached a crisis stage. Governor Clyde had appointed a committee of businessmen and -women in the spring to study the school situation and bring back recommendations that might be implemented, in an attempt to get the school contracts in the various districts signed before school started during the first part of September. The committee met for a period of several months and brought back a recommendation for increased expenditures for schools, which Governor Clyde rejected. As a result, very few contracts had been signed when the schools began that fall, and most of the teachers went back to work without contracts.

Then, at about the time of the primary election, the board of governors and the executive secretary of the UEA called a three-day UEA meeting. All the teachers left the schools. This action was denounced by Governor Clyde as a strike, and John Evans retorted that it wasn't a strike, that they would continue to work for a period of time because they would have a new governor to deal with after the first of the year who might be more reasonable. It was a bitter exchange, and at this same time the National Education Association put Utah under sanctions: no member of the NEA from any other state would come into Utah to teach school. Of course I exploited the situation as much as I could because Melich, after all, was the candidate of the Republican administration and had solid support from Clyde.

I continued to stress both in public appearances and in paid media advertising the four things that we had pinpointed earlier: school buildings for higher education, adequate school finance programs, stepped-up employment through an increase in our tourist promotion budget, and the creation of an industrial development division.

Sometimes in the heat of the campaign you tend to lose your perspective, and this happened to us near the end. It must have been a week before the November election when an anonymous mimeographed letter was scattered throughout the state. There must have been two hundred thousand copies made, as it went into every voting district, so a large amount of money had gone into it. It made a scurrilous attack on me and suggested that the Democrats who had supported Ernie Dean should not vote for me for governor but should write in Dean's name instead. Happening as late in the campaign as it did, this event threw us into a panic. We had a meeting and somebody brought in a picture that he had obtained of Mitchell Melich when he was at a party one night, obviously a little tipsy. A suggestion was made that we should have copies of this picture printed and distributed as a backfire to the thing that had happened to me. We had no knowledge that Melich's campaign organization was behind the Dean write-in letter, so we decided to go home and sleep on it. I talked to the family about the matter that night and my son, Tony, was aghast that I should even think of doing such a thing. By the next morning I had thought better of it. When I met with my committee again, some of the flyers with the Melich picture on it had already been printed up, but we burned them, and I'm glad we did.

The presidential campaign in 1964 was a hotly contested one, too, and would prove to have a definite effect on the senatorial and gubernatorial campaigns in Utah. Lyndon Johnson was running for his first elected term. The Republican candidate was Barry Goldwater, an ultraconservative—at least we thought he was at that time. (The Republican party in Utah became so conservative in later years that Goldwater looked like a liberal.) At any rate, the Goldwater and Johnson campaigns were waged vigorously. The principal thrust of the Johnson campaign was to suggest that Goldwater was so pugnacious and aggressive that he would get us into war. The

Goldwater people, on the other hand, attempted to paint Johnson as a great liberal and a spendthrift who was bound to lead us further into public debt.

In the U.S. senatorial contest in Utah, Ted Moss had the Democratic nomination and was running for his second term. The Republican race in the primary had been between Sherman Lloyd, an incumbent congressman, and Ernest Wilkinson, the president of Brigham Young University and a former Washington lawyer for whom Lucybeth had worked when I was courting her.

This was an acrimonious campaign. The Wilkinson people tried to paint Sherm Lloyd as a moderate, and maintained that he drank. Sherm was a social drinker and said so, and I suppose that even admitting it hurt him a great deal. Although Wilkinson in the early going was considered the underdog because of Sherm's experience in Congress, he emerged the victor in the primary by a narrow margin, and the groundwork had already been laid for the bitter election campaign which followed. Wilkinson and his supporters were vicious in their attacks on Ted Moss. They painted him not only as a big-spending liberal, but almost as a Communist sympathizer.

As election day drew near, both Senator Moss and I were deeply concerned with the presidential campaign, because we knew that we probably weren't going to run much differently in the state of Utah from the way Johnson ran. I did not have any confidence that I would win. The newspaper polls showed that I was running about neck and neck with Melich. They showed also that Johnson was slightly ahead of Goldwater and that Moss and Wilkinson were just about even. When the votes were counted on election day, Johnson received about 55 percent of the vote in Utah to 45 percent for Goldwater, and both Moss and I ran about one percentage point stronger than Johnson did.

On the night of the election Lucybeth, the children, and I did the rounds of the television stations. We had to make an appearance of great modesty as we responded to interview questions, even after I was sure of winning. I was well ahead in Salt Lake and Weber counties and was even close in Utah County. By ten or eleven o'clock at night it was clear to everyone that we were going to win, and then the seriousness of the situation hit me for the first time. I had been engrossed in the campaign, trying to get elected, and now here I was, elected governor, and actually had to do the job. I grew more and more thoughtful as the evening went along and as I reflected on the fact. Mitch Melich called me while I was on one of the television stations and very graciously conceded. We went home that night very happy, but a little concerned also.

That evening, after the children had gone to bed, Lucybeth and I sat by the fire for a few minutes and I had very little to say. Finally, I asked, "What if I let them all down?" And then after a few minutes I replied, "But I won't."

We slept late the next morning and about noon Governor Clyde called me on the phone and asked if I would like to come down on Thursday morning and talk. I said I certainly would, and the following day I went down to his office. Clyde was gracious. He met me at the door and invited me to come in and sit down. The press had been alerted that there was to be a meeting between us and they were all there with television cameras going. During the campaign I had not gotten the same attention from the television people that I was getting now. This was really my first experience with something that I was going to face for the next twelve years. I had to be reasonably careful of my utterances because now I was responsible. In this television interview Governor Clyde and I merely stated that we were going to meet and talk about the transition from his administration to mine. Then we were closeted by ourselves for about two hours while he briefed me on various state matters and I asked him questions.

The first thing I asked was whether I could get some staff for the transition; in particular, I wanted to hire Herbert Smart immediately. I wanted to appoint him as director of finance, and I also wanted him to get busy on the budget. My knowledge of the details of the state budget was insignificant, but Herb had been on the city commission and had managed the city budget. He had also been a member of the tax commission for a period of years before he ran for city commissioner. I asked Governor Clyde if he could provide a salary for Herb for two months. He agreed to do so from his own staff budget. He said he would supplement it from the governor's emergency fund and would put Herb and one secretary on the payroll and give us office space in the Capitol. In addition to that, Governor Clyde prepared a bulletin which went out to all state department heads directing them to cooperate in every way with Mr. Smart and me as we prepared the budget.

Although it had not been a bitter campaign, it had been a tiring one, and Lucybeth and I decided to get away for a few days' rest before I actually entered into preparation for the transition. We went with two friends of ours, Lewis and LaRue Flinders, to Hawaii, where we spent a week in Honolulu.

On returning to Salt Lake, I faced one of the busiest six-week periods of my life. In that length of time I had to prepare three major speeches: my inaugural address, my address to the legislature, and my budget address. Lucybeth worked closely with me on the inaugural address, and it shaped up fairly quickly because it was general in scope and didn't deal as specifically with problems as would the other talks I had to give.

Herb Smart was already well into the budget preparation by the time I got back. Governor Clyde's budget office had accumulated certain requests from the departments, and the tax commission had prepared certain revenue estimates, but I wasn't content with these. I had two economist friends, Whitney Hanks from the University of Utah and Elroy Nelson from First Security Bank, prepare me separate revenue estimates on their own, which they did without charge. We then asked for revised figures from all of the state departments (there were 156 of them at that time) for which we had to prepare line-item budgets—and not just for a year, but for a biennium, because the legislature at that time met only sixty days in every odd-numbered year. I would generally meet with Herb in the morning and we would go over the figures. We met this way every day until almost Christmas, by which time we had the budget fairly well put together, although the budget message was not yet begun.

The state of the state message was tailored for me by the issues I had stressed during the campaign. More than anything else, I wanted to emphasize economic issues: the necessity of getting the economy of the state moving again, of providing jobs for our young people, of settling the school crisis, and of establishing a bonding measure to finance a crash building program on the campuses of the universities and colleges, since we were going to be drastically short of classroom space.

In addition to recommending general programs to the legislature, I also wanted to have a legislative program ready. I therefore had my "backyard mafia" invite about thirty bright young Democratic lawyers to meet with me. We met every evening from about five until seven o'clock, and I outlined the sort of legislation that I wanted. Then these younger lawyers split themselves up into teams and took the responsibility of writing bills, so that I would not be presenting abstract ideas to the legislature, but would have actual bills ready to present. By the time the legislature met on the second Monday in January, the lawyers had prepared 114 separate pieces of legislation, of which all but 12 ultimately passed. I thought this was a very good record, and it indicated that these young men had done their work well.

Sometime in early December I circularized a general letter to all of the heads of state divisions and departments, telling them that I had made few decisions as to personnel changes. I asked them if they would please stay put and do their jobs until I had a chance to get further into this thing, to orient myself and talk to them, and most of them did. A few people quit on the last day of Governor Clyde's term, but not more than two or three of them were in top administrative posts. The rest stayed on and in no case did I let anybody go abruptly. I generally talked to them a month or two before I was going to make a change. As I mentioned, however, there were certain top administrative spots that I wanted to begin filling just as quickly as I took office—in particular the positions for Herb Smart, who was already on board, and Milton Weilenmann.

Within a few weeks after being inaugurated I appointed Milt to head up the Tourism Department. Later we created the Department of Industrial Promotion, which he also took over. As far as my personal staff was concerned, I took as my personal secretary Macel Thurmond, who had worked for me in the law office for about sixteen years. John David Rose, who had handled the advertising for my campaign, became my press secretary, while Glen Hatch, a lawyer from Heber City and a former state senator, became my first administrative assistant. Marjorie Boyd, who had been a secretarial employee of Governor Clyde, stayed on all through my twelve years. This was a small personal staff by choice. There were four of them at the time, and I only had five when I left office.

Others in responsible state administrative positions whom I knew I was going to keep, and whom I had so advised before the transition, were Donald Hacking and Hal Bennett on the Public Service Commission, Jay Bingham in the natural resources field, and Glen Swenson, the executive director of the building board. The director of the State Department of Highways was Taylor Burton, whom I knew very well and trusted. I told Taylor that I was going to replace him before the first of July but would appreciate it if he would stay on in the meantime, and he did stay on for a while.

I was fortunate to be going into the new administration with a Democratic legislature. It's not often that a Democratic governor in Utah finds the majority of both houses of the legislature in his own party. I wasn't so fortunate very often, nor were Governor Matheson or, except during the New Deal years, Governors Blood and Maw. But I did have a Democratic majority in both houses. They were going to organize in the period just before Christmas, and almost all of the various aspirants for leadership positions in the legislature attempted to get my support for their positions. I was warned by Glen Hatch, who as I mentioned had been in the senate himself, that there was no more sure way to get myself into trouble than to attempt to interfere in the legislative caucuses. So I responded to each request with, "That's a legislative matter. I believe in a division of the powers and I'm not going to do anything about it." Bruce Jenkins, a young lawyer whom I knew very well, was elected president of the state senate, and Kay Allen, a businessman who had been in the house for some while, was named speaker of the house. I was to work very closely with these men for two years, and I think our close relationship could not have existed had I attempted to support one of their opponents.

On January 4, 1965, right at noon, I was sworn in as the eleventh governor of Utah. Utah had been admitted to the Union on January 4, 1896, so this celebration took on the atmosphere of both the inauguration of a governor and the anniversary of the admission of the state to the Union. Early that morning Lucybeth, the children, and I got up and had a light family breakfast and reminisced about the house we were then living in, how many years we had been there, and what things had happened to the family. We also discussed the fact that what was going to happen today would make a great change in our lives, but that we were determined it would not change anything between us. About ten o'clock we all got into our 1963 Ford sedan and started for the Capitol.

In keeping with tradition, on the morning of the inauguration there was a breakfast in the governor's boardroom which was attended by former governors and their wives, the heads of all state departments, and certain leaders of the various religious denominations in Utah—a rather chilly breakfast. Bracken Lee and George Clyde were both there, and they had not patched up their differences over the years. Nor was Brack particularly well liked by Herb Maw. There were almost no speeches except those necessary to direct us where to go. Meantime, we could hear the crowd gathering on the main floor of the Capitol.

No one was certain as to how many people would be there. Inaugurations had traditionally not been well attended, but nobody knew what the situation would be with a Democratic administration coming in after sixteen years out of power. When I finally got out into the rotunda, I could see that the entire main floor was full and the balconies were lined about three deep. Later I was to conclude that most of these were job seekers. At any rate, it was a large and enthusiastic crowd.

The breakfast finished by about 11:30, and the people who attended it now proceeded along a narrow aisle through the crowd, down the center of the Capitol rotunda, and up the steps to a temporary stand which had been erected in front of the supreme court chambers on the east side of the rotunda. After all the others had gone by, Governor Clyde and his wife were taken by a military escort to the stand. Lucybeth was then escorted by the assistant adjutant general. Finally, I came up with General Watts, the new adjutant general. As we got to the stand, a battery of guns outside fired a nineteen-gun salute to Governor Clyde, the last he would receive as governor.

Clyde then made a short talk. It was a very proper talk, a bit reserved and chilly, but I was to find out twelve years later just why that was necessarily so. Leaving a position like that after a period of years is a traumatic experience. It was probably much more difficult for him that morning than it was for me. At the end of my third term I was to turn the position over to a member of my own party, a man whom I had known for many years and in whom I had great faith and confidence. On the other hand, Governor Clyde was turning over the governorship to a member of the opposite party whom he'd scarcely known before the campaign started. I'm sure now that it was a very emotional time for him.

Following Clyde's speech, the chief justice of the Utah Supreme Court stepped down and administered to me the oath of office. Immediately after the administration of the oath, there was some military music and then another nineteen-gun salute, this time for me. This was followed by my inaugural address, which lasted about twenty minutes. It seemed to be well received, and it concluded the ceremony. We then went down to the Gold Room for a reception for everybody who wanted to come. This was quite an ordeal – the first of many such receptions in which I would participate. At that time I really wasn't in shape for it. You have to get in training for such things.

The reception broke up somewhere around 3:00 or 3:30, and I went for the first time as governor into the governor's office. My press secretary, John David Rose, had arranged for me to sign a number of official documents, none of great moment, for the press.

I had set a meeting at four o'clock that afternoon for all department heads. It was held in the governor's boardroom, and they were all there. I told them, as I had told them in the earlier circular, that while there would be changes made, I had not had an opportunity to address myself to matters of personnel. Since the election I'd been concerned with the matter of formulating policy to be incorporated in the budget message and the state of the state message. I asked once again that each one of them stay put until I knew what I was going to do.

I was concerned as to how a second thing I had decided to tell this group of state administrators would be received. I had observed, and had been told by legislators, that a great deal of lobbying of the legislature was done by the heads of state departments, often in opposition to what the governor wanted. In fact Governor Clyde in his original briefing with me had said one of the things I would have to watch was that my own department heads did not undermine my own program at the legislature. I knew that if there ever was going to be a time when that would happen this would be it because these department heads had been appointed by Governor Clyde. They knew they weren't going to continue to work for me very long, and there was no basic reason for loyalty to my programs, although their loyalty to the state I never doubted.

I issued at that time an administrative order. Whether I had the authority I do not know, but nonetheless, I issued it. It said in effect that no full-time employee of state government was in any way to lobby the legislature or to initiate an approach to a legislator to affect a piece of legislation under consideration. I told them that if they were approached by a legislator or subpoenaed to testify before a legislative committee, they should give their full and frank opinion without regard to whether it corresponded to my own. But they were not, under any circumstances, to initiate contacts with the legislature. This was received in silence.

I wasn't quite sure what treatment I'd get from the press on this matter because it was a somewhat high-handed tactic, although I felt a necessary one. Both papers the next day almost ignored the inaugural address and covered instead the order I had issued on noncontact with the legislators. The *Tribune* editorial was supportive of my position, and said that they thought it was necessary in order for me to get my program before the legislature and have it successfully passed. The *Deseret News*, while somewhat restrained, was also generally in approval, though it pointed out that this could become a gag rule which, the editor felt, was not good.

After the meeting at the office I went home to prepare for the governor's inaugural ball that evening. There had not been an inaugural ball for twenty-five or thirty years. That we should have one was the brainchild of Wally Sandack of the "backyard mafia." It turned out to be quite a successful affair. The entire Utah Symphony was there to provide music during the earlier part of the evening, and then a dance band took over. I don't know how long the dancing went on, but I remember that night very well. Mother was there, as she had been during the proceedings all day, and it was easy to see in her face her tremendous pride that I had become governor. She was also proud of the fact that my brother Byron, a Republican, had at the same time been elected to the state senate from Davis County. She had a double reason for pride. Byron was at the ball that night, as were many Republican members of the legislature, so it wasn't entirely a partisan affair.

Of the winners in the November elections, not only were the majority of both houses of the legislature Democrats, but so were all four of the other major elective officers: the secretary of state, the attorney general, the state auditor, and the state treasurer. The new secretary of state was Clyde L. Miller, who had been a friend of mine for many years. In 1940 we had run against each other for the position of president of the Young Democratic Clubs of Utah and I had only narrowly defeated him. Clyde was a person who wouldn't hold a grudge at all, and this had made no blip in our friendship over the years. I was delighted that he was going to serve with me. Clyde never claimed to be an intellectual, but he had served in the state senate and had served well. As secretary of state he was in a sense also the surrogate governor; when the governor was out of the state, the secretary of state took over.

Other than that his duties prescribed by statute were rather ministerial. He was in charge of buildings and grounds, and of many records, but so far as the statutory requirements were concerned, his was not a policy-making job. I determined that so far as possible I would change that. Throughout the twelve years we served together, I met with Clyde three or four times a week in addition to our weekly meetings on the board of examiners, and we discussed the administrative decisions that I had made. I don't recall ever discussing these decisions with him from the standpoint of getting his approval. It was more a matter of keeping him abreast of what was happening, because if I were away and something came up, I would certainly want him to be aware of the background of the problem for any decision he would have to make. Furthermore, if something happened to me as governor and I were unable to go on, he would become governor, and I thought it well that he be acquainted with state policy.

Over those twelve years Clyde was a great comfort to me, particularly on the board of examiners, which consists of the governor, the secretary of state, and the attorney general. I was in almost constant friction with my attorneys general, and yet out of the 20,000 or more matters that the board passed on in those twelve years, maybe 500 of them were controversial, and only twice did Clyde vote against my position. I was thus very comfortable with him and felt good about having him in the administration.

It was quite different, however, with the attorney general. Phil Hansen was a lawyer in Salt Lake who had devoted most of his practice to criminal defense work. He was the only Democrat to file for the position in May 1964 and so he won the Democratic nomination by default. Although I tried very hard to find another lawyer to file before the deadline, I was unsuccessful, and I faced the problem of having Phil as my attorney general. During the first few days of my administration I sent a substantial number of questions over to his office for answers. Almost invariably I got back an opinion saying that I couldn't do what I wanted to do. I'm sure there was something more than just legal research involved in his answer. I think Phil had sensed my resentment that he was on the ticket with me and had to run with me. We were almost in a sword's point situation during the four years he was there, and after the first week or two I practically became my own attorney general. I got a set of statute books in the office and did a great deal of research work on legal problems. Practically the only time I sent anything over to Phil for a decision was when I wanted to be told no.

The state treasurer was Lynn Baker of Ogden, also a friend of long standing, and the new state auditor was Sharp Larson, who had been Salt Lake County auditor. Sharp was not a professional auditor but he had the good judgment to employ professional auditors to do the actual work while he administered the office. He was a good state auditor and later, after he was defeated for the position in 1968, I appointed him to the state liquor commission.

The week between the inauguration and the opening of the legislature was a busy one. We continued to live at home, as the Clydes were just in the process of vacating the governor's residence. I now had a brand new Lincoln automobile which we leased from the Ford Motor Company. The very impressive license plate on it read: "Cal 1." I also had a highway patrol aide assigned to me named Mike Gale, who was to be with us for several years until he retired. Mike was an intensely loyal fellow and Lucybeth, the children, and I came to love him very much. He'd pick me up early in the morning at the house, drive me to the Capitol, then take me home in the evening.

During this busy week I devoted myself mostly to legislative matters. I told Macel Thurmond and Glen Hatch that job seekers were to be kept at bay; that task could come later. Although I had my message to the legislature completely outlined before inauguration day, there were still finishing touches to put on it. In addition to that, the hundred or so bills that had been prepared by my lawyers' committees required some revision, and I met frequently with those committees. I also wanted to get better acquainted with the members of the legislature because, after all, whether I was to succeed or fail depended to a great extent on how those men and women looked at the program I was about to present. So I attempted during that week to get as many legislators as I could into my office – and not just members of my own party. We extended invitations to every legislator. I believe at that time there were about twenty-seven senators and sixty-five house members. Most of them came. Depending upon what I wanted to talk to particular legislators about, I would have them in singly or in groups. I think almost without exception, the Democratic legislators came in and talked. Also, at least three-fourths of the Republican legislators came in. I suppose some of them feared, whether rightly or wrongly, that they were going to get a snow job from the new governor, but after this first talk I think our rapport was good. I had previously known about two-thirds of the senators and one-third of the house members, so it was not exactly like meeting a new group of people.

By the end of the week, the message to the legislature was ready. Also ready were the bills for immediate introduction. On the morning of January 11 the legislature convened. It took maybe an hour to get their organizational work done. Then they sent a committee down to tell me that the house and senate were in joint session ready to hear my message. There were three legislators from each house on that committee. They escorted me up to the house chamber, where both the senators and the representatives were gathered. The small galleries were overflowing because there were many people who were interested for one reason or another in what the state of the state message would contain.

It was a long and comprehensive talk. I spoke for an hour, then we took a short recess, and following that I talked for another hour. It was probably the longest speech that I had ever given, and as I came back down from the rostrum and was passing by the senators, Reed Bullen, the senator from Logan, said, "I think, governor, that's the longest speech I ever listened to." I replied, "I'll have to watch that, Reed, because when a Mormon stake president complains about the length of a speech, there's certainly room for concern."

In the speech I dealt mainly with issues that had been the subject matter of the campaign. The first item on which I spent a substantial amount of time was our elementary and secondary educational programs, for which I was prepared to present to the legislature a considerably expanded finance program. In this state of the state address, rather than devoting myself to exact levels of finance, which I preferred to leave for the budget message, I wanted to give the teachers a feeling that the state administration was concerned with their problems. I emphasized that I understood the dignity of the teaching profession, and I understood that since almost without exception they were dedicated teachers, in fairness to themselves and their families they should expect not only a living wage, but a wage with which they could live in dignity.

In the field of higher education I recommended that we give greater emphasis to vocational education and asked for greatly increased appropriations for vocational training both in high schools and in post-high school institutions. I also gave an indication, as I had done during the campaign, that I would ask for a bonding measure for the construction of new buildings at institutions of higher learning, and I suggested the legislature consider a junior college for the Salt Lake City area, which is something they never accomplished.

Next, I requested the legislature to reapportion themselves in accordance with the one-person, one-vote decision of the U.S. Supreme Court, although I was going to have to call them back into a special session in the summer to accomplish that. I asked for congressional redistricting as well. In addition, I suggested legislation that would permit the establishment of metropolitan governments in the state. Although that was something I think needed doing years ago, we really have not gone very far in that direction even today, simply because the idea has not been salable to the people.

Another request I made was for the creation of a committee on the reorganization of state government. Governor Clyde had appointed a similar committee by executive order, but it hadn't done much, and I felt that we had to have legislative participation on the project. Governor Clyde had also created a quasi merit system for the state by executive order. I say quasi because it was always subject to the governor's issuing a modification if he wanted to appoint anybody. I therefore asked the legislature to create a state merit system.

In regard to labor legislation I asked for a repeal of Utah's Right to Work Act. I knew it was a futile gesture but I felt that I should do it anyhow. Furthermore, I recommended beefing up our civil rights laws, particularly in regard to public accommodations; and I asked for a revamping of the juvenile court system with increased appropriations to give us more judges and more supervisory personnel.

The major part of my speech was devoted to the need for economic development in the state, both in industrial development and tourist promotion and publicity. Governor Clyde's poorly funded tourist promotion program was still in place although it needed to be revamped, but there was no industrial promotion program at all. I stressed the need to create new jobs in the state in order to give employment opportunities to young men and women who were coming out of the high schools and colleges. I also placed some emphasis on water development. I'm sure the legislators were glad when I finally finished speaking.

I waited rather expectantly to see what kind of treatment I would be given the next day in the newspapers. The leadership of the legislature was generally supportive in its statements. The Democrats were, of course, very supportive, while some of the Republicans felt it necessary to nitpick at the message a little bit; for the most part, though, they were encouraging. Moreover, I got an excellent editorial in the *Salt Lake Tribune* and a fairly good one in the *Deseret News*.

I don't want to sound too obsessed with the reaction I received in the press. Although it was then and continued to be of great concern to me, I was not interested in self-aggrandizement. The fact is that a governor, if he is to get a program first through the legislature and then have it accepted by the people, must have reasonable support from the press. I felt that I received excellent support from both the print and electronic media throughout my administration. Of course, Jack Gallivan, the publisher of the *Tribune*, had been a good friend of mine for a number of years. The publisher of the *Deseret News*, Bill Smart, had also been an acquaintance of mine for some time, and I got along well with him. He was much more guarded in support of programs I suggested than was Gallivan, but I felt Bill and his political editor, DeMar Teuscher, treated me fairly.

I had a great deal of help in dealing with the newspeople from the press secretaries who served with me. The duties of a governor's press secretary are twofold: one is to conduct relations with the media that cover the governor's office; the other, in a small press section such as mine, is to write or help write speeches that are to be given by the officeholder. In selecting my press secretaries—first David Rose, then Mike Miller, and finally Paul Sheffield—I leaned heavily toward selecting people who had the proper rapport with the press and the electronic media, since I was able for the most part to write my own speeches. In addition, I had in Lucybeth a superb speech writer who probably was more articulate than any press secretary I could have hired.

The week between the state of the state message and the budget message was sort of a regrouping period. I was tired. I was being plagued by job applicants, but I had told my staff that I still wasn't ready to see them. The fact that I had asked for a merit system in the state of the state message was already causing a great deal of concern with some of the party members.

We had a heavy winter in 1964–65. The ski resorts east of Salt Lake City had a great deal of snow, and along with the snow came snowslides. Within a day or so of giving my state of the state message Macel Thurmond came running into my office and said, "Governor, the president's on the phone." This pleased me very much because Lyndon wasn't the kind of guy who went overboard on flattery and I felt that he must feel rather kindly toward me if he would take the time to call me up to congratulate me. Macel put him on the line, and he said, "Cal, I understand that Bob McNamara is snowbound at a place called Alta, Utah." I answered, "Yes, Mr. President, I read that in the paper this morning." The president said, "Goddamn it, get him out of there," and slammed down the phone. I called Nick Watts, the adjutant general, and asked if he had a helicopter in the Air National Guard that could go up to Alta and get the secretary of defense out. Nick said he did not, so I told him to see if he could find a private helicopter service that could send one up there. He called back in a few minutes and said, "I found one. How do we pay for it?" I wasn't quite sure how to pay for it, but I said, "Let's not worry about that. Hire the helicopter and get it up there."

Also during this slow week we moved from our house at 2492 South Twenty-third East into the state residence on Virginia Street near the university, as Governor and Mrs. Clyde had moved out several days previously. There were complaints by some who said that it wasn't a mansion; and certainly that was true. We did not want a mansion. But it was a livable house in which we were comfortable and happy for twelve years.

On Monday, January 18, I had to give my budget message. I had been quite sure that the state of the state message would be well received because, except for a hint of things to come on which people would by and large reserve judgment, I talked about matters that I think most people could agree with. But when it came to the budget and the budget message, I was getting right down to the nitty gritty of government, and I knew this was going to be tough.

Herb Smart had done a magnificent job on the budget. We had increased the recommendation for expenditures for the schools as far as I believed we could go. We had made a recommendation for a bond issue for improvements on the college campuses and expansion of the state park system. The total bond issue was $67 million, of which $2 million was to go for the state park system and $65 million for buildings. Glen Hatch had talked me into the $2 million for the bond issue for the parks because during Governor Clyde's administration the state had bought on contracts a sizable amount of land to create what is now Wasatch State Park. It was farsighted on Governor Clyde's part to do that, although many of these purchase contracts for small sections of land would run for many years in the future and totaled in all about $2 million. Glen persuaded me that we should pay those off with money from the bonding because we were paying a higher rate of interest on the purchase contracts than the bonds would probably require. In addition, I recommended about a threefold increase for tourism, and the creation and funding of the new industrial promotion department.

A budget message is a rather short summary of budget requests, as most of the data is contained in a document of several hundred pages which a governor cannot hope to cover in an address to the legislature. The legislators had clamored to get our budget document ahead of time, but Herb Smart had had experience with this process and persuaded me not to give it to them. So as the legislators filed into the house chamber for the joint session, they received the budget for the first time. The document was close to an inch thick, and they couldn't begin to digest it while I was there. My speech took about twenty minutes to deliver, and then I prepared to leave town.

Two days later saw the inauguration of Lyndon Johnson for his elected term as president of the United States, after having served some thirteen months as president following the assassination of John Kennedy. All the governors of the United States (I believe there were no exceptions that year) were to attend the inauguration and ride in the parade. I had learned from Nick Watts that National Guard planes were available to transport the governor and his necessary official party on official state business, so we arranged to have one of the guard planes, a C-97, fly Lucybeth and me to Washington with various state officials who had official functions to perform at the inauguration or who could do state business there during that time.

However, on the afternoon of the eighteenth, when we were to leave for Washington, a heavy fog settled over the valley and we were unable to take off. I wanted to get away from Salt Lake. I'd delivered a bomb in the budget message and I didn't want to be there when the flak started. We therefore stayed at the governor's residence and got periodic calls from the airport saying we couldn't take off because the fog was too dense. About midafternoon, General Alma Wynn, the commander of the air guard who was going to pilot the plane to Washington, called and said there was a temporary clearing and he could take off almost immediately and land the plane at Hill Field, which was also clear. He believed that the weather was better at Hill Field and we'd be better able to take off from there. So he got the plane up there about four o'clock in the afternoon. We drove up around six o'clock, but by then both Salt Lake and Hill were socked in very badly. We waited on the plane and at the base until a little after six o'clock in the morning, when we finally took off for Washington. It was the first time I was to fly in a military aircraft, although I did it frequently over the succeeding years. We had an uneventful flight and arrived in midafternoon. The city was getting ready for the inauguration, which was to be on the next day.

January 20, 1965, the day of the inauguration, was clear but very cold. There had been rain and some snow, but the snow was largely gone. Our daughter Meg had come down from Harvard for the occasion, and the three of us left together for the Capitol. The air force had assigned us a driver and an automobile, so we had no trouble getting through. We went first to a breakfast in one of the large conference rooms in the House Office Building. We were excited because we were going to meet the other governors. The three of us walked into the room and looked around. There were a lot of people there by then and not a soul did we know. Brevard Crihfield, who was the executive secretary of the governors' conference, had apparently been briefed on our appearance and came over to meet us and make us feel at home.

The breakfast was buffet style. We saw a table across the room with only two men sitting at it, so we walked to the table, sat down, and discovered that the two men were George Wallace and Orval Faubus, the governors of Alabama and Arkansas. Both men were well known nationally for their opposition to civil rights activities, and neither was favorably considered. They were both very cordial, however, and we all made small talk. In just a few minutes two more couples came to complete the seating at the table. These proved to be the new governor of West Virginia, Hewlett Smith, and his wife, Mary Alice, and the governor of South Carolina, Bob McNair, and his wife, Josephine.

After breakfast the governors were taken as a group, in the order in which their states had been admitted to the Union, to the rotunda of the Capitol (which was a madhouse), and from there to the reviewing stand on the east side. Promptly at noon the band struck up "Hail to the Chief," and Lyndon and Lady Bird came down the aisle, followed rather closely by Hubert Humphrey, the vice-president-elect, and his wife, Muriel. Earl Warren was at the time the chief justice of the United States. He stepped up and administered the oaths, first to Humphrey and then to Lyndon Johnson. It was truly a moving occasion.

But the most moving part was still to come. The Mormon Tabernacle Choir was there to provide most of the music for the program. The choir had had a difficult time getting to Washington. The fog which had delayed us had prevented them from taking off from Salt Lake City. Arrangements were finally made for them to take busses from Salt Lake City to Las Vegas, and from there to board airliners for the trip to Washington. The bus trip from Salt Lake to Las Vegas takes eight and one-half or nine hours, and the decision to go by bus was not made until the morning of the nineteenth. It was probably ten or eleven o'clock before the busses were assembled, and the choir members arrived in Las Vegas in the early evening of the nineteenth. There they boarded two planes and flew most of the night to Washington, getting there at dawn on the twentieth and having to perform shortly after noon.

The choir members were extremely tired, and the weather was bitterly cold, but they were all in their places by eleven o'clock. They occupied a large stand in front of and below the area where the president was taking his oath of office. Neither fatigue nor cold appeared to trouble them. They sang three numbers, including "The Battle Hymn of the Republic," and I've never heard them sing more beautifully. Anyone from Utah who was there that day, whether Mormon or not, could not have helped being very proud of that group which performed so well under such adverse circumstances.

After the inauguration ceremonies were completed there was general chaos, with everybody trying to find his or her way to the automobile in which he or she was to ride in the inaugural parade. In 1973 the inaugural parade committee discontinued the custom of having governors ride in the parade, but in 1965 they still rode, with each in a separate automobile. We finally found our open convertible and sat there, quite cold and wrapped up in blankets, for probably thirty minutes before we were given the signal to go.

Meg had been given permission to ride with us. As we went down the streets people were banked deeply on each side. We frequently heard comments: "Here comes the Mormon governor with his old wife and his young wife." I'm not sure anyone meant it seriously, but I'm not sure, either, that someone there didn't believe it.

When I got back to Salt Lake City the legislature was just completing the second week of its eight-week session. I was pleased to see how smoothly everything was going. Most of the smaller, housekeeping-type bills which had been prepared by my lawyers' committees were introduced and had been referred to the legislative committees, and there appeared to be no particular opposition to any of these. The Republican opposition had concentrated principally on the bonding bill, and also on the school finance bill and two or three others. Some major legislation, such as the freeport bill, which exempted from Utah taxation all inventories stored in Utah for transshipment out of the state, and the bill creating an industrial promotion department, had pretty general support in both houses. The right-to-work repeal, however, appeared to be dead. I had felt sure it would be voted down on the floor and I expected it to be bottled up in committee. At any rate, I thought the legislature was doing well.

As the session went on, party lines tended to draw rather tightly around the controversial measures. We had a very narrow majority in both houses. As I recall, it was fifteen to twelve in the senate: if I lost two senators on the Democratic side, we would lose our majority. In the house of representatives it was thirty-nine to thirty. We could lose only four Democratic legislators and still pass a measure on a party-line vote; therefore, it was most important that we try to keep issues from taking on a partisan tinge. I had to caution the legislative leadership many times not to do anything to stir partisan opposition on the floor, and particularly to avoid attacks on the Clyde administration or anything of the kind that would cause the Republican legislators to oppose a piece of legislation on the grounds that it was partisan.

I was pretty sure of the majority hanging together on most issues in the senate. My brother Byron occupied a rather delicate position, of course, since he was a Republican. Although we have had opposing political positions all of our lives, the Republican caucus looked on Byron with some skepticism, particularly when discussing strategies within the caucus that they wouldn't want revealed.

Near the end of the legislative session, my mother became very ill. She was a diabetic, and when her medication got out of balance she would get desperately ill and would have to be hospitalized for two or three weeks at a time. Often during the hospitalization it would be sort of a desperate situation as to whether she was going to make it. One of these periods occurred during the closing weeks of the legislature. I would get reports from the hospital three or four times daily on Mother's condition. Since Byron was up in the legislature where the doctors couldn't reach him on the phone, I would generally send a note to him by one of my office aides, informing him of the latest information on Mother's condition. His Republican colleagues, most of whom were unaware of Mother's illness, couldn't help wondering aloud sometimes what was the content of these frequent notes that were coming to him from the governor's office. This suspicion was fueled when Byron voted with me on three or four crucial measures, including the bonding act, where his vote came near to providing the margin of victory. I'm sure the feeling among Republicans that Byron had been more supportive of my programs than he was of the minority position contributed greatly to the fact that he lost in the primary when he ran for reelection in the fall of 1966.

The Republican opposition to the bonding bill arose largely from the fact that two years previously, in the 1963 legislature, the Republicans had adopted a proposal of their own to meet the school building need on the college campuses. This proposal had provided for the earmarking of a one-half percent increase in the sales tax. The problem I had with the idea was that it wouldn't do the job fast enough. We had to get the buildings planned and construction started right away if we were going to meet the population's needs. The Republican plan would have spread the construction period over nearly a decade. Furthermore, all of the economic indicators said that inflation was going to increase, which meant that every year we delayed, the cost of construction of a building would increase 5 to 10 percent. And although interest rates were low at that time, they showed every prospect of increasing. If we were going to have to bond I felt that this was the time to do it.

There was also another reason why I wanted the bonding bill. I needed the one-half percent from the sales tax which the Republicans had earmarked for building purposes in the general fund to meet the ongoing financial needs of the state. Without that money going into the general fund, it would have been necessary to recommend more of an increase in other taxes, either the sales tax or the income tax, than I was already proposing to do. The Republicans were quick to play on the fact that I was using this money for ongoing maintenance and operations and that it really constituted a tax increase because we were going, at some time in the future, to have to pay the principal and interest on the bond out of tax revenues. Of course, that was true.

Nonetheless, the bonding bill moved steadily ahead through both houses. It passed the house of representatives the first time fairly easily, then went to the senate, where it was amended. It had to go back for a conference, where it was not amended as to any basic part, but only as to certain details, and after much legislative shuffling, the bill passed in the final days of the legislature with the senate amendments intact.

The adoption of the bonding measure, which made $65 million available for school buildings and $2 million for the acquisition of land for state parks, proved to be a fortuitous thing. When the bond came up for sale around July, we were able to get a very good rate. We got bids and sold the bonds for an interest rate of 2.92 percent. This was the last major bond issue in the United States to go at under 3 percent. Furthermore, although we had the money available immediately, we did not spend it immediately. The interest rate on money in the general market was increasing quite rapidly and we were able to invest the unused portions of the fund for the period that we held them for rates up to 7 percent. As a result, the effective rate of interest that the state had to pay on the bonds over their fifteen-year life was only about 1.42 percent.

The school finance bill which I proposed called for an increase in state spending in the high school and elementary schools program of almost $17 million for the biennium. Two other school bills had been introduced and were moving through committee toward consideration on the floor. One of these was introduced by Senator John Bernhard, a Brigham Young University professor. It called for almost the same amount of money that I was proposing but would have distributed it in a different way. The additional money that I was going to put into the school program would have gone largely to teacher salaries. It was my feeling that Utah's salary scale had fallen so far below the national average, and particularly below the average of surrounding states, that we had to use our limited resources to get the teachers a basic living wage. Senator Bernhard's bill would have put part of the money into a general across-the-board increase of teacher salaries, but would have put about one-third of the money into an incentive program where certain meritorious teachers would get a substantially greater increase than others.

This merit system in the public schools had long been debated and there was a great deal to say in favor of it. However, I did not favor Senator Bernhard's bill for two reasons: first, I thought we had to get the general average salary up substantially, and, second, nobody had come up with an acceptable formula for distributing incentive or merit money. Most of the formulae that were presented or debated relied so heavily on subjective considerations on the part of the school administrators that it was obvious such a system could have become subject to abuse.

The third proposal could be regarded as the UEA proposal, although I'm not sure that the UEA as a body ever endorsed any one of the three. An Ogden member of the house endorsed this proposal, which would have given the same amount that I recommended for general across-the-board increases. In addition, it would have laminated on top of that the incentive and merit programs, thus costing substantially more in the biennium than I proposed: an increase of around $23 or $24 million. I did not see how we could meet that much of an increase. I knew we couldn't on the tax schedule that I had presented to the legislature, and if we were going to get that extra $5 or $6 million it would require some tax adjustment.

The school finance matter went down almost to the final day before the administration bill was passed. There were some amendments to it, but it passed by and large in the form in which it had been introduced.

We also had introduced three civil rights bills: a housing bill, a public accommodations bill, and a fair employment practices bill. The fair employment practices bill and the public accommodations bill passed with comfortable majorities in both houses, with some of the Republicans coming over to vote for the bills and very few Democrats voting against. However, a substantial surprise attack was made on the housing bill near the end by real estate interests in downtown Salt Lake City. I was quite unprepared for the attack because I thought the three civil rights bills would go through all right; but the housing bill didn't make it through the legislature.

The state merit system bill caused a substantial amount of controversy as well. I had problems with the Democratic majority because many of them saw it as freezing into office state employees who had been hired during the Lee and Clyde administrations, which, in truth, it did. However, I did not believe that any substantial number of these people had been employed on a strictly partisan basis. In the years since 1946 the need for technically trained people in state government had increased. We almost had a de facto merit system, if not a de jure one. No new governor was going to take the chance with the complicated machinery of state government to turn out competent people and replace them with people with no training merely because they had the right political credentials.

The merit system bill was passed. This, however, was a matter that was giving me increasing problems with my own party—not in the legislature particularly, but in the basic party structure throughout the state. More and more I was becoming the subject of critical comment by party officials, and probably this rose to a crescendo when I appointed Republican A. Pratt Kesler to the tax commission. It had to be a Republican appointee because the statute required a bipartisan commission, but many people could not see why I would select such a target of their wrath as a former Republican attorney general and state chairman for this job. However, I felt that Kesler was well qualified. He wanted the job, and I was glad to get him.

I was considering appointments to the Board of Regents of the University of Utah when I was first contacted by LDS Church officials trying to influence state policy in areas that the church could not reasonably consider moral. These positions were actively sought by prominent citizens in the community because they carried with them considerable prestige. I received a call from Hugh B. Brown, the first counselor in the first presidency of the LDS Church. I had known President Brown for many years. He was an active member of the Democratic party and a man I loved and admired very much. Brown approached the subject rather gingerly, saying, "Governor, I have been asked by my associates to call you and tell you that we would regard it as a great favor if you would reappoint Brother Derrick as a member of the Board of Regents of the University of Utah." The man referred to was Royden Derrick, a Salt Lake industrialist. I knew Royden well, liked him, and felt that he was a good appointee, but for certain reasons which I related to Brown, I didn't plan to reappoint him. I said, in effect, "President Brown, Mr. Derrick was an excellent member of the Board of Regents for a number of years. He's been chairman for several years. But in the last three or four years Western Steel, the company of which he is president, has been getting construction contracts all over the United States and, in fact, all over the world, with the result that Mr. Derrick is gone from the state a large percentage of the time. And recently, I'm informed, he has been a very infrequent attendee at the meetings of the board. Although he is a good man and an able man, recently he has not been contributing. Furthermore," I continued, "he is one of the people the Republicans are considering running against me in 1968. Given those facts, what would you do?" Brown replied, "I wouldn't appoint him."

Along other lines, I had asked the legislature to provide for a committee to study the organization of the executive branch of state government and make recommendations for revision. This was done, and the committee was to be called the Little Hoover Commission. There was some controversy, however, as to how many members of the study commission should be appointed by the governor and how many should be appointed by the leadership of the legislature. Everybody agreed that it should be a bipartisan body. I was not really concerned about the appointive powers to the commission, but I wanted the power to appoint the chairman and I wanted enough people as members to give their work an administrative voice. Ultimately, though, their recommendations would be ineffective unless there was general legislative approval. So the greater participation by legislators or legislatively appointed members of the commission, the greater the chance for legislative acceptance. After a little pulling and tugging, the membership of the Little Hoover Commission and the power of appointment were decided upon.

The budget, which is the backbone of any program, was passed almost without change from what I had recommended. The chairman of the joint appropriations committee was Senator Ernest Mantes, a Democrat from Tooele County. Ernest had been in the legislature a number of years. He was a successful businessman, having for a long time conducted an automobile business in Tooele. He was well trained in finance and he generally agreed with me on most items in the budget. In fact, during the preparation of the budget Herb Smart, who did most of the work for me, had worked very closely with Mantes. The budget required an increase in sales tax. It also required an increase in the percentage of both the individual and the corporate income taxes, and this part of the plan did get some opposition. I lost three or four Democratic members of the house on these taxation measures; fortunately, I also picked up some Republican support.

At that time, the law provided that the state could levy a property tax. This tax was to be fixed not by the legislature, but by the tax commission, which meant in practical effect by the governor. Over the years, beginning in the early forties, the property tax on a state basis had been increased periodically until, when I became governor, there was a 9.7 mill levy on property. I promised the legislators that if they would give me the increases I asked for in sales tax and income tax, I would set about lowering the state property tax and would eventually eliminate it. That gained me enough Republican support to pass the revenue measures that were a basic part of the budget. I kept faith with this promise. I reduced the property tax the first year from the 9.7 mills to 8.6 mills, and we cut it down almost every year thereafter until about 1970 when it was entirely eliminated from the state financial structure. Since that time the state has made no levy against property, leaving that major source of revenue to the school districts and local units of government which depend largely on it for their survival.

The legislature ended after its sixtieth day on what I thought was a note of good feeling. The Republicans, of course, felt they had to criticize some things. Governor Clyde gave a critique of the legislative action and was generally in approval, although he was very critical of the passing of the bonding program. The *Salt Lake Tribune* on the morning after the legislature ended had a large black headline on the front page: "Legislature Adjourns in Administrative Triumph," or words to that effect. This gave me some concern because I'm sure the legislators felt, as I did, that it wasn't an administration triumph; it was a triumph of good people working together, and I tried to play down the role of the governor in what had been accomplished in the legislative session. I knew if I played it up it would come back and haunt me later and cost me in future legislative support. Fortunately, both the *Deseret News* and the *Salt Lake Tribune* editorialized on the accomplishments of this legislature and the legislative leadership, and they tended to play down the contribution of the governor.

I felt that this was an excellent legislature, and I used the veto power sparingly after this particular session. Two of the bills which I vetoed after the session ended were just minor bills and were vetoed because of technical defects. I've been a legislature watcher in Utah since the 1940s, and I believe that this was the best legislature Utah has had. In fact, that summer at a meeting of the National Legislative Conference, Governor Anderson of Kansas, the chairman of the National Governors' Conference, cited this Thirty-sixth Legislature of the state of Utah as the outstanding legislature in the United States that year.

Within a few days after the close of the legislative session the members of the Little Hoover Commission were named. This was to be one of the most important commissions ever appointed in Utah, and their work has contributed immensely to the development of state government in the last few years. I made four appointments and the president of the senate and the speaker of the house each made four appointments. They were to be bipartisan appointments, evenly balanced politically. I appointed Joseph Rosenblatt, a Salt Lake City industrialist; Thorpe B. Isaacson, an insurance executive who was also assistant to the Council of Twelve Apostles in the LDS Church and later became a counselor to the first presidency; Dr. Merle E. Allen, who at that time was at Weber College; and John Rackham, an economist.

I designated Joe Rosenblatt as chairman of the commission, and he proved an excellent choice. Joe spent almost forty hours a week for a year giving the state his services without any compensation at all. He worked hard as the leader of the commission. Joe set up a staff and the commission began its meetings quickly after the legislative session ended. We had an appropriation for the Little Hoover Commission of $150,000.

We knew that we needed a consulting firm. We had presentations by several firms and the one Joe selected, with my concurrence, was the firm of Booze, Allen and Hamilton. They sent in several people, headed by a man named Gordon Smith, who had been with a number of national accounting firms and had previous experience in auditing state and county books. Gordon stayed with us for just about a year. He returned to California after he had completed his work with the Little Hoover Commission and in the spring of 1967 was appointed by the new governor, Ronald Reagan, as comptroller of the state of California. His service in overhauling the fiscal system of California was based, I'm sure, in large part on his experience with the Little Hoover Commission in Utah.

Soon after the close of the legislative session there also came the first of what would prove to be many invitations to Washington, D.C., for briefings of the governors by the president on state-federal relationships. We began our stay with a White House dinner, which was the first time Lucybeth and I had been to the White House, except to stand in the visitors' line. Forty-two of the fifty governors and their wives were there. The Johnsons had a reception line in the East Room where the governors walked through with their wives, and each had a moment to spend with the Johnsons.

I hadn't seen Mrs. Johnson to talk to her since 1938, when she and Lyndon were newlyweds. That was on the evening I was inaugurated as the speaker of the Little Congress, and Lucybeth and I weren't yet married. As we came through the line Lyndon, of course, remembered me. I don't know how Mrs. Johnson could possibly have remembered, but evidently she had been briefed. She is an extremely gracious lady, and she called attention to the fact that we had met all those years ago. We became very fond of her on the occasions that we were to be in her company during the next four years.

The next day the forty-two governors were briefed by the president and members of his cabinet on the Great Society program, which he was getting ready to send to Congress. Most of this program had actually been proposed earlier by President Kennedy. But Kennedy, although a great innovator, did not have the ability to work with Congress that Lyndon Johnson had.

Also at this briefing session we were advised concerning the administration's Vietnam policy. At that time the Vietnam policy, as the president saw it, was much less important than it later came to be. It is my belief that Vietnam undermined the Johnson presidency, and it is equally my belief that Johnson early on had no intention of getting involved in Southeast Asia to the extent he did. He just got caught in a situation from which he couldn't extricate himself without a disastrous retreat and complete abandonment of U.S foreign policy. The things we heard at the briefing that day were dramatically different from those we were to hear at subsequent briefings over the next three or four years.

I had by now made most of my appointments to the part-time policy-making positions in Utah government. These positions were generally much sought after, even though they carried with them only a small per diem. In most cases, the appointments of the administrative heads of the various departments were made by these part-time commissioners, with the concurrence of the governor. This meant, of course, that I would confer with the policy-making boards before a selection was made.

In the month or two following the close of the legislature, two major changes were made. Taylor Burton, who had been the director of the state road commission for a number of years, came to see me immediately after I was elected and said he was willing to leave office then or, if I wanted, to remain until the first of July. I asked him to wait. I had appointed to the part-time policy-making board of the state road commission two new people: Weston Hamilton, a Salt Lake banker, as chairman of the commission, and Clem Church, a man from Panguitch, as the second member. Three holdover members made up the rest of the five-man commission.

The chief engineer of the road commission under Burton had been Henry Helland, who had previously been employed by the state highway commission of Montana and by the Bureau of Public Roads of the U.S. government. I knew Helland and thought he would make an excellent director of highways. I discussed it with the highway commission and we agreed that Helland would become the director. This left vacant the office of chief engineer. There was an engineer in the state highway department named Blaine Kaye, a career employee whom I had cross-examined a number of times on the witness stand when I had represented landowners in condemnation actions. I appointed Kaye to the position of chief engineer and later, when Helland retired, advanced him to the position of director.

Jim Cannon stayed on as director of the Tourist and Publicity Council until after the legislative session ended. After he and I had a talk, and he knew that I was going to appoint somebody else, he left. I appointed in his stead Manny Floor, a young businessman in Salt Lake who had been actively engaged in public relations work. The budget of the Tourist and Publicity Council had been increased manyfold, and so when Manny took office he could make plans for the vastly increased programs that we were going to establish with the new funds.

Another change I made concerning a full-time directorship caused me some pain. This was in the position of director of the state parks service. The director under Governor Clyde had been Aldon Hayward of Bountiful. Our families were close and I had known Aldon well all the while I was growing up, even though he was ten years older. Nonetheless, Hayward was not a professional parks man and I felt he was unqualified. At about that time, a man named Felix Koziol had resigned from a position with the forest service. Koziol was a superbly qualified man, albeit nominally a Republican and known as such. After consultation with the parks department policy board, I appointed Koziol, much to the dismay of my Democratic friends.

As a result of the policies that I had adopted regarding personnel appointments, my relationship with a fairly sizable portion of the Democratic party was deteriorating rapidly. In the early summer of 1965 we had a state convention to elect the new state officers of the party. The preceding state chairman did not choose to seek reelection, and there were two aspirants for the job: one was Ray Pruitt, who had been both the Democratic party chairman and the surveyor of Tooele County; the other was Ed Flynn, an industrial relations man with Kennecott Copper in Salt Lake. I let it be known, quite clearly, that I would prefer to see Flynn elected, because Pruitt was a leader of the group that was highly critical of my personnel policies. The convention vote was close, but Pruitt won, which meant that I now had a hostile state chairman. I did as much as I could to make a rapprochement, but he insisted that the state Democratic committee should have control of patronage appointments in the state. That was a position I couldn't accept and one on which we continued to differ.

Things got so bad that in August of that year at the meeting of the central committee, a resolution was actually introduced

censuring me for ignoring the wishes of the Democratic party in regard
to public appointments. The resolution did not pass, but the fact that
it was introduced and seriously considered indicates how severely my
relationship with the party had deteriorated. It really didn't get back
to a reasonable level again until the election of 1968, when it was
quite apparent to the dissident group that I was going to be the nominee for governor again. They had either to get behind me and support me or take a chance of losing the governorship for the party. Our
differences were to some extent ironed out, and from that time my
relationship with the party leadership was reasonably good. This position as titular head of the Democratic party of the state, which automatically goes to the governor, was one I didn't particularly enjoy and
an activity in which I didn't engage too well.

During the first session of the legislature I became more
and more aware of how different the problems faced by rural Utah
were from those faced in the more urban areas along the Wasatch
Front. I had traveled throughout Utah during the campaigns, but
largely I had grown up and lived in or adjacent to the major center of
population. The problems presented by the rural legislators often were
not as familiar to me as they should have been. Lucybeth and I talked
about this quite a lot. We decided that during the remainder of 1965
we would visit each county in the state for at least one day. We made
a public announcement of our intention to do this, which was greeted
with some enthusiasm and some skepticism on the part of the rural
areas. It was apparently believed that we would soon tire of this activity and not complete it. Nonetheless, we started out in the late spring
and early summer of 1965 on these county visits.

On a typical visit, we would go into the county either early
in the morning or late the previous evening and stay there overnight.
In the morning I would meet with the county commissioners. There
would then be a period for officials of cities in the county to come in
and chat. Just before noon, I would meet with the school people to
discuss the needs of that particular school district. The afternoon I
reserved as a period for individual citizens to come in and meet with
me. These meetings were generally well attended. Even in the smallest
county we would get twenty or thirty people who wanted to chat with
the governor for a moment. That would take up all of the afternoon,
generally, in ten-minute appointments. I took not only my own per-

sonal staff on these trips, but also, depending upon what I believed might come up during the meetings, personnel from the administrative departments that I thought needed to hear the proposals, and oftentimes, complaints.

In the evening I would be available for a meeting or a social gathering with local Democratic party members. I did this for two reasons: first, I didn't want the party to feel that I was ignoring them entirely; and second, I was having growing trouble with the grassroots party members because of patronage problems. In a number of counties the situation got bad enough that the local Democratic county committee would decline to sponsor an event, in which case I would ask the public officials if they wanted to have a social event in the evening. So always we would have some kind of a social gathering to which the general public would be invited, although they knew it was to have political overtones.

Our first visit was into the Uintah Basin, where we had set aside three days: one for Duchesne County, one for Uintah County, and one for Daggett County. The Duchesne County visit was our first one and we were trying out our format there. Lucybeth decided that as I was meeting with the city and county officials in the morning, she would meet with some of the women. Her meeting was announced in advance, and a rather sizable group of women showed up. By way of getting things started, Lucybeth asked how many of them were from the various Duchesne County towns, and it turned out that almost all of them were from the two small towns of Hanna and Tabiona. One of these women stood up and announced, "We're here about the road." She proceeded then with an emphatic description of that road between the two towns, and an equally emphatic demand that something be done about it.

The road between Hanna and Tabiona really was a disaster. The towns were about ten miles apart, and as the high school was in Tabiona, the students from Hanna had to be transported by bus. The road was so bad, the women said, that the students had to get out and push the bus part of the way. I had heard some talk about this problem from the county officials during the morning meeting, but the women descended in force upon the citizens' meeting in the afternoon. They let me know, without any chance of misunderstanding, that so far as they were concerned this was the county's top priority.

This road was part of the state road system. It shouldn't have been, but an enterprising legislator some years before had decided that the state might as well maintain that road rather than Duchesne County, and so he had passed an act putting it on the state road system. The state had largely ignored it, but there wasn't much I could do to ignore these women, so when I got back to Salt Lake I told Henry Helland that he had to rearrange his budget and do something about that Hanna-to-Tabiona road, even if he had to defer certain sections of I-15. He did. We fixed the road up before that fall, and I'm glad to say that it was appreciated out there.

We met the next day in Uintah County. I knew the problems there a little better because I had been in that county many times trying cases. On the third day we went up into Daggett County. The social gathering that evening was in the home of Heber Bennion, who had been secretary of state a number of years before, and whose campaign for the governorship I had managed in 1952.

A few weeks later we left for a series of county meetings in south-central Utah. Our main point there was Panguitch, in Garfield County, but we also visited in Wayne and Piute counties. After the meeting in Garfield County, a mutton fry was arranged for us at the home of Billie and Wally Miller on Panguitch Lake. This mutton fry came to be an annual event for the rest of the time we were in office. They were wonderful occasions. The Millers would cook mutton and sourdough biscuits in dutch ovens around a big campfire, and we would spend the evenings singing.

On this first occasion, a county commissioner of Piute County named Basil Lay approached Lucybeth. Mr. Lay was concerned about an Anasazi Indian village that had been excavated in Boulder, a rather remote town in Garfield County. He knew she had an interest in anthropology. He wanted Lucybeth to intercede with Dr. Jesse Jennings, the head of the anthropology department at the University of Utah who had done the digging down there and was a former professor of hers, to bring enough of the artifacts back to make an exhibit. It would be necessary, though, to provide a building of some kind in which to house the artifacts. Mr. Lay had prepared a list of materials that would be needed. It wasn't an impressive list. He had priced the materials out, and his total figure was $1,500. Lucybeth talked to me about it, and it certainly seemed like a reasonable proposal. Felix Koziol was with us on that trip, so I said, "Kozy, I think this is a worthy project. Let's do something about it." I don't know whether Kozy felt I was more devoted to the project than I actually was or whether he, himself, was caught up in it, but the next thing I knew they had plans for a museum down there which was to cost not $1,500, but, originally, more than $40,000 and eventually almost $80,000. Nonetheless, the museum was built and it is beautiful.

The 1965 session of the legislature had reestablished the State Industrial Promotion Department which had been abandoned some sixteen years earlier when Lee became governor. The appropriations for the new department would not become effective until July 1, so as that month approached I made the appointments for the part-time policy-making board. I appointed men from around the state who were interested in, and knowledgeable about, industrial promotion. I tried to get the appointments geographically well scattered and, of course, I was required by the law to make them bipartisan. I had had Milt Weilenmann standing by since the election to take the chief administrative position in this new department. When the law became effective he came to work for the state and stayed the remaining eleven and a half years I served as governor. He continued as director after the Tourist and Publicity Council, the Department of Industrial Promotion, and a number of others were grouped together under the Department of Developmental Services.

In the spring of 1965 an organization of businessmen, called Pro-Utah, was formed by Gus Backman. Gus had been the executive secretary of the Salt Lake Chamber of Commerce for about twenty years, up until the time Max Rich had taken over the job in the fall of 1964. He then became, for a period of time, the manager of the Hotel Utah. Pro-Utah had great difficulty getting funding. This problem was corrected when the new Department of Industrial Promotion came into being, as it brought with it a budget. Gus was only too eager to combine the efforts of the state department with the efforts of the private sector, as this was the reason for the existence of Pro-Utah. And, although the major part of the burden rested upon the state government, we were delighted to have Pro-Utah's efforts.

We immediately began a program of taking groups of Utah businessmen into various financial and industrial centers of the United States. Generally in these areas we were able to find sizable numbers of business leaders with Utah backgrounds who were willing to set up meetings for us with the leaders of industry and finance in their adopted towns. One of our first trips was to New York, where there was a large group of men with western backgrounds who called themselves the Lochinvar Club. The club set up a meeting and a dinner in the Waldorf-Astoria Hotel. I flew back in the National Guard plane with Milt Weilenmann, members of the staff, members of the advisory committee, and various Utah industrial leaders. I was scolded for using the plane several times by the National Guard Bureau, who were questioning whether this was a public purpose; but I adhered to my policy and continued to follow it. As a matter of fact, the crews of our Air National Guard had to spend a certain number of hours each month in the air, and if we didn't use them for this purpose, they would just fly around in routine patterns. So I felt we were not taking advantage of a situation.

At each of these industrial promotion gatherings we would have a person from Utah, generally somebody from the tax commission, explain the state tax structure and why it was helpful to business and investment. We would conclude with a slide presentation covering all of the advantages of the state from tax structure, to cultural advantages, to our school system. We always had our guests paired off on a one-on-one basis with people from Utah or with Utah roots. From these meetings we were able to get prospects that we could follow up.

Industrial promotion, quite unlike tourist promotion, is not something that yields quick results. If you put an ad in a national magazine for tourists, people planning their summer vacations will see it and you will begin to feel the results rather quickly. Not so with someone who intends to open a new industrial plant. Sometimes it would be a year or more before a particular contact would begin to bear fruit. But I feel that these trips we made – and we must have made close to a hundred of them, often going back several times to such places as New York, Los Angeles, San Francisco, and Chicago – bore fruit. The proof of this was in the fact that during the early seventies Utah's unemployment rate began to drop, until it was below the national average. The Utah press supported us. They put the nickname "Rampton's Raiders" on these groups of businessmen that went with me. And far from ducking this program, which I regarded as a civic responsibility, business and industrial leaders seemed to welcome the opportunity not only to go on these trips but also to be dubbed "Rampton's Raiders."

A problem that would constantly nag at me for the rest of my period as governor—and I'm sure it was a problem for my successor, Scott Matheson—was the equalization of assessments of property valuations throughout the state. Even though we were gradually doing away with the state property levy, the level of property assessments in the counties was of serious import to the state government because of the school equalization fund. Under our school program as it then existed, each school district, whether countywide or smaller, was required to apply a certain minimum levy. The state then assured that if this levy did not yield so many dollars per classroom, the state would make it up from the uniform school fund. We were at a point where the uniform school fund was supporting about 65 percent of the school programs, and that percentage was rapidly increasing. Over the years the county assessors had played a game to see who could keep their assessments at the lowest level in order to get the best break they could from the uniform school fund.

There were certain types of property in the state that weren't assessed locally, but by the tax commission. These were the mines and the utilities, which were assessed at about 25 percent of their true value. In some of the school districts other assessed valuations—such as homes, farms, and commercial properties—were down to 5 or 6 percent of their true valuation and, as a result, the money from the mines and utilities was flowing into these counties to support the school districts. Before I became governor the utilities and the mines had commenced litigation to require the state to equalize this burden in order to make sure that all properties were assessed at the same percentage of their reasonable market value.

Governor Clyde had tried to remedy the problem with spot checks, but that didn't get far because he didn't have enough staff members. So during my administration the legislature made an appropriation for the tax commission to go into these counties to require the county assessors to bring the assessed levels up. Our first target was 20 percent. If the county wouldn't do it, the state tax assessors would do it themselves.

This caused a great uproar in the counties because it increased the valuation of all homes within the counties that had been underassessed, as well as all business properties except mines and utilities. It was something that had to be done, however, and we pressed ahead with the policy. I had many irate county commissioners in to see me, but all I could say was, "I'm sorry you feel this way about it, but it's what the law required; and not only that, it's the fair thing to do." You can make the most logical argument in the world to a taxpayer or a county commissioner as to why the taxes or the assessments in their county have got to go up, but regardless of how logical you may be, you just can't win the argument.

By the time I had finished my third term as governor, we had the assessments relatively uniform. The problem was, however, that we were doing these assessments in five-year cycles: one year we would do certain counties, selecting those that were most out of line first, then another year we would do another group. By the time we got through the first five-year cycle inflation would have raised the market values of these properties, although their assessed valuation was still at the old level. While it might have been at a level of around 20 percent five years before, when we had completed the reassessment procedure it could be back down again to 15 percent, and so we had to start over. It's a continuing process and I assume it's going to have to continue because the local officials won't do it themselves.

In 1965 we were fairly successful in getting contracts in most of the forty school districts. The exception was the Box Elder County School District, where there was an impasse between the school board and the teachers' association. I didn't want to get personally involved in the problem if I could avoid it. I got in touch with Ted Bell, who was then the state superintendent of public instruction. Ted had been in that position for two or three years when I became governor, and had been at sword's point with Governor Clyde during most of the school crisis of the preceding year. Ted was a good school man and a good administrator. He and I had already worked together closely, so I asked him to intercede in the Box Elder dispute. I had Ted, along with Darrold Long, the executive secretary of the Utah School Boards, and John Evans, the executive secretary of the Utah Education Association, come to my office. I told them that while this was a local matter, I knew very well that there was pressure coming on both sides from the state level—on the one hand, from the UEA, and on the other hand, from the Utah School Boards—and I wanted that stopped. I sent Ted Bell up to see if he could negotiate it.

While there was some movement in the negotiations, we were getting close to the opening of school and nothing substantial was happening. I ultimately did make several personal trips to Box

Elder County and we finally got the thing together. After the dispute was settled, Ted Bell said, "You've discovered one of the secrets of mediation. You get each side so angry at the mediator that they cease to be angry at each other and settle."

An event of considerable importance to the people of the Salt Lake City area that occurred in the fall of 1965 was the opening of I-15 from Sixth South to 33rd South, and of I-80 from its intersection with I-15 east through Parley's Canyon. The interstate highway had been started during the Eisenhower administration with the establishment of a federal gas tax, the funds of which were distributed to the states to help build the interstate highway system on a matching basis. At that time the State Highway Department, with Governor Clyde's concurrence, made a wise policy decision. They decided to spend the first interstate funds allocation putting highways in and through the major cities. There were two reasons for this decision. The first arose from the fact that highway construction per lane-mile is more expensive in urban areas, both because of the numerous structures involved, and because of the higher cost of obtaining rights-of-way. The Clyde administration felt that inflation was going to impact highway cost in future years, and so good planning dictated that the most expensive sections should be put in first. Second, it was obvious that the Salt Lake City streets and minor state roads leading from the city out into the suburbs were becoming badly overcrowded, and that I-15 and I-80 were going to form major links in the Salt Lake Valley transportation system. This policy brought some criticism from the rural areas, but in my opinion it has proved to be a wise one.

During the summer and early fall of 1965 Lucybeth and I began to get acquainted with governors from the other states. Our first Western Governors' Conference was held in Portland, Oregon, in June, and the National Governors' Conference was held in late August or early September, in Minneapolis. I enjoyed the Western Governors' Conference very much, and to this day, most of those fellow governors are good friends with whom I continue to associate. I, John Love of Colorado, Stan Hathaway, later to be governor of Wyoming, and our wives meet about once a year for what Stan calls the "Exhausted Governors' Conference."

At the National Governors' Conference in Minneapolis we became acquainted with governors whose names were well known nationally. This was where we first met Nelson Rockefeller, who had been governor of New York for some time, and who was clearly a leader among the national governors. I never was able to get close to Nelson. Later, we got acquainted with his brother, Winthrop, who was elected governor of Arkansas, and we found him to be entirely different. Winthrop was a charming and warm person. Other nationally prominent governors whom we met and liked were Bill Scranton of Pennsylvania, John Connally of Texas, and John Chafee of Rhode Island.

An interesting part of the Minneapolis conference was a visit we made to Waverly, Hubert Humphrey's home, which is located twenty-five or thirty miles out of Minneapolis on a lake. We had known Hubert before, having campaigned with him, but I believe this was the first time we met Muriel. Our love and affection for these two people continued until Hubert's death, and we were pleased when Muriel was remarried to a childhood friend of hers and Hubert's.

Over the years we never missed a governors' conference, either national or regional, that we could possibly get to because we felt they were very worthwhile. I'm not sure that any momentous decisions ever came out of these conferences, but it was valuable to know the other governors on a first-name basis. Governors have to deal with each other fairly frequently—most commonly in extradition matters, but on many other matters as well. While I was governor I had occasion fifty or sixty times a month to talk to the governor of some other state about something that was of importance to both our states. To have these contacts on a friendly basis, to know and understand the man or woman to whom you're talking, is very valuable. Furthermore, the conferences are places for letting off steam. The governorship is a lonely position. You're the only person in your state—except for any still living ex-governors—who can appreciate the problems you have. But when you get together with forty-nine other men and women who have the same problems, you quit feeling sorry for yourself. You get a better perspective.

Overall, things went well with the state government during 1965. The Little Hoover Commission was working hard and making progress. I was getting periodic reports from Joe Rosenblatt, and although these were not generally made public, the newspapers made occasional reference to the commission's progress. There seemed to be a favorable response among their readers. I knew that I was going to have to call a special session right after the first of 1966 to get the

Little Hoover Commission recommendations under way, if for no other reason.

Through the balance of the fall months we continued our county trips and our out-of-state industrial promotion trips, and I settled into the enjoyable job of running the state.

CHAPTER FIVE

IN THE LION'S DEN: UTAH'S GOVERNOR

I had already called the senate into a special session in October 1965. This was the first special session of the senate that had been held in the state of Utah. Quite accidentally, as I was reading through the constitution one day on an entirely different subject, I came to the section on legislative sessions and found that the senate could be called into special session to do what is called "executive business." Because I had made a substantial number of appointments that needed confirmation, and because I wanted to get these appointments before the senate as quickly as possible, I issued a call for this special session.

It was not, therefore, a precedent-setting measure for me to call another special session just after the first of the following year. There were several matters that I felt needed to be addressed before the regular biennial session of the legislature, which would not occur until the spring of 1967.

The most significant thing that happened during this special session was the presentation to me and the legislature of the report of the Little Hoover Commission. This commission had been at work for almost a year and had written a very comprehensive report, together with a minority report that was endorsed by two members of the commission who had reservations about some of the proposals. The Little Hoover Commission report called for a thorough overhauling of the executive branch of Utah government. Joe Rosenblatt presented the proposals to the legislators. We were not expecting them to act that session because we knew that this matter was going to require a long study by the legislature. The plan was to start implementing the report in the 1967 general session.

The Little Hoover Commission found that there were some 157 different departments, agencies, offices, and divisions of state government that had grown up without any planning, and each one of them reported directly to the governor with no intervening supervision. The commission proposed to unite these into ten or twelve departments with department heads reporting to the governor, and with subdepartment directors reporting to the department heads. A small office director who previously had access to the governor now had access only through an intermediate administrator.

There was a great deal of protest. Most of it came from the legislators and from the constituencies of the various departments of government among the general public, as the third- or fourth-level administrators didn't want to arouse my ire by coming out and opposing me publicly. There were a few that did speak out, naturally, but I never took adverse action against them. I imposed no sanctions.

However, I did find it necessary as we approached the new session of the legislature and as the debate over the Little Hoover Commission report continued to wax strong, to impose the same sort of rule that I had imposed the year before. As the legislature started considering these recommendations in their interim committee meetings and called for reactions to certain proposals from within the administrative sections of the government, the officer called should testify truly and accurately as to his or her point of view without regard to whether it conformed to mine. This cut down some on the public controversy. While the debate on the Little Hoover Commission proposals subsided somewhat a few weeks after they were presented, it continued to occupy the attention of the public and the legislators during the balance of 1966.

Near the end of the session Utah made its presentation to the U.S. Olympic Committee, seeking to be designated as the U.S. nominee for the 1972 Winter Olympics bid. The committee meeting was held in Chicago, and a number of other U.S. cities were making bids. Lake Placid, New York, was the principal bidder against Utah. We had done a considerable amount of lobbying with the Olympic Committee, however, and Utah received the designation as America's nominee. We immediately began preparing for our presentation to the International Olympic Committee in Rome the following spring.

In February 1966, the U.S. government decided to divest itself of Fort Douglas. The original proposal included the entire fort, but there were some facilities that I wanted to stay in federal hands. However, a great deal of the land could be well used by the University of Utah. We therefore decided to make a study of the Fort Douglas property and present a proposal to the Department of the Army for the transfer of this property, or such part of it as we wanted, to the state of Utah. I appointed as head of the study committee my former law associate, David Watkiss. The committee's report was submitted to the state and federal governments and, to a substantial extent, has been followed. This was the beginning of Research Park at the University of Utah, which has contributed greatly to both the state and to the university.

I continued to make personnel changes at the state level. In late February the Utah Fair Board, at my request, removed Theron Garrard from the chairmanship. Mr. Garrard had done a responsible job; however, he did not agree with my concepts of what the fair should be and I felt I had to have somebody there who was more amenable to my ideas. A short while after Mr. Garrard left, I appointed Hugh Bringhurst to be fair manager. He turned out to be a wonderful manager, and he served in that position from early 1966 through the last of my administration and into Scott Matheson's administration, retiring only when he reached his sixty-fifth birthday. Hugh was a rare public official. He was sometimes a little unorthodox in his ways, but he endeared himself to everybody who used the fairgrounds, and the fair prospered under his administration.

When the first special session of 1966 adjourned in late January, I had not planned to ask the legislature to act on the major recommendations of the Little Hoover Commission in another special session. By spring of that year, however, I had decided to call a short special session to provide for the constitutional amendments that would need, if the proposals were approved by the legislature, to go on November's ballot. Otherwise, if the legislature waited until the 1967 session, they couldn't be put on the ballot until November 1968.

Moreover, as the time approached for the special session, I began to have concerns about what was happening to the Democratic party both in Utah and nationally, and about what kind of a legislature I would have in 1967. On the local level, we were having a great deal of trouble in Salt Lake County. The three county commissioners—Bill Larson, Marv Jenson, and John Creer—were continually squabbling, and people were disgusted with them. This infighting was hurting the Democratic party. The party was already in disrepute, particularly in Salt Lake County, but those sentiments now carried over throughout the state.

Even more worrisome was a division that appeared to be coming in the national party over two issues: one was the Vietnam War and the other was the rising environmental movement. Generally in Utah the people seemed supportive of the Vietnam War, as was I. I could see that if a major section of our party took a firm stand against the war in the 1966 elections, it wasn't going to do us any good. It seemed that the environmental movement was also unpopular in Utah, and while I certainly was in favor of many of the ideas that were being advanced by environmentalists, I felt that some of the positions taken were extreme.

It began to appear as early as the spring of 1966 that we were going to have a difficult time in the election that fall; and so, rather than have the major recommendations of the Little Hoover Commission go over until the regular session of 1967, when they might face a hostile legislature, I decided to put the entire Little Hoover Commission report on the agenda of a special session to be called in May.

This caused considerable comment in the community. Republicans were not in favor of considering the entirety of the Little Hoover Commission report in a special session. Some former legislators brought an action to block the special session. Their contention was that the legislature, not having properly reapportioned itself, should not be permitted to consider such an important matter as the complete overhaul of the administrative government of the state. The action was brought in the U.S. District Court and was heard by a three-judge court, as federal rules at that time required. The judges were David Lewis, Willis Ritter, and Sherman Christensen, and they declined to issue any kind of an order preventing the legislature from meeting. The Republicans then attempted to get a writ of certiorari direct from the U.S. Supreme Court, but the application for a writ was turned down by Justice Byron White, who was then the supreme court justice with jurisdiction over the Tenth Circuit.

The legislature thus met in the second 1966 special session on May 16. However, they did not want to go as far as I had asked, and I guess I can't blame them. They'd only had the report for a few months, so rather than make actual statutory changes as I had recommended, they passed a resolution authorizing me as the executive to make certain changes and certain groupings of state agencies. After I had done that, I was to report back to the regular session, which would meet right after the first of the year. Then the legislature would make a decision as to whether they would go further. I wasn't happy with what I got, but it certainly was better than not moving at all on the recommendations of the commission.

Meanwhile, it had come time for Utah to present its bid for the 1972 Winter Olympics. The International Olympic Committee meeting was held in Rome on April 26. We chose a group of about fifteen people who had been active in the Olympics for Utah program to make the trip to Rome. Max Rich was chairman of our Olympics committee. Others who went along were Jack Gallivan, Gene Donovan, Felix Koziol, Devereaux Jennings, and Will Lucas. We had raised enough money to pay our air fare from Salt Lake to Rome, and I was able to get the permission of the National Guard Bureau to carry the sets for our presentation on a National Guard plane that was flying to Frankfurt on a training mission. They also authorized the plane to do the extra trip from Frankfurt to Rome and back.

In Rome there were two other principal competitors: Helsinki, Finland, and Sapporo, Japan, both of which gave excellent presentations. However, I felt that our presentation was as good as either of theirs. The members of the International Olympic Committee looked over the presentations and heard the dog-and-pony shows that were put on by the three delegations. After the judging was over, the decision was made to award the Olympics to Sapporo. In retrospect, it was probably the best thing that could have happened to Utah. Sapporo put on a good Winter Olympics, but it almost bankrupted the city and they had to have help from their national government to bail them out. Utah would have been in the same position, I'm sure, and it would have been difficult for us to get any help on a national level. At the same time, the fact that we had been chosen as the U.S. nominee and had made such a good showing gave a boost to Utah skiing unequaled before or since.

The day after the judging, the Western Governors' Conference was to convene in Las Vegas, Nevada. I caught an airplane that morning in Rome, and got to Las Vegas in time for part of the banquet. I was very tired, of course, having traveled all that distance.

The meetings on the following day gave rise to some controversy. Mark Hatfield, the governor of Oregon who was soon to become senator, was the chairman that year. My business development committee had recommended a bill to set up a western tourist council. Mark took it upon himself not even to present our recommendation to the governors for their acceptance or rejection. I was offended by this, and he and I had a confrontation in the open meeting. Finally, I was able to get a motion passed calling it up, and it was adopted. It left an estrangement between Hatfield and me that persisted for a long time.

Early in June 1966, Ted Moss was able to get through the Senate a bill affecting the reliction lands—that is, the lands from which the Great Salt Lake had receded since statehood. The lands were the subject of a controversy between the state and the federal government. Various industries wanted to build around the lake, but as long as the title to the shorelines was in dispute, they didn't know from whom to lease or whether anybody could give good title. We were effectively blocked from exploitation of the mineral resources of the lake. The Moss bill provided that the state could go ahead and lease these lands, treat them as if they were the state's. The money received for the leases would be placed in escrow, and when litigation finally decided who owned the land, the money would go to the owner. The leases of the state would be recognized by the federal government should it turn out to be the owner of these reliction lands.

The Department of the Interior felt that the bill Moss had succeeded in getting passed undermined their authority, and they were pressing the president very hard to veto the bill. Ted wanted me to get in touch with the president and urge him not to do so. I can recall that when the call came through from Ted I was down in Ephraim at the home of Floyd Holmes, the president of Snow College. I tried to get President Johnson on the phone, but he was in the air between Washington and his home in Texas. Finally, they patched me through to the airplane, and although the connection wasn't the best, I urged the president not to veto the bill, pointing out to him that we needed to have some stability and that the case in the courts was not going to be decided for months and possibly even years. The president said he would take it under consideration. Ultimately, he signed the bill, and we were able to move ahead with the leasing of the shore lands. That opened the way for the H. K. Industries to develop their magnesium properties on the southwest shore of the lake and also enabled Great Salt Lake Minerals to move ahead with their lithium operation just west of Ogden.

On June 29, just two days before the beginning of the new fiscal year, I exercised the power the legislature had granted me to consolidate some of the agencies of state government. By executive order I created six consolidated departments. Ward Holbrook became chairman of the health and welfare grouping; Herbert Smart, who had been my budget director, was made head of all budget services and the general service agencies; Jay Bingham, who had come to my administration from the Clyde administration, became head of natural resources; Felix Koziol of the state parks service became head of recreation; Raymond A. Jackson, a friend from Nephi, was put in charge of all of the public safety areas; and Lynn Baker, the state treasurer, was placed in charge of revenue services. This was the group with which we faced the first attempt at modernization of state government in many years.

Early in July, Lucybeth and I went to the National Governors' Conference in Los Angeles. Governor Pat Brown was the host governor, and the meeting was held at the Century Plaza Hotel, which was just opening up for business. It was at this conference that a bipartisan resolution was passed by an overwhelming vote to endorse the positions of the Johnson administration concerning the Vietnam War. I favored the resolution and voted for it. At that time not only Johnson but the bipartisan group of governors, who I'm sure represented overwhelming public opinion, still supported the position of the administration regarding Vietnam.

In August 1966 a project began that would affect the remainder of my administration. The Arizona Public Service Company, Southern California Edison, and San Diego Gas and Electric had decided to build the Kaiparowits Power Project. This would be a coal-fired power plant that would produce three thousand megawatts—the biggest power plant ever built in the country. Generally everyone I had talked to in Utah or elsewhere was for it. People were not yet caught up in the environmental movement which would later defeat the project. Kaiparowits was under study, and tests had gone on for a period of some ten years. It really didn't fold until my last year in the governorship.

In mid-September, Lucybeth and I attended a meeting of the Education Commission of the States at Newport, Rhode Island. We flew into Boston. Both of our girls were in school in that area then: Janet was attending Jackson College and Meg was at Harvard. They met us and together we drove down to the meeting at Newport.

On the way, an interesting thing happened. The preceding Fourth of July there had been an article in a little newspaper called the *Sandwich Times*, which was published out on Cape Cod. This article told of an old inn there known as the Daniel Webster Inn. An inquiring newspaper reporter had noted a flag hanging in front of the inn with only forty-five stars. He inquired of the owner where the old flag came from, and he was told that it was the flag that had flown over the Capitol in 1896 on the day that Utah was admitted as a state. The newspaper man asked him if he didn't think he ought to send that flag back to Utah, and he said he didn't know whether he should, but if the governor of Utah ever happened by Sandwich, he would give him the flag as well as a whale steak.

We knew we were going within a few miles of Sandwich, which lay between Boston and Rhode Island, and so I had written this fellow at the Daniel Webster Inn to tell him I'd come by to get the flag. When we got to Sandwich that day there was a big crowd of people. They had arranged a big luncheon at which to present us with the flag. All of the local officials were there. John Volpe, the governor of Massachusetts, was in bed with a cold so he had sent the lieutenant governor, Elliott Richardson. We were given the flag and the whale steak (which I can't recommend). We brought the flag back to Utah, where it was to hang from the balcony of the capitol rotunda on Statehood Day each year.

In September, Lucybeth and I flew down for the dedication of the Glen Canyon Dam. Governor Clyde went with us, as did a number of other people. Lady Bird Johnson was there and gave the dedicatory speech. They called on me to talk and I responded, not thinking until later that I should have deferred to Governor Clyde, because really he was our water expert and had headed up Utah's effort in regard to the dam.

Through the fall months, and particularly during October, the coming election was hanging over us. I was not optimistic about the chances for the Democrats. It seemed particularly significant that early polls showed Sherman Lloyd, who was trying to return to the House after losing a Senate bid, was leading the Democratic incumbent, David King, by several points. All in all it seemed to me that we were building up to a situation much like we had had twenty years before when so many Democrats were defeated.

Those of us who weren't running pulled out all stops to try to help those who were. Vice-President Hubert Humphrey came to the state. Ed Muskie campaigned here. I spent most of the two weeks before the election on a campaign tour throughout the state. But we were unable to stop the Republican tide that was building up, and on election day our fears were justified. The Republicans swept the state from one end to the other. We had only five Democratic state senators out of twenty-eight, and only ten representatives out of sixty-nine. I thought this was particularly unfortunate because the Democratic legislature, most of whose members were running for reelection, had done an admirable job. But that really didn't seem to make much difference. Not only did we lose in the legislature, but we lost both congressional seats and the county offices in almost every county.

I didn't have much time to lick my wounds, however, because the legislature was going to meet in January and I had to do three things: I had to finish getting a new budget ready; I had to prepare my state of the state message; and above all, I had to establish contact and rapport with the new Republican legislature. Even though I had opposed them I was faced with the practical problem that they were there, and if the state was going to avoid a period of deadlock, I had to take the first step toward making sure that we would have the proper cooperation between the administration and the legislature. I made every effort in the weeks preceding the legislative session to approach the various legislators who had been elected on the Republican side and see if I could come to some point of understanding with them.

The Republicans held caucuses to choose their new leaders sometime late in December. There were several prominent Republican state senators who were vying for the presidency of the senate, and each was able to attract a certain following. The result was a deadlock in their caucus, and they selected as the president of the senate Haven Barlow, a compromise candidate. I had known Haven for many years. He was from north Davis County, and I felt that I would get along well with him. Incidentally, for many years there had been an unstated policy in the senate that a president would serve for only two years and then, even if his party stayed in power, he would be replaced by another member of the party. Haven was to fool those who thought he was just a stopgap president, however, and he remained as president of the senate for the next six years.

At any rate, I felt that my relationship was all right with the senate. It was fine with Haven, and it was also good with Warren Pugh, Wallace Gardner, Hughes Brockbank, Charles Welch, and a number of others. On the Democratic side, the five senators that we had were well established, and the fact that they were so much in a minority gave them a spirit of cohesiveness, not just among themselves, but also with me. I knew that I wouldn't have the intraparty division in the Democratic ranks that I had had previously.

The situation in the house, however, was entirely different. I had feared that the speaker of the house might prove to be Franklin Gunnell. He was a representative from Cache County who had been in the house three or four terms prior to his election as speaker. I never liked Gunnell. I didn't trust him. He was fairly bright, though I suppose the term should be devious. Everything that happened between Gunnell and me during the 1967 session, his every reaction to my proposals, was based entirely on what it would do for him, not on what it would do for the state or even for the Republican party. It was common knowledge that Gunnell wanted to be the Republican nominee for governor in 1968, and so it was obvious to me that I faced a serious problem with the house if we were going to get any kind of meaningful legislation through that session.

The one thing that a legislature must do every session is establish a budget for the state, and unless the governor and the legislature can get together on a fiscal policy, the state will have a very difficult situation. After the 1966 election I pretty well redid the entire budget that had been in process since September. I wanted to make sure that I could present to what was obviously a conservative Utah electorate a very sparse budget, a very conservative budget. I wanted to make sure that when my budget message came in, the members of the legislature, and particularly Gunnell's partisans in the house, couldn't pick it apart and show that I was going to increase taxes or that I was giving unreasonably large increases to social programs. I was determined to move ahead with the school program that we had set in motion two years previously, because I'd made a promise that I would take a number of annual or biennial steps to bring the Utah student expenditure up to the mountain states' average.

There were other programs, however, that I would like to have pushed ahead, such as outdoor recreation and natural resource programs, that I felt I would have to leave for a later time. In the public appearances I made between the election and the beginning of the legislature, I stressed time after time that there would be no need for a tax increase from the next legislature. We would end the biennium with a surplus of several million dollars, as opposed to the $6 million deficit with which we had ended the previous biennium. I kept talking on the subject of fiscal responsibility, and I attempted to present a budget to the legislature that reflected that viewpoint. As a result, I got strong support from the newspapers in the state, and strangely enough when my budget message was presented to the legislature I didn't get very much flak, even from the Gunnell faction.

Not so well received, however, were my recommendations in regard to the reorganization of the state administrative structure. I reported the changes I'd made following the special session in 1966 to this new legislature, and recommended that those changes be made permanent.

Other than the appropriations bill, not much of significance came out of the 1967 legislature. I tried to get passed an open housing bill, but it was defeated. I tried several other reasonable pieces of social legislation which were summarily rejected. After the legislature left, I vetoed some twenty-two bills. One day, in exasperation and frustration, I said something in a speech that I regretted almost immediately—though I meant what I said at the time. I stated that in some twenty-five years of watching the state legislature, this house had been the worst legislative body I had ever seen. The senate, on the other hand, as I expected it to be, was reasonable.

I had asked the legislature for an air pollution control bill, because it was obvious that the degree of pollution we were getting along the Wasatch Front was a cause for serious concern. This was before much had been done nationally concerning air pollution, but I knew something would be done eventually and I wanted to get ahead of the problem. The legislature, however, watered down the bill. I signed it (Senate Bill 36), but in signing it I issued a statement that it was a weak bill and wouldn't take care of the problem, and that in the near future we would have to come up with a much stronger measure.

The most controversial bill remaining was the Sunday Closing Act. We had had Sunday closing acts before, but they had been declared unconstitutional. In this bill, the sponsors attempted to meet the problems that had caused the courts to set aside the previous legislation. The LDS Church, of course, wanted me to sign the bill. Ordinarily the church leaders left me pretty much alone, but on this particular bill I received a number of calls from church leaders of all ranks, including general authorities, urging me to sign it. I didn't like the bill because, although I wished every store would close on Sunday, I didn't regard it as a proper matter for the state to require that they close. Furthermore, I was still concerned about the constitutionality of certain items in the bill.

I finally decided to give everyone an opportunity to express an opinion on the bill, and I held a meeting in the governor's boardroom that lasted several hours. I heard from members of the public, both for and against the bill, and after hearing all of their arguments I decided it was bad legislation and vetoed it. I wrote a rather lengthy veto message in which I attempted to analyze dispassionately all of the aspects of the bill.

I didn't expect the fact that I had written a treatise at the time I vetoed the bill to take the heat off me, and it did not. The *Deseret News* ran a front-page editorial implicitly accusing me of going back on an agreement. Certainly I had never made any agreement that I would sign the bill, but the *Deseret News* editorial was highly critical and I thought a bit unfair. As might be expected, the *Tribune* editorial supported me.

The 1966 election had not only brought into power a Republican legislature, but had also seen a substantial number of Republican governors elected in the other states. I met many of them for the first time immediately after the adjournment of the legislature, as we had been summoned to Washington for a briefing on the Vietnam War. Some of them I would have a great deal to do with in the succeeding four years. Among the new governors were Ronald Reagan in California; Tom McCall in Oregon; Lester Maddox in Georgia; and David Cargo in New Mexico.

The governors were almost unanimously in support of the administration's Vietnam policy. The so-called domino theory stated that if we did not prop up South Vietnam, the other countries inSoutheast Asia would fall like dominoes to the Communists, without any military aggression. This theory was well accepted, not only among the governors but by the country as a whole. Still, these sentiments were beginning to break down, and the remainder of 1967 and into 1968 would see a drastic change in the attitude of public officeholders and of the people generally toward our involvement in Vietnam.

In early April 1967 it came time to elect new officers of the Democratic party. The chair and vice-chair were not my supporters. Ray Pruitt, the state chair, and Sevilla Reese, the vice-chair, although friendly on the surface, felt that I wasn't sufficiently partisan. I asked Wally Sandack, a lawyer in Salt Lake, if he would run for the state chairmanship. I told him that if I was going to run for reelection in 1968 I couldn't do it with a state chair who was always sniping at me. Sandack agreed to run. At first Pruitt stated that he would run against him, but by that time I had repaired some of my problems with the grassroots party people. It was obvious that with my support and the support Ted Moss was also giving him, Wally Sandack was going to win, and so Pruitt dropped out. Sandack was elected without opposition and Norma Thomas was elected as vice-chair.

Among the delegates at the Democratic state convention was a man from Ogden named Bart Lower. Bart was a peculiar individual. He asked for the microphone while Sandack was being nominated —supposedly for the purpose of seconding Sandack's nomination— but when he got it he delivered an anti-Jewish tirade. Sandack, of course, was Jewish, and Lower said, "We can't have a Jew heading the party in this state, especially in a year when George Romney is running for President"—an awful tirade. One of the delegates was Charles Romney. Although Charles was a Democrat, he was also a younger brother of George Romney, the Republican governor of Michigan. Charles jumped from his seat and came running down the aisle, challenging Lower to physical combat. That was put down as the sergeant-at-arms restored order, but it was an unpleasant and disturbing thing, although Sandack was well able to handle it.

In May 1967, the governors of the Rocky Mountain states met in Salt Lake to form an organization which we called the Rocky Mountain Federation. This was to be a partnership between government and the private sector. Hopefully the governors would take the lead in the organization, but the board of directors contained many leaders of industry, agriculture, and mining from throughout the West. This organization existed for about eight years. It was succeeded by an organization called WESPO—Western Governors' Policy Office—

which is still in existence. The Rocky Mountain Federation hired a staff, and a man from Denver named Donald McMahon was the first director. We had a budget that was contributed to both by appropriations from the state legislatures and by dues that were charged to the private sector. The Rocky Mountain Federation contributed a great deal toward working out economic problems that were common to the mountain states.

The Western Governors' Conference meeting was held at West Yellowstone in Montana, beginning on June 25, 1967. Governor Tim Babcock of Montana was the host. The ranks of the Democrats had been depleted in the previous election, so of the thirteen governors present, only John Burns of Hawaii and I were Democrats. Although I'd seen most of these governors a few weeks previously at the White House, this was the first chance I had to get acquainted with some of them.

Among them was the new governor of California, Ronald Reagan. He was an unknown quantity. At the meeting in Washington he had spoken up several times with what I regarded as rather mundane and innocuous statements, and I wasn't very impressed with him. At the West Yellowstone meeting he didn't show up for the first session at all. The second day he came in with an entourage of reporters and television people, sat down for a few minutes, and then asked to make a speech. He was told that he could if he'd just wait until it came the right time.

Finally he was permitted to talk and he got up and started reading a prepared speech about the Wholesale Meat Act. All of the governors sat there looking perplexed as to what he was talking about, and finally Tom McCall, the new governor of Oregon, stopped him and asked, "Ronnie, are you by any chance talking about the Wholesome Meat Act?" That was the act Congress had just passed, under which the federal government took over the examination and inspection of certain meat products. Reagan stopped, went back through his text, and said, "Oh yes, yes, the Wholesome Meat Act," and then went on as if nothing had happened. I discovered that it was almost impossible to embarrass the man.

As I dictate this story, he is the president of the United States. I'm aghast still that a man of his shallowness of intellect can be the president of this country. He indeed has a facile tongue. He is a great communicator, but he's almost devoid of ideas. I believe he has no basic principles that guide him, and I feel he is greatly influenced by those around him. He did, as governor of California, have the ability to appoint good people, and to some extent has shown that ability while he has been in Washington. Of course, this is one of the marks of a good administrator and I'll have to give him credit for that; nevertheless, he is not the caliber of man you would expect to be governor of a large state, let alone president of the country.

Tom McCall, on the other hand, was a very interesting man. He had been a newspaper reporter and a radio and television commentator. Tom, to my great regret, has since died of cancer. He had a keen sense of humor, a very biting one sometimes. Although he was a Republican, as was Ronald Reagan, he delighted in puncturing Reagan's balloon. In 1977 a banquet was held in Washington state for Dan Evans, who was retiring as governor. I went, as did many governors who had worked with Dan. Reagan was there and Tom McCall was the master of ceremonies. He introduced Reagan as "Ronald Reagan, a man who is a legend in his own mind."

Another leader who came from the broadcasting industry was Jack Williams, the new governor of Arizona. Jack was not as flamboyant as Tom McCall, but a sound man and a good governor, and one with whom I established a fast friendship. A number of years later when I-15 was under construction and we had built the road to the Utah border, the so-called Arizona strip was still unfinished. Of course it did no good for us to bring I-15 to our border and for Nevada to bring it to their border unless the short section across the Arizona strip was completed. This didn't mean much to Arizona, as this particular area is cut off from the populated areas by the Grand Canyon. Both the governor of Nevada and I asked Jack Williams if he wouldn't expedite construction of this section, and we made available to him certain of our credits from the federal gas tax. Arizona did move up completion of the Virgin Narrows strip by about three years, and enabled us to gain the use of I-15.

By mid-1967 Utah, as well as the rest of the nation, was beginning to suffer from recession, and I was confronted with a problem of deficient revenues for the first time since I had been in the governorship. In the previous biennium we had had a growing economy. Sales tax and income tax had come in well over estimate, and so we had surpluses that we could put into buildings. However, early in the biennium, which began on July 1, 1967, but for which appropriation

had been made the previous January and February, it became evident
that revenues were not going to hold up to the estimates we had made
at the time the appropriations bill was passed. I didn't want to call a
special session to meet this problem because I still was fearful of what
this Republican legislature would do if they got another chance. But
there was a provision in the Utah law, little used, which allowed the
governor to cut back expenditures if he could see that he was going to
run into the red, since our constitution prohibits running a deficit. I
decided I would use the executive power.

The one thing I didn't like about this executive power was
that I had to make the cuts across the board, except for the school
fund. It couldn't be selective cutting. I think that's proper because it
probably would have been an unconstitutional delegation of legislative power to the governor if he'd been able to make selective cuts. I
ordered a 4 percent cut in the spending of all departments of government to which my authority extended.

The cries that went up from the state departments were
anguished. The loudest wails came from the universities. Jim Fletcher,
the president of the University of Utah, was sure that he couldn't run
the university through the year if he had to cut back 4 percent. Many
of the state department heads came to see me to ask if there wasn't
some way that they could be exempted from the cut. I wanted to exempt
the welfare department, but I didn't have the authority to do that,
and so the cutback went across the board.

Although it was badly received by the state employees, to
my surprise it was received with great acclaim by the people generally
and by the press in particular. If I were to select one thing that occurred
during my first term that boosted the approval of my administration
most among the people, it was this original cutback which was without precedent in the history of the state. I believe the tremendous
majority I received in the 1968 election, while the Republicans were
carrying the state for most other offices, resulted from this cutback
which had received such genuine popular approval.

Another matter that occupied a great deal of my time in
the fall of 1967 was the Kennecott Copper strike. The employment
contracts of the major copper companies in the United States then
ran on a three-year cycle, and the contract came up for negotiation in
1967. As I recall, the workers labored for a period of time without a
contract and then all of the mines in Montana, Utah, Arizona, and

Nevada were shut down and remained down. The governors of the four states met in Salt Lake City at my invitation, but there wasn't much we could do except pressure both labor and management. Finally the talks shifted to Washington.

As the months moved on toward the close of the year, a great deal of speculation came up, as it always does, regarding the 1968 election. The Republicans were canvassing all of their prospects for the governorship race, hoping to come up with a natural candidate to run against me. There were about ten or twelve of them who were considering it. In the state senate were Hughes Brockbank and Warren Pugh, and there were a number of other Republicans who had been active in the party, Vee Cummings among them. Also, there were just beginning to be rumblings about the man who ultimately did become the Republican nominee, Carl Buehner. Mr. Buehner had just retired from being a member of the presiding bishopric, one of the general authorities in the LDS Church. The prospect of his being a candidate caused me some concern. He was a quiet and retiring man, but I was uncertain just what the effect of the church's involvement would be on my candidacy if a former member of the general authorities were to run.

As the year drew to a close I was being subjected to conflicting pressures. The national party wanted very much to get the seat in the Senate held by Wallace Bennett, who would be up for reelection in 1968. I was getting urgings from Washington—continual urgings—to abandon the race for the governorship and run for the Senate. On the other hand, the party at home felt that it was more important for us to keep the governorship as a base for building a party structure. I was torn between the two prospects. I'd always wanted to be a U.S. Senator and I certainly had an opportunity at this time, although I didn't feel that Senator Bennett would be an easy opponent to defeat. The newspaper polls taken at that early time showed that I was running ahead of him, while other Democratic potentials ran behind. There were a number of others looking at the race too: Phil Hansen, the attorney general; Milt Weilenmann, head of the promotional activities of the state; and political science Professor J. D. Williams of the University of Utah.

On the national scene the general assumption among the people was that Johnson would run for a second full term. Senator Robert Kennedy was positioning himself to make a run as well; he would certainly run if Johnson didn't and probably even if he did. On the Republican side, George Romney had announced his candidacy for the presidency in a dramatic statement, claiming that he had prayed all the night before and had received assurance that he should run.

At this time there was also considerable pressure on me from some sources to bring the legislature back into another special session, mostly to take care of some housekeeping bills that I felt could wait. I would have been willing to call a special session if we had found an agenda on which the Republican leadership could agree. It didn't make sense, though, for me to call a special session before the end of the year if I was just going to give the Republican majority a sounding board for the coming election and accomplish none of my own goals. So I decided not to call a special session in December 1967.

The first three months of the new year were busy ones for me. I wanted to get the county trips out of the way before the election campaign began in earnest. Even though it was difficult sometimes to make these visits during the winter months, I decided to continue them, and so we completed our round of county trips for that year during the first four months of 1968. I also continued my trips to other states with "Rampton's Raiders" during the spring months for the purpose of attracting industry to the state. I wanted to get these tasks behind me because had I done either the county trips or the out-of-state trips while the campaign was on, I could rightfully be accused of using them for campaign purposes. It would certainly have reduced the effectiveness of what I was trying to accomplish.

The Kennecott strike was still hanging on, although by now talks were in progress. The other governors and I were bringing all the pressure we could on both management and the unions to settle the strike, but it still wasn't settled at year's end, and the economic outlook in Utah for the following year was clouded. I kept the 4 percent cutback I had made earlier in effect, but at the first of the year it appeared that unless the Kennecott strike was soon settled, another cutback would have to be made, and that I didn't want to do.

Finally, President Johnson decided to step in. The negotiations were going on in Washington, and in early or mid-March I went back for several days in an attempt to further pressure the negotiators and rouse the president to keep doing the same. We were finally successful, and the copper strike ended that month.

While I was in Washington I had gone to the White House hoping that I could see the president, but he was giving a talk in the East Room when I got there. I talked with Marvin Watson, Johnson's aide, for half an hour until the meeting was about to break up. At that point Marvin said, "Stand by the door and when the president comes out he'll see you. I believe he has some free time and he'll probably ask you to come in." So I waited by the door. The meeting broke up and when the president saw me he took me by the arm and we walked into the Red Room, which is just off the main hall running from the East Room. We talked there for almost an hour, and I felt closer to him than ever before.

He was obviously feeling the pressure of the Vietnam War. He knew that the protests being raised against the war were dividing the country and he was very troubled. Then he told me that he had about made up his mind not to run in 1968. He said the decision would be announced by the first of April, which was about two weeks away. "I'm almost certain the decision is going to be not to run," he said, "but I don't want you to tell anybody about this. I don't want it mentioned at all." I promised him that I would not talk to anyone about the matter.

I went on home to Salt Lake. With the copper strike settled things had quieted down a bit. About the first of April it was announced that the president was going to make a speech on the Vietnam War. We were having dinner at the governor's residence early in the evening when I got a call from Washington. It was Marvin Watson calling to say that President Johnson was going to announce that he would not run, and that the president had asked him to call me and half a dozen other governors before the speech went on. That speech was one of the most dramatic that I've seen on television in my lifetime. Probably the only more dramatic speech I've heard was a number of years later when Richard Nixon announced his resignation from the presidency.

I was disappointed that Johnson would not run. Although the political pundits have said that he pulled out because of a fear of defeat, I think there was nothing to that at all. The president was running well in the polls then and I'm convinced, and most of the other governors that I know, including Republican governors such as Jim Rhodes and John Love, are convinced that if he had run again he would have won. I believe that his reason for withdrawing was to reduce the divisiveness in America and to allow him to make decisions concerning the Vietnam War that would not be affected by his candidacy for reelection. Of course the withdrawal of the president created a great deal of furor. Bobby Kennedy had announced that he was going to run two or three weeks before. I don't know whether he was aware that the president was going to withdraw, but I doubt that he was because the president and Kennedy were not close.

Things were also happening on the Republican side. The polls, which had showed Romney the leading candidate immediately after he announced early in the year, now showed him continually slipping away. Nixon went into the lead in the polls, and was followed by Rockefeller. As they approached the New Hampshire primary, Romney was in third place. Romney had made a trip to Vietnam, and when he came back he made an unfortunate statement, explaining why he had changed his position from supporting the war to opposing it. He stated that he had been brainwashed by the administration and the army people. The political writers immediately picked that up and made fun of Romney as being a weak character who could be brainwashed. This contributed to his decline until finally, in the spring, Romney withdrew, leaving Rockefeller to challenge Nixon.

As things progressed Nixon pulled further and further ahead, until Rockefeller also withdrew, leaving Nixon almost a clear field. Although Bill Scranton did get into the race late and Barry Goldwater made some noises as though he might run again, it was pretty well assured by early summer that Nixon would be the Republican nominee.

I soon announced my candidacy for a second term. This was followed about ten days later by an announcement from Carl Buehner that he would seek the Republican nomination for governor. Because we didn't expect opposition from the Democratic party, the people on my committee, with my concurrence, decided to keep the campaign at a very low key until after the primary in September.

The spring months were full of political activity nonetheless. Both J. D. Williams and Phil Hansen announced for the U.S. Senate on the Democratic side, to oppose Senator Bennett. I felt that neither of these candidates could hope to beat Bennett, and I actively sought to get another candidate into the race on the Democratic side. Milt Weilenmann, who had worked with me for three years, decided shortly before the filing deadline to run. Soon after he announced that he would take a leave of absence from his state job during the time he was a candidate, and later he did return to the state position.

Although Vice-President Humphrey had not yet announced his candidacy for the presidency, I had made known the fact that I expected him to run and that I intended to support him. That caused concern among some Utah Democrats because there was a significant amount of support in the state both for Eugene McCarthy and for Bobby Kennedy. During the later part of May Kennedy was in the state, but for some reason we didn't connect. I did receive a phone call from him, however, just as he was leaving the airport. Although he knew I was not supporting him, he was very courteous about making the call. Kennedy's visit here was a day or two before the Oregon primary, which he lost to McCarthy, they being the only two on the Oregon primary ballot.

Then, June 6, I was awakened by a phone call very late at night or early in the morning at the residence. It was the highway patrol calling to tell me that they had just received word that Senator Robert Kennedy had been shot. The death of Kennedy put a damper on the presidential campaign for a little while, but not for long. It was within the next two or three weeks that Gene McCarthy came to Salt Lake campaigning. He had taken most of the Kennedy support in the state of Utah. When he came to Salt Lake, he called me personally to see if I would introduce him at a rally his supporters had planned at Liberty Park. I had known McCarthy for some time; I liked him and I told him that I would come, although I reiterated my preference for Vice-President Humphrey, who had just announced and who had substantial support in Utah.

I went to Liberty Park and introduced McCarthy. I got considerable criticism from his supporters because in introducing him I made it quite plain that I was for Humphrey. McCarthy had not, up to that time, given the assurances that others had given—principally Humphrey—that they would support the Democratic nominee for president, whoever it might be. I told McCarthy during the introduction that the Democratic party of Utah would support him if he won the Democratic nomination, and that I felt he should give us the assurance that he would also support the nominee. This caused additional criticism.

It is difficult to appreciate the bitterness that existed in the Democratic party at that time, caused mostly by the continuance of the Vietnam War—although Johnson, after his withdrawal from the campaign, was making every effort to bring the war to a close. Johnson made it known that it wasn't going to end merely by withdrawing our troops and sacrificing what we had stood for in the war. The amount of dissension over this war had split the country and the Democratic party in a way that was hard to believe. This breach was apparent long before the Democratic National Convention in Chicago, and although Humphrey had not been in the forefront of the administration's effort in Vietnam, since he was running with President Johnson's approval, he tended to attract the opposition of the protesters.

The issue of selling liquor by the drink in restaurants had meanwhile again raised its head. Jack Gallivan, the publisher of the *Salt Lake Tribune*, had long been a supporter of a law in Utah that would permit the sale of liquor by the drink. For a long while the only way to purchase liquor in the state had been to purchase it from the state liquor stores and then to drink it at home or in a private place. The legislature had never shown any inclination to support a liquor-by-the-drink bill, and, of course, the LDS Church was opposed to it. This was one of the areas where the church felt it had a legitimate role in government, and it had actively opposed liquor by the drink on numerous occasions over past years. I don't recall whether the LDS Church actually opposed people signing the petition that Gallivan had initiated that year to put the liquor-by-the-drink question on the ballot. My recollection is that they stayed pretty quiet during the petition drive. Nonetheless, the required number of signatures was secured, and in mid-July those signatures were filed with the office of the secretary of state. Following this the church did mount overt opposition, and it appeared that liquor by the drink would be an issue in the campaign.

This gave me a problem. I was ambivalent and indifferent on the question of liquor by the drink. I didn't care whether we had it or not. In my opinion, the existing liquor law had not prevented our industrial growth or the growth of tourism, as some people had stated.

Still, I didn't feel that liquor by the drink, whether it passed, was a matter of concern to me as governor, and yet I was continually faced with this problem during the campaign. Every time there was a Democratic rally or a debate of any kind, the Republicans had people there to ask me my opinions about liquor by the drink. Also, they would always ask me about my support for the repeal of the right-to-work law, which had been on the books in Utah since Governor Lee's administration. I must have answered those two questions fifty times during the course of the campaign, and always in the same way. I said I favored the repeal of the right-to-work law and, although I had never been able to get sufficient support in the legislature to repeal it, if the legislature saw fit to change the law I would not veto the bill. In regard to the sale of liquor by the drink, I answered each time that I did not care whether it passed or not, that I would vote on the issue at the voting booth, and that my vote, like anyone else's, was private.

Near the end of July, both parties had their state conventions. Two additional candidates had filed to run for governor on the Republican side: Lamar Rawlings, the Salt Lake County auditor, and another man whose name I do not remember. The third candidate didn't attract much attention, but it still had to go before the state convention. As expected, Buehner came out high, and although Rawlings got enough votes to appear on the primary ballot, he lost in the primary by about a three-to-two vote.

At the Democratic state convention, the principal contest was for the U.S. Senate nomination. Milton Weilenmann received the high vote—something over five hundred votes. The other two candidates, J. D. Williams and Phil Hansen, were very close together at somewhere around four hundred and fifty votes each, with Hansen leading by just a few. So the way was open for a primary campaign between Weilenmann and Hansen. Once again I knew that this was going to cause me some trouble within the party because my support of Weilenmann was well known; the close vote at the convention indicated that the Democrats in this state were not necessarily going to do what I asked them to do, and the primary for the U.S. Senate seat would be a close one. I became involved in his campaign, and Weilenmann did defeat Hansen by a narrow margin in the primary, although he lost the election to Senator Bennett. I inherited many political scars as a result of my support of Weilenmann, both at the convention and later in the primary.

This convention also selected Utah's delegates to the Democratic national convention, which was to be held in Chicago. I was elected as a delegate, as was Senator Moss. We had a split delegation, but more than half of us at that point were for Humphrey.

The Republicans held their national convention about two weeks before we did. They selected Richard Nixon as their nominee on the first ballot over Nelson Rockefeller. That was good news for the Democratic party nationally, but bad news for us in Utah — Rockefeller was liberal and not very popular in this state. At that time Nixon, although he was not well loved as vice president, had not shown the traits of character that would later lead to his resignation from the presidency. On the other hand, on a national basis it was generally felt by Humphrey's supporters that he would have a better chance of defeating Nixon than Rockefeller. This was largely because of the influence of the Vietnam War at that time. Nixon was a hawk on the Vietnam issue, and while Humphrey would not repudiate the Johnson position, he was more moderate in his attitude toward the war than Nixon was. So with the growing interest in the war — and with opposition to the war and particularly to the bombing of North Vietnam increasing — it appeared that Humphrey probably would run much stronger against Nixon than against Rockefeller.

The Democratic convention met in Chicago amid scenes of rioting and other violent kinds of demonstrations against the Vietnam problem. The convention was scheduled to go four days, beginning on Monday. Monday was largely an organizational day, and as I had things to do in Utah, I didn't get into Chicago until that night. The street scenes there were almost indescribable. The protesters held large demonstrations even at the airport, because delegates were still coming in. The demonstrations were even more violent on the city streets as we drove from the airport into town. I didn't go to the convention hall that evening. I went to my hotel and stayed there because it was fairly late.

The next day we were to take up the platform at the convention, and the principal plank was a repudiation of the Vietnam War. It called for U.S. withdrawal. This, of course, was what the demonstrators were aiming at, and their demonstrations during the second night of the convention were stepped up even more.

The oratory on the floor was impassioned and sometimes intemperate. The news networks appeared to be trying to force the passage of the Anti-Vietnam War Resolution. Whether that represented the prevailing attitude among the press or whether they figured it was the most newsworthy story, I don't know. Covering our delegation was a roving correspondent named Sandy Vanocur. He covered our delegation and several near to us, and on anything that had to do with the issues, Vanocur would walk past me or Ted Moss or Cal Rawlings and pick out for comment those in the Utah delegation who were known to favor Gene McCarthy or George McGovern (who had been a late entrant to the contest), and particularly those who were known to be against the war.

The vote on the Vietnam resolution was surprisingly close. I had expected it to be defeated by two-to-one or better, but it was not. The vote rejecting it was only about 55 percent against and 45 percent for the resolution. This did, however, indicate that in all probability Humphrey was going to win the nomination on the first ballot, because nearly everybody who voted against the Vietnam resolution would be Humphrey's supporters, while Eugene McCarthy and George McGovern would split between them the anti-Vietnam vote.

Wednesday was the day for the nomination of the candidate for the presidency. Riots and disturbances were still going on in the streets. The nominations started late in the afternoon because they wanted to get on prime time television as much as possible. Nominating speeches, demonstrations, and seconding speeches were expected to consume two or three hours. The aim was to have the first vote completed around nine or ten o'clock, Chicago time, and that's the way it turned out. Humphrey won the nomination by a substantial majority, taking an almost two-to-one victory over the combined McGovern-McCarthy vote. He was declared the nominee by midevening, and the convention recessed until the next day.

I had not been back to my room in the Morrison Hotel very long when the phone rang. It was Bill Canelle, who was Vice-President Humphrey's administrative assistant. He said, "Hubert would like to have you come over to his room in the Hilton Hotel. He wants to talk about the selection of a candidate for vice-president as his running mate." I said, "I'll be over just as soon as I can get there." I dressed, and because the distance was not far and the taxicabs were afraid to go on the street that night, I started for the Hilton on foot. I picked my way through the back streets, because the streets around the Hilton, where it was known that Humphrey's headquarters were located, were

filled with protesters. Across the street in Grant Park there was a substantial amount of violence going on. The police were there with clubs.
The protesters had adopted a tactic of getting a piece of plate glass,
about as big as a dinner plate, and sailing it like a saucer toward the
police. Obviously these pieces of flying glass were very dangerous and
a number of policemen were cut. The police reacted accordingly, and
many people were injured in the park that night.

I got into the Hilton Hotel through a back door and identified myself to the security men. Security was extremely tight, but I
made my way up to Humphrey's room. It was a large room, and I had
supposed there would be a great many people there. Actually there
were not many. Besides Hubert and Bill Canelle and myself, there
were John Connally, Bob McNair, Hewlett Smith, Charlie Terry, and
Larry O'Brien. I was a bit surprised at O'Brien's presence there because
John Bailey was the Democratic national chairman at that time; however, that was sort of a tip-off that Hubert was going to change national
chairmen, which he did immediately after the convention.

Hubert started by going around the room, asking each of
us whom we favored for the vice-presidential position. There was at
first no consensus. Then the governors seemed to lean toward Cyrus
Vance, but for some reason Hubert was not buying that. It soon became
evident from the conversation that he had not really called us there
for advice, but to tell us who his choice would be and to try to get our
support. His choice was Ed Muskie. I had met Muskie up to that time
only infrequently; I didn't know him well, but I felt I could support
his nomination. John Connally was very much opposed to Muskie, as
was McNair. They had a sort of anti-Yankee feeling against Muskie.
All the while this discussion was occurring on the fifteenth floor of
the Hilton, the demonstrations were happening across the street in
the park. The protesters had loudspeakers and were shouting out
unrepeatable obscenities. Generally it was a scene of violence. Our
meeting broke up about one-thirty or two o'clock in the morning, and
the demonstrations were still going on.

On the fourth day of the Democratic National Convention the vice-presidential nomination was made, and Hubert's recommendation of Ed Muskie was accepted. The two made their acceptance speeches and the convention was over by early afternoon. But
the problem in the streets still persisted. Although the violence of the

demonstrations had toned down from the night before, there were still scattered bands in Grant Park and downtown Chicago. Charges were made of police brutality, including one claim by the McCarthy supporters which was never verified that police followed some demonstrators into the Hilton Hotel and physically abused a number of them in the hallways and in their rooms. The party left Chicago badly splintered, principally over the Vietnam War issue, and there were also a few overtones of the environmental protest movement, which would be taken up seriously by activists over the next several years.

After returning home from Chicago I became busy dealing with state affairs, since I had been absent a lot during the summer months. I was also getting ready for the fall campaign. When the primaries were over I wanted to start the campaign in earnest. It appeared certain that my opponent would be Carl Buehner.

The fall campaign was difficult for me because as governor I had to run the state, and the amount of time I could spend on the campaign was limited. Usually the lack of time is compensated for by the fact that the incumbent traditionally has more public recognition. The challenger has got to become known, which takes time, so the incumbent starts out with a considerable advantage if he has a good record, and a disadvantage if he has a bad record. I felt that my record in the four years I'd been governor was acceptable. I was, however, concerned because Buehner, in his capacity as a general authority for many years, had made speeches almost every weekend at various ward houses throughout the state. As a result of these activities, Buehner was probably as well known, or better known, than I was among the Mormon people. And I was uncertain about the influence of the church on Utah voters as well. No member of the general authorities had run for public office since Reed Smoot was defeated by Elbert Thomas in 1932, so there was no recent track record to show whether the general church membership would feel an obligation to vote for Buehner.

I was also apprehensive because obviously, with the split in the Democratic party, Nixon was going to carry Utah quite heavily against Humphrey. At that time we were using paper ballots almost exclusively. The mechanical setup of the ballot, in which a person may vote for the entire ticket of a particular party by marking a circle under the party emblem at the head of the ballot, gave a considerable advantage to the candidates of the party whose presidential nominee was carrying the state. If a person wanted to vote for Nixon for president, he or she would simply mark the circle above Nixon's name. It was easier to mark than was the little square opposite Nixon's name; and a mark in the circle would count for every candidate in the Republican party, unless the voter crossed over and put a mark opposite the name of the candidate of another party. This was a big advantage.

The newspaper polls that were taken earlier in the year had given me an advantage over Buehner, but not an overwhelming one. It was something like a 54–46 edge and, of course, these polls in no way measured the advantage that a candidate would get from the format of the actual ballot. It was going to be a difficult election, and all things being equal, I felt that I would be lucky if I pulled through. My campaign advisors and I agreed that we should engage Buehner in debate at every opportunity. The experience I gained during my four years as governor should have given me a knowledge of state affairs that a newcomer could not hope to equal. If in the debates we could focus on rather narrow and technical issues in state government, it might very well be that I could overcome some of the advantages Buehner appeared to have.

Buehner had a rather slow, folksy style of speaking that I thought was effective in groups of two or three hundred people. His speeches tended to be stereotyped or almost memorized, but still, he did rather well with them. Nevertheless, we issued a challenge to hold a series of debates, and it was accepted by the Buehner people. We scheduled a series of about twenty-two debates over the next six weeks before service clubs and other groups throughout the state.

The first of these public appearances occurred around mid-September in the Northwest Community Center in Salt Lake. Not only Buehner and I, but all of the candidates of both parties for major office, took part at this meeting. Among the people appearing was a person by the name of Mark Anderson, who was the leader of the John Birch Society in Salt Lake, and who was an independent candidate for the U.S. Senate. The crowd which appeared, as might be expected from that particular area, was largely Democratic and not particularly friendly to the Republican candidates.

I got into an altercation with Mark Anderson. He said something derogatory in his speech about Lucybeth's activity with liberal causes and practically implied that she was a Communist, and we came close to blows. Some very pointed verbal exchanges took place. The crowd became excited and there was shouting and I'm sure that this experience shocked Buehner. This wasn't the type of crowd you found at a quarterly stake conference and it wasn't the kind of confrontation he was used to. He made a short perfunctory speech and sat down.

A few days later we were to debate before the Utah Public Employees' Association. This was actually a debate format, with only Buehner and me appearing, and we had an opportunity to ask each other questions. I had heard Buehner say on a radio spot near the end of the primary campaign that if he were elected governor he would reduce state expenditures by 30 percent. I asked him how he expected to cut state expenditures by 30 percent when a huge percentage of the money went for personnel, and these people out in front of us were the people who would have to be laid off if the expenditures were cut. Buehner denied that he'd ever said such a thing, and I said, "Yes, you did. Just give me a moment." I turned on a recording I had of the radio message and the audience heard just exactly what I told them Buehner had said. I believe that Buehner had just been reading texts and had no concept of what they meant. When he heard his own voice saying what he had a minute before denied he had said, he turned rather pale, and that was in effect the end of that debate.

That was the end of all the debates as it turned out. At the next two or three joint meetings we had planned, Buehner failed to appear. Then we received a letter from his campaign committee saying that all future debates were canceled. We, of course, made all we could of this, and stated what was already beginning to appear to people—that Buehner had no concept of what state government was about or what the issues were in the campaign.

Although there were no joint appearances during the last five weeks of the campaign, the campaign still became rather vicious. I don't know to whom to attach responsibility, but I had never before, nor have I since, been engaged in a campaign where the underground rumors were spread as they were in this one. Lucybeth and I were depicted as confirmed alcoholics. Bill Smart, the editor of the *Deseret News*, called me up one day and said that an anonymous tip had just come in that Lucybeth had been driving while drunk and was in a bad automobile accident and that the affair had been hushed up. In truth, Lucybeth hadn't been in any automobile accident, and she never got drunk.

There was also a story that I had formerly been married and that Lucybeth was a second wife. Although that probably would not have been damaging in most states, the feeling in Utah was that a divorced person wouldn't run well. The rumor was rampant. We heard it from many people, and each time it seemed that the first wife's name was different, so someone didn't get his story very straight. Furthermore, rumors had it that Lucybeth and I were having domestic trouble.

It was a bad campaign and one which I resented. Buehner himself engaged in this sort of thing on occasion, although I can't believe that he did it of his own volition. He was a kind man, but he was fed this line. At one talk that he gave he repeated the rumor that I was addicted to alcohol. This was more than I felt I should have to take, and so I wrote a very strong letter to N. Eldon Tanner, who was a counselor to President McKay in the first presidency of the LDS Church, telling him that I didn't intend to put up with this sort of thing. Although Buehner was no longer a general authority, he was running under the mantle of his former position. I told Tanner that I felt the general authorities should take steps to make certain that this campaign was put back on the right track.

Tanner, on receiving the letter, called me and said that he and others were disturbed by the tone that was being taken by the opposition in this campaign and that indeed he would take such steps as he could to correct the situation. The situation did get better, at least on the surface, although I'm sure the sub rosa comments were still occurring. What hurt Buehner worst was that he wouldn't appear in debate, and we exploited that matter through letters to the editor and by other means.

Shortly before the election the *Tribune* endorsed me editorially, which they had not done for a candidate for many years. The *Deseret News*, although it made no endorsement, had a number of what I would regard as favorable editorials regarding my administration. At the same time, the newspaper polls showed my lead over Buehner had gone up to somewhere around 60–40.

The other campaigns within the state were, at the same time, escalating. Milt Weilenmann was deep in the race for U.S. Senator against Wallace Bennett. Although the original polls showed

Weilenmann running far behind, as they approached the election it was obvious that Weilenmann was the better campaigner. By the time they reached the last poll before the election it was about 52 percent for Bennett, 48 percent for Weilenmann. In my opinion, had it not been for the influence of Nixon as the head of the ticket, Weilenmann would have defeated Bennett. As it was, Bennett defeated Weilenmann by less than 12,000 votes statewide. Weilenmann actually carried Salt Lake County by a rather sizable majority.

The Democratic and Republican presidential candidates both came to Utah. Nixon was permitted to appear in the Salt Lake Tabernacle, as had been the custom, since that was the only hall in the community large enough to accommodate the crowd that would want to hear a president or a presidential candidate. Hubert had been in touch with me saying that he wanted to make a major speech somewhere in the West, preferably before the end of October. If we could arrange for an appearance in the Tabernacle, he would try to make it here. We were able to arrange for the Tabernacle, but Hubert's schedule was difficult and it wasn't until about three days before the tentative date that we actually had confirmation that he would be here. We therefore had difficulty making sure that we would have a crowd at the Tabernacle, as you just don't get a spontaneous crowd of five thousand people to show up for anything. At any rate, Hubert did come; we arranged a parade, and he spoke around noon.

We took him first to see the general authorities of the church, and he was very graciously received. Then he went to the Tabernacle, which was filled, and gave the speech that most people regard as the turning point in the presidential election of 1968. Without actually repudiating the Johnson stance on Vietnam, Hubert took an entirely different track. I am sure it had been his position all along, but being a good team player, he had played it down. In effect he said he would stop all bombing of Vietnam and attempt to negotiate and scale down hostilities just as rapidly as possible.

I thought it was a good speech, a diplomatic speech, and indeed it was received well around the country. Generally, political pundits say that if Humphrey had made the Salt Lake City speech two weeks earlier, or if the election had been two weeks later, he would have won. He never could have carried Utah, of course, but nationally the polls showed a rapid closing between Nixon and Humphrey during the last two weeks with the result that Nixon just barely defeated

Humphrey in the popular vote. One can't help wishing that the Salt Lake City speech had been made two weeks earlier, if that would actually have changed the tide. The country six years later might have been spared the ordeal of Watergate.

Ed Muskie also came into the state campaigning. I had met him once or twice before the Democratic convention, and of course I met him on the final convention day, but I got better and better acquainted with him as this campaign went on. We struck up a close friendship that has endured to this day, although I don't see him as often now since he left government. Right up to the time that he left as Secretary of State after Carter's defeat, I would see him whenever I went to Washington, and whenever he was in the West he would drop in to see us.

The election of 1968 in Utah was predominately in favor of the Republicans, although not overwhelmingly so. I was able to defeat Buehner by a vote of almost two to one. In addition to that, Clyde Miller, who ran for reelection as secretary of state, won. This was a very important position as far as I was concerned because the secretary of state and the attorney general sit along with the governor as members of the powerful board of examiners that must pass on all state claims. If a governor had a secretary of state and an attorney general both working against him and attempting to thwart what he was doing, he would be in a very difficult position. I was pleased that Miller won because during the previous four years Phil Hansen, the Democratic attorney general, had been pretty well against me on anything I wanted done, while Clyde had been supportive. During the final days of the campaign when Clyde had run out of money and our campaign was comparatively well financed, we spent some money in support of him. The Republicans, however, won the office of attorney general, with Vernon Romney as the successful candidate. I didn't know at that time that he would be my foremost source of trouble in the administration over the next eight years.

After the election and a short rest I got actively into preparing for the legislature, which would meet in January 1969. As before, it was necessary for me to prepare a budget, an address to the legislature on the affairs of state, and an inauguration day message for the first Monday in January. I got ready to give the speeches, and I approached the second term with more confidence than I had approached my first term as governor.

In preparing for the second term I was more concerned with consolidating the gains that we had made in the first four years than I was with any new goals. We had made a great step forward in funding for the school programs and the social programs. Although we had had a very good period of time in 1967 and 1968 as far as state financing was concerned, I wasn't certain how things would go over the next four years. Above all, I didn't want to have to retreat from anything we'd done because we couldn't finance it. I therefore proposed some substantial tax increases in my state of the state message and in the budget message. I asked for an increase in sales tax from 3 to 4 percent and for increases in several license and franchise taxes so that we would have enough leeway to carry forward the programs that we had already undertaken.

I felt that I could propose tax increases more effectively coming in as a freshly elected governor, even though I didn't have a Democratic legislature, than I could at midterm when I didn't know what was going to happen. The legislature, although still Republican, was less Republican than it had been in 1967. Furthermore, the leadership was more to my liking than that of the previous two years had been. Since there was still a tug-of-war between the liberals and conservatives in the senate, Haven Barlow, falling as he did in the middle, was reelected president of the senate for the second time in a row.

What delighted me most, however, was that Frank Gunnell had been defeated as speaker of the house in the Republican caucus. The new speaker was Lorin Pace, who had been in the house for about six years. He was a lawyer from the south part of Salt Lake County. I was never close to Lorin, either before or after he became speaker, but I felt that I couldn't do worse than Frank Gunnell. Pace made the ordinary noises that a partisan political leader is supposed to make, but at no time did I feel that he was being irrational in his opposition, and when he did oppose me it was on a matter of principle.

Generally, the legislature supported me. I felt that if my proposed tax increases were necessary, and I was reasonably sure that they were, then we should have them. On the other hand, if they proved to be unnecessary and if as a result of their imposition we built up a surplus, then I was going to propose to the legislature that we reduce the property tax levy on a state level again. Both Haven Barlow and Lorin Pace gave initial approval to my proposals, and also both city newspapers went along with favorable editorials. The *Tribune* was quite enthusiastic in their endorsement. The *Deseret News*, as usual, was more restrained.

As the initial days of the legislature began, Lucybeth and I prepared to do something that I was not enthusiastic about: attend the inauguration of Richard Nixon as president of the United States. We flew in the National Guard plane from Salt Lake to Washington, taking a number of staff people with us. At that time we were flying the C-97 plane, which would go from Salt Lake to Washington non-stop. We had expended some $3000 – money that was raised by some friends – to build a bedroom and a galley in the plane. In Washington we were joined by Max and Billie Rich and Lew and LaRue Flinders, who had flown back in a plane belonging to Bill Kibbe.

We arrived in Washington a day or two before the inauguration, but already I didn't like the way things were developing. Naturally I wasn't happy about Nixon, whom I didn't know; but from what I had learned from the press and other sources, I thought I wouldn't like him. I did not like his replacing Johnson in the White House, and so admittedly I was not prepared to be fair to Nixon and his people. Nor was I prepared for the carnival atmosphere that seemed to be settling over Washington. I suppose, in retrospect, that it was justified. The Republicans had been out of office and frustrated for eight years, but it seemed to me that the people we were seeing at various places were a pretty sleazy bunch.

The day before the inauguration I called my friend, Benito Gauguine, who had been in the European theater with me during the war. Benny, who practices law in Washington and is more Republican than Democrat, was a very astute observer of the current scene. He had been around Washington seeing congressmen and administrative officers come and go for all the years from 1946, when he got back from World War II, until 1969, so he knew the town well. I recall his saying, "Within two months everything in this town is going to be for sale." I thought at the time it was a little cynical, but the more we went through that weekend the more I thought about Benny's remarks and wondered whether we weren't moving in the direction he suggested. Of course by the end of the first year of the Nixon administration it was quite obvious that that was true. The influence of money was impossible to believe.

The inauguration itself was downbeat for me. As usual, the governors sat on the inaugural stand immediately behind and to the

left of both the incoming president and vice-president and the outgoing president and vice-president. Nixon's entrance was very dramatic.
He came in and waved, flung out both his hands as the orchestra
played "Hail to the Chief," took the oath, and gave his inaugural speech.
In retrospect it seems an ironic speech for him to have given, as it
contained the admonition, "Let us lower our voices." I suppose voices
were never raised more in partisan clamor than they were during the
Nixon administration.

I was interested in some people who were sitting around me
in the stands while we were observing the inauguration. Immediately
behind me were President Marcos of the Philippines and his wife,
Imelda. I'd always regarded her as a very beautiful woman and it was
difficult for me to accept the fact that up close she really wasn't. She
was hard and painted, like a hard copy of the Dragon Lady from the
"Terry and the Pirates" cartoon. Also in the row behind me sat General Omar Bradley, with whom I later had an opportunity to talk for a
few minutes.

We rode in the inaugural parade, sat in the reviewing stand,
and that evening went to the inaugural balls, but all in all, I was glad
to get out of there and get home again.

In February I returned to Washington for the regular midwinter National Governors' Conference. We were told that we would
have several sessions at the White House to get acquainted with the
new administration. About fifteen governors had been invited to a
morning meeting during my first visit. We met in the cabinet room
with Nixon and Agnew and two or three of the newly appointed cabinet members. Nixon went around the table shaking hands with everybody. When he came to me he called me Cal and slapped me on the
shoulder, although he'd never laid eyes on me before, and I was offended
by such phony camaraderie. But I applauded Nixon's effort to culti-
vate the governors, and so was willing to forget partisan differences as
much as I could.

What bothered me more than anything else at that time
was that Nixon was even outdistancing Johnson as far as support of
our involvement in Vietnam was concerned. During the last part of
1968 Johnson had certainly been having second thoughts about Vietnam and had been getting ready to back off and try to find some
accommodation. After the election was over he had said he would
seek a truce. In his Salt Lake City speech Humphrey had also said he

was in favor of bringing the Vietnam War to a close on any basis that we reasonably could. But here was the Nixon administration attempting once again to whip up the fervor of the people in support of an extension of the war.

There was another meeting in Washington at about that time for which we were all invited to the State Department. A number of officers from the president's cabinet, or subcabinet, gave speeches in support of stepping up the effort in Vietnam. Mel Laird, who was then either the secretary of defense or the designee, gave a speech telling why we had to make more effort in Vietnam. Among other things, he claimed that an oil pipeline had been laid in North Vietnam to bring oil supplies from Communist China and North Vietnam to the Viet Cong troops. His point was that this showed an increased effort on the part of the north, and we must meet it. He claimed that the piece of pipe which he held in his hand—maybe a six-inch or eight-inch pipe—was a piece that had actually been brought back after one of our bombs had hit the pipeline.

But the press revealed on the next day that it was not from an oil pipeline: it was a piece of pipe that apparently had been given to Laird by somebody at the Pentagon along with this fancy story. It was merely a prop for his speech. I can't believe that Mel Laird, if he knew the facts, would have misrepresented them. I've become fairly friendly with him over the last several years since. We golfed together in a tournament at Sun Valley. I also knew him when he was in Congress and regarded him highly. I don't think he would have done that. It just indicates how far the Nixon people would go at that time in their attempt to step up support of the Vietnam War.

The two days of meetings and briefings were brought to an end by a dinner at the White House. We had been there on many occasions when the Johnsons were our hosts, but this was the first one with the Nixons. The last one, six years later, was to be a tragic affair. Nobody could have known in 1969 what was coming, but I still didn't feel good, never did feel good, about the Nixon administration. I still was having a hard time getting used to Nixon as president, and was unable to warm up to him at all, in spite of the fact that he made such a great effort to be a good fellow—too great an effort, I'm afraid. I was uncomfortable with his gushiness.

The Utah legislature finished its regular session in the middle of March. This was the first year in the history of the state that we had made a budget for one year only. The legislature two years before, in accordance with a recommendation from the Little Hoover Commission, had passed a resolution proposing an amendment to the constitution providing for a regular session of the legislature to meet as always on the second Monday in January of odd-numbered years, and to stay in session for sixty days; in addition, a budget session was proposed to meet on the second Monday in January of even-numbered years and to stay in session for twenty days. The budget session was supposed to consider only budgetary matters unless other matters were approved for inclusion on the agenda by a two-thirds vote of the legislature. We had not yet had a budget session when the 1969 legislature finished, but there was one in prospect for the following January.

The 1969 legislature was probably as harmonious as any I've experienced. They didn't rock the boat; I didn't have any big battles with them. By and large they adopted my budget, and they approved with only minor variations the tax increase proposals that I had made. Actually, because of those tax increases we had built up a surplus of funds and, as I expected, we were able to continue our reduction in the property tax levy on the state level.

During the summer of 1969 I proceeded with my travels to the industrial centers of the country, and made one trip to the Hollywood, California, area to court the movie industry. We had city elections coming up that year, but during the summer and fall the political activity was at a minimum, so it was rather an easy and enjoyable time for me.

The new governor opens a new ski lift at Park City, 1965.

Rampton with State Senator Omar Bunnell of Price at Scofield Reservoir.

The governor opening a new section of the interstate in Salt Lake City in 1965.

Governor Calvin Rampton and Lucybeth with Senator Frank Moss, viewing the New York World's Fair from the Unisphere on Utah State Day, July 24, 1965.

*LDS President David O. McKay, his son Robert, and the governor at the
dedication of the Zion's First National Bank in the Kennecott Building,
November 1965. Ernst Wittke photo.*

*The Democrats assemble in 1964.
Congressman David S. King, Governor Calvin L. Rampton, Hubert H.
Humphrey, Bill Bruhn, and Senator Frank E. (Ted) Moss.*

*Senator Edmund S. Muskie of Maine with the governor
at the Salt Lake City airport, October 27, 1968.*

*Senator Edward Kennedy of Massachusetts and the governor
confer during the campaign of 1968.*

The future governor of Utah receives the support of President Lyndon B. Johnson. Cecil W. Stoughton photo.

The governors of Arizona and Utah meet near St. George to open the new interstate through the Virgin Narrows. Arizona Highway Department photo.

CHAPTER SIX

BREAKING A PRECEDENT: UTAH'S FIRST THREE-TERM GOVERNOR

During the later part of the summer of 1969 something happened that changed the course of the Democratic party. I first learned of it in a very small front-page box in the *Tribune* one morning, which said that Senator Edward Kennedy had accidentally driven off a bridge at the little island of Chappaquiddick in Massachusetts, and that a young woman who was in the automobile with him was missing and assumed drowned. That first day it was a small article, but during the next weeks it ballooned into the major interest of news reporters in the country. Mary Jo Kopechne was dead, having been unable to get out of the car, although Kennedy claimed to have dived in several times in an attempt to rescue her. The problem was that not only had Kennedy been driving with the woman under questionable circumstances, but after the car went off the bridge he left the scene of the accident and didn't report the matter until the next day. The justified supposition was that he had panicked and run.

This conduct would most definitely defeat his efforts to become a presidential candidate for the Democrats. Each time he made an effort to run the issue would be revived. Americans were pretty well disenchanted with Jimmy Carter in 1980 when he was seeking the Democratic nomination for a second term. The polls indicated that Kennedy would run far ahead of Carter if he were to become a candidate. Kennedy therefore became a candidate, but as soon as his candidacy was official, the newspapers revived Chappaquiddick and his standing in the polls plummeted. He was never able to make a serious challenge to President Carter. In 1983 Kennedy indicated that he would not be a candidate in the 1984 presidential election. Ostensibly it was because of his concern for his family and the families of his brothers, but I guess that he is realistic enough to know that anytime he attempts to run for the presidency Chappaquiddick will be immediately revived by the press and defeat his chances.

I say that Chappaquiddick has had a great influence on the course of the Democratic party because Kennedy was the natural leader of the liberal wing of the party, and probably would have been able to make liberalism the party's dominant position. There has been no other candidate around whom the left has been able to coalesce. Fritz Mondale, who ran for the presidency in 1984, was really more liberal than Carter, but he wasn't about to fire the imagination of the liberals as Kennedy was able to do.

I was saddened to see this happen to Ted Kennedy. I had liked and still like him very much. I hadn't known John Kennedy except to meet him in a reception line two or three times, and I really didn't like Bobby Kennedy very well, although he had been our houseguest on at least two occasions. We had Bobby's whole family there on the Fourth of July in about 1966 or 1967, and the next year when he was there with one of his aides he stayed overnight. He was a difficult man to talk to, but Ted Kennedy was delightful company. He stayed overnight at our house with his wife, Joan, sometime before the Chappaquiddick incident, and we enjoyed them very much.

Not long after the Chappaquiddick incident the University of Utah School of Business invited me to go to Wiesbaden and be the commencement speaker at the graduation exercises of their MBA program with the Air Force. Soon after our return from Europe, Lucybeth and I left for Seattle and the Western Governors' Conference. I was elected chairman of the conference that year and Stan Hathaway was elected vice-chairman to succeed me in the following year. A few weeks later in early September, we went to Colorado Springs for the National Governors' Conference. John Love was elected national chairman. It was the Republican's turn for it that year, as the position alternates between the parties.

The Utah economy during 1969 had done well. The tax increases which the legislature had enacted in the spring yielded us a substantial surplus. We would go into the budget session in good financial condition. I had to prepare a budget for that session, which was to meet on the second Monday of January 1970, and I wanted to be sure that whatever surplus we had was either kept intact or put into one-time expenditures, such as buildings. I didn't want it folded into the operating budget for the following year because doing so can give government an appetite that's hard to satisfy after the surplus is gone.

By this time Wallace Gardner, a state senator from Utah County, had become chairman of the Joint Appropriations Committee of the senate and the house. Wally had succeeded Ernest Mantes when the Republicans assumed control of the senate. He was a very good legislator and a fine gentleman. During all the while that he served as chairman of the appropriations committee, through about three sessions, we never had serious friction between us. If we had a problem where we appraised a matter differently, we could generally sit down and talk it out. I feel that I owe a great deal to that man because he helped me make my administration a financially responsible one.

Other Republican senators on whom I depended at that time were Warren Pugh, Hughes Brockbank, and Karl Snow, who had moved from the house to the senate. So although the senate was overwhelmingly Republican, it revealed few partisan overtones. And although I never got close to Lorin Pace, still I think he treated me fairly, and my relationship with the legislature was good.

We reached the end of the year and got ready to face a new campaign the following year. The most important office at stake would be that of U.S. senator. It was pretty well assured that Ted Moss would run for his third term, and it was doubtful that there would be any opposition from within the Democratic party. The probable nominee for the Republicans appeared to be Lawrence Burton, who was congressman from the First Congressional District. Burton had been in the House of Representatives four years at that time and was rather popular. Everyone assumed that he would be the Republican candidate, and although my brother Byron ran against him, he was unable to get much support, and Burton easily won the Republican nomination.

On the second Monday of January 1970, the legislature met in the first budget session in the history of the state. Because this was the premiere session and it was short, only twenty days as compared with the general session's sixty, we were not sure just how it was going to work out. The constitutional amendment that instituted the budget session also provided that nonbudgetary measures could only be considered during a session if the introduction of these measures was approved by a two-thirds vote of both houses. It was hoped that this would cut down on the number of nonbudgetary matters that would be considered. As we might have foreseen, however, there was a lot of back scratching and logrolling in regard to nonbudgetary matters. As a result, early in the session the calendar was bogged down with nonbudgetary measures—many more than the legislature could hope to address in twenty days if it was also to consider the budget.

Fortunately the budget was not as hard to take care of that year as it would be in others because we were having reasonable growth in the state, and since we had had the tax raise a couple of years before, the state's resources were in good shape. Even before I presented my budget message to the legislature I had gained the concurrence of the Republican leadership that it was generally acceptable to them. They also agreed to appoint a sifting committee at the end of the second week, where only those bills that we both felt were essential would be considered. I told them if they passed a lot of bills that shouldn't be in a budget session, I was going to veto them. They agreed that that was a reasonable approach.

During the legislature, the *Tribune* ran a poll on the governorship to determine whether the people of Utah felt I was doing a good job. The unusual thing about this poll was that I received a slightly better rating from the Republicans in the state than I did from the Democrats. Seventy-one percent of the Republicans polled said that I was doing a good or excellent job, while only 69 percent of the Democrats felt that way. Only 23 percent of the Republicans thought I was doing a fair or poor job.

I'm sure this resulted from several factors. The breach with the party leaders that I had had during my first term was being healed slowly, but there was still some opposition from the more liberal members of the party. However, I think the two things that really caused me trouble with the Democrats were the Vietnam War (although by this time I was thoroughly disabused of any notion that we should continue in Vietnam if we could possibly get out) and the environmental movement. Since I had during the preceding several years been a vocal supporter of the national government's program in Vietnam, I wasn't going to change my stripes all of a sudden and say, "Well, now that we have a Republican president, I'm no longer supporting our presence in Vietnam, and therefore we should get out." I thus had little to say about Vietnam after I changed my viewpoint. However, there was an element in the party that was violently opposed to further Vietnam participation, and this group felt that I should be out beating the drums to get the troops home.

The second group who were on the liberal side of the party and who viewed me with some suspicion, were the active environmentalists. I believed that there was a middle ground between the views of the militant environmentalists and the views of those who were willing to develop at any cost. I was attempting to find this ground, and it caused unhappiness on the part of those Democrats who were aggressive conservationists.

When we were about a week into the legislative session, the state was saddened by news of the death of David O. McKay, the president of the LDS Church. President McKay was ninety-six at the time of his death and had had a number of sinking spells over the preceding years. I usually tried to get in to see President McKay five or six times a year, if I possibly could. I suppose during my lifetime there has been no more deeply loved president of the church than McKay. He was a large man with a great shock of white hair and a commanding presence. But more than that, he was a kind man. He was a spiritual leader, as opposed to some presidents of the church, such as Heber Grant and George Albert Smith, who had not been warm personalities. Everybody, Mormon and non-Mormon alike, loved and respected President McKay.

Joseph Fielding Smith was set apart as the president a few days after President McKay's death. Smith was ninety-three at that time. His health appeared to be fairly good, but he had trouble with his attention span. I think everyone felt that Smith's tenure as president of the church would be short and that it would be more or less a caretaker situation, with Harold B. Lee as the heir apparent making most of the major church policies. This proved to be true, except that N. Eldon Tanner continued to be the business head of the church.

One of the nonbudgetary matters that the legislature had considered during the budget session was another Sunday closing law. This caught me in a bad spot. In the previous session when I vetoed the Sunday closing act, I had written a long message outlining exactly the things that I felt were most objectionable in the act. The new act, which was passed by the budget session in 1970, had successfully met every one of the constitutional objections that I had raised in the first veto message. I couldn't deny it, but I still didn't like the bill. I didn't like the idea of attempting to legislate morality. However, I had many times stated that I would not let the matter of whether I liked a bill be the deciding factor on whether I would veto it. In other words, I wasn't trying to be a third house of the legislature. I tried very hard to find some constitutional objection to the new bill, but couldn't. Finally I decided that while I couldn't sign it, I couldn't veto it, either, and it became law without my signature.

Near the end of February Lucybeth and I went to Washington for a midwinter governors' meeting. As usual, we had dinner at the White House. This wasn't a particularly momentous conference, and there was by that time a schism growing between the governors and President Nixon. None of the governors, not even the Republicans, felt close to him.

It was becoming more and more difficult for me not to be publicly critical of the Nixon administration. I felt that he should not be in office: but there he was, and as he was president and I was governor of a state, I should not be unreasonable in my criticisms. But pressures were building. For instance, most of the governors were offended by Vice-President Agnew's activities. Agnew had been governor of Maryland for two years before Nixon selected him, and so we all knew him well. I had rather liked Agnew as a governor. We were on a number of committees together and at various times had played golf together. But his role—I guess the role assigned to him as vice-president—was that of hatchet man for the president. His speeches were strident, intemperate, and offensive even to the governors who liked him.

At the same time that Agnew became vice-president, Wally Hickel, who had been elected governor of Alaska in 1966, was appointed as the secretary of the interior. I knew and respected Hickel and felt that he was a very good appointee. Before long, though, Hickel couldn't take what was happening in the Nixon administration. He became quite vocal in his criticism of Agnew, and it wasn't long before that criticism—in fact criticism of the whole approach of the Nixon administration to the problems of youth in the country—caused the president to remove him.

Another sacking by the Nixon administration that disturbed me a great deal was that of Jim Allen as the commissioner of higher education and assistant secretary of HEW. When I was chairman of the Education Commission of the States, Jim Allen, who was the superintendent of public instruction of the state of New York, had been the vice-chairman, and so we were close and very friendly. He was sacked because he had become critical of the Nixon policy on education.

In the meantime, resistance to U.S. policy in Vietnam was growing, particularly on campuses. Then a tragic thing happened in early May 1970. Four students at Kent State University were killed by national guardsmen. A number of colleges across the country where there had been a particularly great amount of agitation actually closed. In mid-May, the president called a conference in Washington. All of the governors were worried, and we went back to discuss what we should do to defuse the thing. I really can't fault the president's performance at this conference. He didn't appear with the governors very often, but he seemed genuinely concerned. However, Vice-President Agnew offended most of the governors by saying, "This has got to be put down. The first thing we have to do is to restore authority on the campuses, and we have to do it by whatever means necessary." This, just after the events at Kent State, didn't go down very well with the governors.

We had some instances of unrest and militancy even on the Utah campuses, which had been relatively tranquil until Kent State. At the University of Utah, fire was set to an old abandoned bookstore. I think the setting of that fire did more to restore order on the campus than any exertion of authority could have done, however, because even though no great damage was done by the fire, the more responsible students were shocked that someone would engage in arson.

In another incident a building adjacent to the campus that belonged to the National Guard and was used by both the National Guard and the ROTC program was bombed. The day after the bombing Jim Fletcher, the president of the university, called me on the phone and asked if he could come over. We never had been close. Fletcher was an austere man. I'd made efforts to get close to him, as I was to Daryl Chase and later to Glen Taggart at Utah State University, but I'd never succeeded. This morning, however, he was very shaken. He came into the front room of the governor's residence and he and I sat on the sofa and talked for about two hours.

Fletcher was considering resigning because although we had not had a great deal of violence on our campus, there had been a steady tension. He felt that he was unable to handle it, and he was very disturbed. His wife, Faye, was also greatly upset by what was going on, and by criticism in the press of Fletcher and the university administration, alleging that they were unduly tolerant of the dissident groups on campus. I wouldn't have believed that Fletcher was able to shed tears until now. I found myself bucking him up, encouraging him to stay. He left feeling much better, and I felt much more kindly toward him than I had ever felt before.

Then early in July, a group of governors went on an exchange trip to Japan. Lucybeth and I were members of the party, and later, when we got back to the Salt Lake airport, we received word that there was a group of hostile student protesters who were going to come to the airport and picket when our plane came in. They hadn't got there yet when we arrived, and the airport authorities asked us if we would please leave, because they didn't want any disturbance that might interrupt the ordinary use of the airport. We drove directly home. Evidently the student protesters went out to the airport, found that we'd gone home, and started for the governor's residence. We were very tired, having traveled nonstop from Japan, and I decided to take a bath.

Just as I was getting in the tub, Lucybeth knocked on the door and said, "There are some Salt Lake City police out front with several canine corps dogs waiting for the protesters. What shall we do?" I said, "Ask them to go. We have a couple of highway patrolmen here who are perfectly capable of providing security if we need it, and I doubt that we do." A few minutes later I heard activity out in the other part of the house, and Lucybeth came in and said the students were there and she had invited them in. I got out of the tub, put on some casual clothes, and went out.

There were thirty-five to forty students sitting around the living room, most of them on the floor, some of them on the couches, drinking soda pop that Lucybeth had given them. The two highway patrolmen were making themselves inconspicuous. I went in, sat down on the step leading into the living room, and asked them what they wanted to talk about. We had a good exchange for a few minutes. Finally, one of the leaders of the protest group said, "Would it be all right if we got the photographer from the *Chronicle?*"—the student newspaper. The *Chronicle* people came over and took some pictures, and we had a good time. The students left and that seemed to be the end of the campus problems.

Not long afterwards, Jerry Rubin, who was a nationally known student agitator, appeared on the campus and gave a speech — and he was almost laughed out of town by the students.

On the campaign front, with Republican Lawrence Burton giving up his seat in the First Congressional District to run for the Senate, the Democrats saw a good chance to capture that congressional seat. An early announced Democratic candidate for the position was Keith Melville, a political science professor at Brigham Young University. Keith was a fine fellow, but he'd run for office before and was not an aggressive candidate, and the feeling in the party was that he just couldn't make it. I was approached by a number of party leaders to see if I would make an effort to get my administrative assistant, Gunn McKay, to run for the position. Gunn had been working for me for about two years, after my first administrative assistant, Glen Hatch, had decided to return to his law practice.

At the time Glen had left, the assistant attorney general assigned to my office had been Allan Howe. Allan had actually worked for Phil Hansen, but had an office with my other staff people, so he knew the governor's office and its routine. I had some reservations about appointing Allan to the position of administrative assistant. He had not been satisfactory as an assistant attorney general as far as I was concerned, but Glen's departure had caught me quite unaware. I had to have somebody almost immediately, so I appointed Allan.

Allan stayed in that position about a year and a half, but he never seemed to get anything done. Every project he undertook was left up in the air. I had been looking for some way to move Allan out without causing too many hard feelings among the party members, with whom he was quite popular. The chance came when a position opened as director of the Four Corners Regional Commission. This was before the 1968 election, so the Democratic president was still in power and this would be a Democratic position. I was pleased when Allan showed an interest in the job, and perhaps it wasn't fair of me, but I agreed to endorse him for the position, and he was appointed. That was when I appointed Gunn McKay as my administrative assistant.

Gunn had been, during the 1965 session of the legislature, the majority leader in the house. At first he and I didn't get along very well. He had been an active supporter of Ernest Dean in the 1964 primary, and I'm not sure he'd ever fully adjusted to my being governor. Gunn had lost his seat in the 1966 sweep and had been out of office for two years. He was a schoolteacher, lived in Huntsville, and was a grandson of David O. McKay's brother. Being a large man with thick hair, he looked quite a lot like President McKay. Gunn was a good administrative assistant—rather slow and plodding, but with a sense of what needed to be done. He worked well with the staff and with me, so I had no hesitancy about urging him to run for the congressional spot when it became obvious that it was going to be open.

The Republican nominee that year was Richard Richards, who had been the Republican state chairman and who had managed Carl Buehner's campaign in 1968. Richards was later to become the national chairman of the Republican party. It was felt that the First Congressional District was Republican and would go Republican again, and I'm sure that Richards was confident he would win.

On the national level, it became evident as the campaign progressed that the Utah seat in the U.S. Senate was being eagerly sought by both political parties, and during the year a series of highly placed Republican federal officials came to Utah to talk for Lawrence Burton. Several senators and as many as five or six members of Nixon's cabinet came, Spiro Agnew was through once or twice, and finally Nixon himself arrived. At a strategy meeting, the Moss Committee managers realized that they couldn't possibly match the parade of speakers that the Republicans could bring in for Burton, and so they decided to bring in no one. Thus, other than two or three senators who came in for fund-raising affairs, we did not bring outside office-holders into Utah to campaign for Moss. The committee had assigned me the task of answering each of the federal officials as they came into town, and I really got more coverage than was warranted since I made the same basic reply each time—that these people really didn't know what Utah needed in a U.S. senator. This reply seemed to work with the public, because they also felt the Republicans were bringing in too many outside people.

As late as mid-August, Burton was leading Moss in the polls. I suppose the strategy of the Republicans was: if it's working to bring in these big names from outside—the cabinet members, the vice-president, the president—then let's pile it on. When Burton and Moss had first announced in the spring, Moss had a little bit of a lead over

Burton in the informal newspaper polls; but during the late summer and early fall when the first flood of outsiders began to come in for the campaign, Burton began to move ahead. By the primary elections he was leading Moss substantially. Among the most effective people the Republicans sent in was David Kennedy, the secretary of the treasury under Nixon. Kennedy was a Mormon, had been born and raised in Woodruff, and it was difficult to raise the outsider charge against him. But the Republicans continued to bring in other outside people until it had clearly become counterproductive. Moss began to move up in the polls rapidly, until by mid-October a poll showed the two candidates to be running about neck and neck.

The president's visit to Utah in the campaign of 1970 had some interesting aspects. Because he was the president and he was visiting my state—even though I knew he was coming on a political trip, which he had indicated to the press was not to be political—protocol required that I meet him at the airport. I went there with Lucybeth, assuming that we would be moved up through the crowd to be the first to greet the president as he came off the plane, and then I intended to get out of the way immediately. However, the Secret Service had been told by the Republican campaign people that that was not to be, and so I was not allowed to go out to greet Nixon. I didn't really feel very bad about it. We waited until the president drove uptown in his motorcade and then we left, but the members of the press had noticed that I was there and that I was not allowed to greet Nixon as protocol required. There followed a great furor in the press to the effect that the president and his aides were not sufficiently sensitive to the needs of protocol to recognize the presence of the governor of the state.

Another rather amusing thing happened during the Nixon speech in the Tabernacle. The presidential seal had been hung up on the podium in front of the president, as was customary, and Mr. Nixon began his speech on a nonpartisan presidential note. About ten minutes into the speech, however, he shifted tone and started on a heavy partisan harangue in favor of Burton and against Moss. And just as he began this harangue, the presidential seal became detached and fell onto the floor with a crash.

There was an aftermath of the president's visit, though, that for a while was somewhat sad for us. I knew that the president would use the Tabernacle for a political harangue. I had talked for some time to President N. Eldon Tanner about this and he agreed that there was a problem. He informed me that if the president asked to use the Tabernacle for a speech the church really couldn't refuse him. There was a long-standing policy that the president of the United States or presidential candidates of either party should be allowed to use the Tabernacle. However, Tanner said he would make every effort to assure that the affair was conducted in a way that would not indicate church approval of the candidate being supported by the president.

We got home from the airport in time to tune in on television to Nixon's speech, and saw at once that the Mormon Tabernacle Choir was there and all of the general authorities of the church were on the stand. This displeased us greatly. In fact, it made Lucybeth furiously angry, and she dispatched a very spirited critical note to Tanner. He didn't personally answer the letter, but his secretary did answer in kind with an equally spirited defense and a statement to Lucybeth that said in effect: "This is none of your affair." This created a split between ourselves and the Tanners which we didn't like because we were very fond of them.

I found out later that President Tanner had raised the question of the presence of the choir and the general authorities at the Nixon speech, but he had been told by others of the general authorities, principally Harold B. Lee, that assurance had been given that this would be a presidential speech on policy and not a political talk. Based on this understanding, Tanner, the choir, and the other general authorities were there.

The split with the Tanners was unpleasant because we were frequently in their company, and two or three times a month we sat at head tables together. One evening there was a function in the Lafayette Ballroom. The head table was long, stretching clear across the east end of the ballroom. Lucybeth and I were sitting immediately to the right of the podium and the Tanners had to pass very close behind us going to their seats. Just as President Tanner came by Lucybeth he turned, put his arms around her, and kissed her on the cheek; she started to cry, and it was a touching scene. I'm sure that as far as President Tanner and Lucybeth were concerned this patched the thing up.

Meantime, the duties of the governorship went on and the political work I was doing had to be in addition to those duties. We'd had a slight downturn in the economy in Utah in the spring of 1970, and it had become evident by the time we reached July that the revenues were not going to equal the estimates we had made when the legislature was in session. I was afraid that if we went too far into the fiscal year before taking action the cutback would have to be too severe, and so shortly after the beginning of the fiscal year I ordered a 2 percent cutback on all appropriations. Once again this caused considerable furor, particularly with the colleges, who felt they had more right to criticize as they were rather insulated from my administration. My appointed officials usually took the cutbacks quietly in statements to the press, whatever they might have said in private.

In late July there was a serious racial disturbance at the Job Corps Center at Clearfield, during which a man was stabbed. I don't recall whether the man stabbed was white, black, or Hispanic, but at any rate, it was racially motivated. Law enforcement officers had been placed around the Job Corps Center because adjacent communities were concerned that a riot there might spread into Ogden and Clearfield. I was asked if I would come up. My security people were nervous about my going into this situation, but I didn't feel that I was particularly threatened. I asked the security people to stay out and I went into the area. The leaders of the various groups called their people in and we sat down and chatted for a while. It seemed to help, and things settled down. I had feared that this incident might lead to the closing down of the Job Corps Center, which I would have regarded as a very unfortunate result. I'm sure the corpsmen feared this, too, as the matter quickly subsided.

There was at this time serious overcrowding at the state prison, and we needed to relieve the pressure. Then, in late August, one of the perennial tempests in a teapot occurred—this concerned the location of a halfway house for prisoners about to be released from prison. The halfway house concept had worked well in other states, and it seemed a good idea for Utah, so I tried it out on the legislative leaders and the press. Everybody was enthusiastic until it came to the matter of selecting where the halfway house would be located. We had explored several possibilities in the Salt Lake City area, where it had to be situated in order to be near workplaces of most of the prisoners on work release. We finally decided to take a long-term lease on the Lake Hills Motel on West North Temple. Immediately the community groups on the west side began shouting that we were always putting undesirable facilities in their area. Why didn't we put it somewhere else? We had a number of hearings, but finally, after all the hearings, it was evident that we weren't going to find a suitable place that would be totally acceptable.

This was one of the few times that Vernon Romney went along with me on a controversial matter. The board of examiners voted unanimously to place the halfway house at the Lake Hills Motel. We were careful about the prisoners we put there, and we made every effort to exclude violence-prone persons. We also tried to avoid putting persons there with drug or drinking habits. The inmates got along pretty well, and the neighborhood resistance eventually softened. However, this problem came up again and again in my administration, and Scott Matheson had the same problem with the location of various facilities during his years in office.

As everyone had expected, Gunn McKay had defeated Keith Melville in the primary election in early September. This was really the only extensively contested primary battle in the state. From then on the election race really heated up. After the Republicans turned off their invasion of outsiders, they started a media campaign, trying to build Burton into a personality of his own. They made one of the most incredible gaffes that has occurred in Utah politics. They wanted to show Lawrence Burton as a regular fellow, just a regular he-man from the West. There had been some rumors of Burton's excessive drinking. Although it had not really become a campaign issue, many people knew about it, and the media planners wanted to counter this image by giving him the aura of a healthy outdoorsman. They launched a campaign spot on television entitled "A Man to Match Our Mountains." It showed Burton on a horse, engaged in the roundup of some cattle. He was so obviously ill at ease on the horse that it looked ludicrous, but for some reason they kept running it. I thought that after seeing the first spot they would have pulled it. They must have run that ad for a week, until Lawrence Burton and his horse became a household joke.

From that point on it was all easy going for Moss, and he won the election by a comfortable majority. Gunn McKay won the House seat. Sherman Lloyd, the Republican nominee in the First Congressional District, won reelection over Bob Nance, a Democrat who was a newcomer to Utah and to politics. Nance was superbly qualified, but he wasn't very outgoing. Nonetheless, he ran Sherm Lloyd a close race.

I was delighted that the Democratic candidates for the legislature did well. After the disastrous defeat in 1966, and without much of a comeback in 1968, the Democrats again carried the house of representatives. The holdover majority of the Republicans in the senate kept us from gaining control there, but we still increased our strength. I was certain that with the personal friends I had on the Republican side in the senate the 1971 session of the legislature would be a good time for some more constructive proposals that might stand a chance of acceptance. The election of McKay to Congress meant that I had to have a new administrative assistant, and I hired my former press secretary, Ronald Swenson. Mike Miller, who had gone down to the Four Corners Regional Commission with Allan Howe as a pressman, came back to be my press secretary.

I now had to get ready for the meeting of the legislature on the first Monday of January 1971. This was a general session, so I had to prepare both the state of the state message and the budget message. The legislature was rapidly organized. The house was Democratic, and Lorin Pace had been selected as minority leader. Once again, the Republicans in the senate had elected Haven Barlow as president, and the Democrats, with their increased minority strength, had selected my friend Omar Bunnell from Price as minority leader. All in all, the upcoming legislative session looked good. During December, as I was getting my budget message ready, I met frequently with the legislative leaders of both houses. I was attempting to frame both my budget and my substantive legislative recommendations on a consensus basis, and this largely came about.

The 1971 session of the legislature was pretty much a housekeeping session. The budget did not require any requests for major increases in taxes, and the substantive bills I put in my message on the state of the state were, except for some civil rights measures, not greatly controversial. I did, however, want to raise more revenue, and I decided that this might be the time to increase the severance tax. For a number of years we had had a very low severance tax — 1 percent on metalliferous minerals and 2 percent on oil and gas. We had had nothing at all on coal. The coal industry had been generally depressed, and I was not sure that it was time yet to attempt to get a severance tax there. Since the copper industry that year was prosperous, I wanted an increased severance tax on it, although without at the same time laying an additional burden on lead or zinc mining, which were also in a depressed state.

This offered a constitutional problem, because it was difficult to get a classification of metalliferous minerals that would include copper and yet eliminate lead and zinc. My proposal to the legislature was that there be a graduated severance tax; that is, the tax should increase depending upon the size of the company and its production. I felt this was defensible legally because it worked on the same principle as the graduated income tax.

Needless to say, this proposal in the budget message caused a great hue and cry. The copper people claimed that in spite of the fact that the price of copper was high and the profits were good, this was temporary and an increase in the severance tax could well strike a long-term blow to the copper industry. I didn't believe that. Jack O'Keefe, who was the head of the Utah Copper Division of Kennecott Copper Company, was a good friend of mine. Nonetheless, we engaged in a very spirited controversy over this matter. He was making speeches critical of my proposal and on one occasion I wrote an open letter to O'Keefe setting forth the basis for my recommendation to the legislature. The *Deseret News* took a position against me. The *Tribune* remained neutral, although I believe Jack Gallivan did so more because he was my friend than because he favored what I was doing.

The matter came up in the house first, where the Democrats now had a majority. My friend Richard Howe, the older brother of Allan Howe, was the speaker of the house of representatives, and as Dick had been supportive of the school program, he was also supportive of my efforts to increase the severance tax. The bill did pass the house by a narrow margin. However, the Republicans still held a majority in the senate, and the bill was defeated there. I lost some of my close Democratic friends in the senate. Omar Bunnell, who would support me on most issues, would always steer clear of any increase in the severance tax because he felt it might open the door for the imposition of a severance tax on coal. Omar told me many times privately that there was a lot to say for putting a severance tax on coal but he wasn't going to say it. It is quite understandable he would not, as he was the state senator from Carbon County.

With the beginning of the new U.S. Congress, John McCormack, who had been the longtime speaker of the House of Representatives, was retiring and Carl Albert of Oklahoma was taking over as the speaker of the house. That would move Tip O'Neill of Massachusetts up to the position of majority leader. I knew both these men well because I had appeared before various committees in Congress and they were friendly to me. I wanted to see what I could do to help Gunn McKay get a good committee position. Gunn wanted to be on the Interior Committee, so I called both O'Neill and Albert and told them that I'd surely like to see Gunn get on that committee. They said they'd see what they could do, but it didn't look too promising. Sherman Lloyd was on the Interior Committee, and he wanted to stay there because he had some three or four years seniority and certainly didn't want to give that up. With Sherm on the committee it would be rather difficult for Gunn to get the assignment.

Gunn's second choice was the Military Affairs Committee, because Hill Field was under the jurisdiction of that committee, as was the Tooele Ordnance Depot. This would offer Gunn a substantial opportunity to do things for his district. But once again they said that it would be difficult because it was a popular committee. In fact, there were some people with seniority in Congress who would give up their present committee positions to get on the Military Affairs Committee. But once again both men said they'd see what they could do.

About a week before the session began, Carl Albert called me on the phone and said, "We've got something that may interest you." I asked what it was and he said, "They have decided to expand the Appropriations Committee by four members." I said, "That's not going to do us any good. I know the senior members of the Congress well enough to know that the Appropriations Committee is the choice committee of the whole Congress and that men with great seniority, even chairmen of other subcommittees, would resign their positions to take the Appropriations Committee opening." Carl said, "That's true, but a rule has been passed by the majority in the House saying that of the four new members, two must be freshmen—one Republican and one Democrat. We've been sort of pushing you around on McKay, but I like him. Do you think he'd accept that position?" I said I was sure he would. I don't recall who the Republican freshman was, but as I understand it, this was the first time in the history of the Congress that a freshman had got on the Appropriations Committee.

And to make things even more inviting, Gunn was appointed to the subcommittee of appropriations on military installations.

Gunn did very well in the Congress during the years he was there. He had the ability to ingratiate himself with the seniors in Congress, establishing a camaraderie with them without undue familiarity, and they liked that. Many times Carl Albert, and later Tip O'Neill, told me just how much they liked Gunn. When Gunn lost the 1980 election, Tip O'Neill told me that that hurt him as much as the loss of any of his colleagues in the Congress could have done.

Although it was a year and a half before the 1972 Democratic convention and more than a year before the first primaries, the candidates for the Democratic presidential nomination began to announce themselves. The earliest to announce were George McGovern and Ed Muskie. McGovern really wasn't given much of a chance to get the nomination at that time, because although he had been active in Democratic party affairs, he was not a forceful person. He did not have an impressive way of speaking, although he was a very bright man. I was, however, pleased when Muskie announced for the presidency. The newspaper polls showed him far ahead of other potential candidates for the Democratic nomination, including Hubert Humphrey, who hadn't yet announced but was expected to.

The year 1971 was one of frantic political maneuvering, not only on a national scale, but also within the state. Every day or two a piece would appear in the paper speculating whether I was going to run for a third term. I still hadn't made up my mind. I felt that I would, but I didn't want to make an announcement until later. It would probably not be until April 1972, because if I announced that I wasn't going to run I would pretty much lose my control of the Democratic party; and if I announced that I would run, the campaign would begin right then, and I didn't want to campaign for eighteen months. So whenever I was asked I said that I would not make up my mind until sometime in the spring of 1972.

The Republicans were desperately seeking to get a candidate whether I ran or not. Those on whom speculation centered were Vernon Romney, the attorney general; Hughes Brockbank, a state senator; Reed Bullen, another state senator; and Rendell Mabey, a second cousin of mine and the son of former Governor Charles Mabey. Rendell had at one time been speaker of the house of representatives and had lost the Republican nomination for governor to Bracken Lee many years before.

I hoped that Romney would be the candidate. I felt that I could beat him, but more than that, I wanted him to run because I didn't want him again for attorney general. He gave interviews to the newspaper about twice a week gratuitously criticizing as a matter of policy the things that I had done. I'd had it with him. Had he announced he was a candidate, I certainly would have made my decision and started the campaign earlier because I would have enjoyed the fight.

Finally, though, Romney announced that he would not run for governor, but for reelection as attorney general instead. Rendell Mabey, Reed Bullen, and Hughes Brockbank all in turn dropped out of the race by the early spring of 1972. In the meantime, Nicholas Strike, a Salt Lake businessman, announced that he would be a candidate for governor. I think this took the Republican party rather by surprise. While Nick Strike had a good reputation as a businessman, he had never held any political position. He decided on his own that he was going to run, and when the filing date arrived in May 1972 he was the only Republican candidate, thus winning the Republican nomination by default.

At the Republican state convention in the summer of 1971, Kent Shearer was elected as the Republican state chairman. I had been with Kent in a reserve army unit for several years and we got along fairly well. However, he was cynical, had a sharp tongue, and was given to overstatement on almost any subject he talked about. I was sure that with Kent as a spokesman for the Republican party, it would be a nasty campaign. He would be slashing in his attacks, making broad accusations which wouldn't be pleasant to run against.

On the other hand, I was certain that Kent would overstate himself and that pretty soon he would lose credibility, which is exactly what happened. During the campaign the following year, when he had Nick Strike sort of thrust upon him as a candidate, Kent took it on himself to lead the campaign. He made speeches about how I was an ultraliberal – a radical – and how I had set up a state machine which he called the octopus. He adopted a slogan which he thought would take, but which I think backfired on him: "We're going to have an

election, not a coronation." I don't think I had ever appeared imperi-
ous, so it just didn't sell.

An embarrassing event occurred while I was in Washington on state business in the fall of 1971. Ed Muskie had asked Ted
Moss and me if we would go on television with him and endorse him
for the presidential nomination. A number of senators had endorsed
Muskie before that time, but no senior governors had yet done so,
and he felt this was important. Apparently it was newsworthy because
all of the networks were there for the announcement. Each of us gave
a short talk. It was about a two-minute segment and it went on television at six o'clock that night on all three channels. The problem was
that on that very day George McGovern was in Salt Lake speaking at
the University of Utah. The television hadn't yet come on, but the
radio had picked up the item and it was generally known, as George
made his speech with Lucybeth sitting in the background, that I had
just endorsed Muskie for president.

I don't know how the mixup occurred. I can't believe that I
would have made the announcement at that time had I realized that
George was going to be there. I certainly wouldn't have done it had I
known that Lucybeth was going to appear on the platform with George
when he made his speech. And although Lucybeth didn't mind my
endorsing Muskie, since she was for him too, she didn't appreciate the
timing. Apparently some other people thought it was rather unusual
because television station KUTV awarded me the "Lemon of the Week"
for my blooper.

In the summer and fall of 1971, we again set about doing
our county trips. I wanted to get into every county that year and spend
at least a day in each. As before, I knew that in an election year my
county trips would be suspect and therefore not as effective, and I
really didn't want to exploit them for political purposes, so we did all
of them in 1971. In addition to that, I attempted to get as much industrial promotion work behind me as I could so that next year, if I were
a candidate, I would not have to spend too much time out of the state.

As a senior governor completing two four-year terms I was
taking part more and more in the activities of the National Governors'
Conference. For a number of years in a row I held the chairmanship
of the Fiscal Affairs Committee, which was one of the more important committees, as it dealt with budget and management of state government. For the most part, the governors I knew during my time in

office were individuals of great ability. I would say that on an average they ranked substantially above the members of Congress in dedication and ability. There were some exceptions on both sides though, and it's dangerous to generalize.

When I first became governor in 1964, Carl Sanders was serving out the last two years of his four-year term as governor of Georgia. Sanders I liked very much. I thought he was a very able fellow. However, the Georgia constitution prohibited a governor from immediate succession; he could not run for reelection in 1966. Elected to succeed Carl was Lester Maddox. Lester was not a very imposing physical specimen. He was small and a little bit strutty, had a bald head and a high squeaky voice. He'd made a career out of being a bigot. He ran a restaurant in Georgia and had hit the headlines when he, in spite of the Federal Civil Rights Law, refused to admit blacks to his restaurant, which he called "The Pickwick." He threatened them with an axe handle, saying he was going to hit any black who tried to come in. This is the type of man he was. He never did command respect from his fellow governors.

Then, of course, when his four-year term was up, Lester was ineligible to run again. Everybody assumed that Carl Sanders would be a shoo-in for reelection to a second four-year term. Declaring against Sanders was Jimmy Carter, who had been in the Georgia legislature and apparently had some backing, although in the early going it didn't appear that Carter was going to give Sanders a very serious challenge. However, during the time he had been out of office, Sanders had carried on a successful law practice in Atlanta, and I believe had inherited some wealth. At any rate his campaign was quite ostentatious. He had big billboard pictures of himself flying his plane all around Georgia. Carter came in quietly as the poor boy with a somewhat demagogic manner, although I think it was permissible politics, and he won the election.

Carter was popular with his fellow governors during his first two years in office. He was a small, rather quiet man who made an effort to be pleasant with everyone. He smiled readily, learned people's names, and sought to become active in the governors' conference. My problem with Carter was that when he received these assignments, he didn't do them adequately. As time went on I began to get annoyed with him, although we were good friends and up to this point had not had any real trouble.

Another governor I became well acquainted with was Winthrop Rockefeller. Winthrop, during the two years that I served on the Executive Committee, was also a member of that committee. The committee met five or six times a year to discuss business matters of the National Governors' Conference. Winthrop was a different type of individual from Nelson. Nelson was an extrovert who tried to be a good fellow. Winthrop, when he hadn't been drinking, was quiet and pleasant. He was substantially larger than Nelson, both taller and heavier. He had a great deal of ability and was generally regarded well by his fellow governors. But he did have a weakness for drink. The consumption of liquor made an abrupt change in his personality.

In 1965, when I first took office, the governor of Louisiana was Big John McKeithen. He had been in office for about a year, and was a real character. He used to come into governors' meetings trailed by two bodyguards, one of whom would carry his glasses. As he sat down, one of them would hold his chair and the other would hand him his glasses. It was quite an amusing sight, but he was apparently liked in Louisiana, as he did serve two terms. McKeithen was frightened to death of a politician in Louisiana named Jim Garrison, who was the prosecuting attorney. Garrison also was a colorful character, and everything McKeithen did seemed to be in an attempt to get one up on Jim Garrison.

After McKeithen had served two terms and couldn't run anymore, Edwin Edwards, who had been in the U.S. House of Representatives, was elected governor of Louisiana. Ed was a peculiar fellow. He was a small man, dapper, smooth, articulate, but apparently facile and shallow as well. He had a great deal of courage but not much sense. He had no compunction about admitting that he was subject to being influenced as a politician by the power groups. He appointed his wife, Elaine, to the U.S. Senate for a period of time. After she left office we found that she had been given $10,000 as a gift by some foreign interest. That just rolled off the Edwardses' backs— didn't stop them at all.

I served with four governors of Illinois. During my first term, Otto Kerner was serving his second term and was in office two years with me. I liked him very much; he was a good golfer, and we played together frequently. He had married a daughter of Anton Cermak, the former mayor of Chicago, who was killed in Florida in 1932 while campaigning with Franklin Roosevelt during Roosevelt's first try for the presidency. Otto resigned the governorship to accept an appointment to the U.S. Circuit Court of Appeals, and he had a very sad career from then on. He was charged with and convicted of taking a bribe while he had been governor and went to prison.

The 1972 meeting of the legislature was a twenty-day budget session. By this time the legislators had become used to the mechanism of a budget session and were much more restrictive in the type of nonbudgetary matters that were put on the agenda. The legislators could see that such matters tended to make a general session out of a budget session and cut down the time for consideration of budgetary matters to the extent that the twenty-day session was not enough. Wally Gardner was still the chairman of the Joint Appropriations Committee, and as had been true in the past, he and I worked well together in getting the budget ready. It was not a hectic or unpleasant session. It was, of course, the gubernatorial election year, so I took some chaff from the Republican leadership in both the senate and the house on the day of my message, but generally the appropriations were passed without major changes.

Following that session of the legislature, I announced my decision to seek a third term. Since only I on the Democratic side and Nick Strike on the Republican side filed, there would be no gubernatorial primaries. A limitation of around $100,000 had been placed on gubernatorial campaign expenditures. I made a determination—in view of the fact that we did not have a primary campaign and I could get all of the exposure as an incumbent that I needed—that we would spend none of that money during the summer months. The state committee had its own funds to take care of the organization, so we did not have to support them. Actually, we collected more than $100,000, and after the campaign was over we had in excess of $12,000 on hand. We decided to make a prorated refund to all contributors with the exception that we wouldn't refund less than $1 to any person.

At the Democratic state convention I was nominated to run for governor. We had a substantial number of the left-wing people in the party who were delegates, and they had been elected specifically to elect delegates for McGovern to the national convention. They adopted a platform that I disagreed with on several matters. It had always been my position that the candidate for office on a party ticket had an obligation to support his party's platform unless he announced ahead of the election that he would not do so. If he were silent, then the public was entitled to assume that he supported all of the planks of the platform.

About two weeks after the convention, I had a press conference and selected seven planks in the Democratic platform that I said did not represent my point of view and which I would not support into legislation if I were reelected. This raised considerable concern among the left-wing group in our party in the state and there was a goodly amount of sniping at me from that side, as well as from Kent Shearer and Nick Strike on the Republican side. And although it didn't look like a campaign that I was going to lose unless the effect of the straight ballot defeated me, I still didn't like to have this opposition from the Democratic party itself.

Near the end of July, Lucybeth and I went to Miami to attend the Democratic National Convention. I had been elected a delegate. This was an unhappy convention for me because Ed Muskie had dropped out of the race. The early polls had shown Muskie running substantially ahead of Nixon in a one-on-one contest. He was the only Democrat who even ran near Nixon, and there was every reason to believe that he would sail into the Democratic nomination.

But anyone who remembered the unfortunate things that happened to front-runners in the past, including George Romney in 1968, should have foreseen that there was trouble ahead. The political pundits of the press seem to take a delight in shooting down the front-runner because when he comes out far ahead at the convention, it's hard to make news. Every time Muskie made a speech, he was criticized. He continued the effort to win the nomination from the spring of 1971 until April 1972. It was the constant carping by the press that seemed to pull him down, rather than any one thing.

The final blow, however, came just before the New Hampshire primary election. There was a terrible fellow named Loeb who ran a newspaper called the *Manchester Guardian*. He was an arch-conservative and a man, as far as I can tell, entirely without scruples. He ran a very critical article about Jane Muskie, accusing her of being a drunk and a vulgar-tongued woman. I knew this wasn't true because Jane had stayed with Lucybeth and me in Salt Lake. We were incensed at that kind of treatment and, of course, Ed was very angry. He got on the bed of a truck in front of the *Manchester Guardian*'s offices to make a defense of Jane. He became overwhelmed and broke down and cried, and the television cameras made much of this. I didn't think it was such a bad thing. I thought it was a normal thing for a husband to do when his wife had been treated in that manner. But the press poked great fun and a few days later in the New Hampshire primary Ed did poorly. It wasn't long after that primary that he decided he wasn't going to make it and withdrew from the race. George McGovern thus received the Democratic nomination at the Miami convention.

Back home, the Republicans, evidently remembering the fiasco of Carl Buehner refusing to debate me four years previously, now issued challenges to debate. I told them that I would do it, but I was going to wait until after the primary. Therefore the first two or three times that Strike and I appeared together were before various civic clubs where we each gave a speech and there was very little give and take. But it was apparent to me that he hadn't done his home-work and that he hadn't been properly briefed on state subjects, so I determined that our first television debate would be a real debate.

Strike was totally unprepared. He criticized me for complet-ing I-70, a highway in southern Utah that runs from Green River west about one hundred and ten miles to Salina. Strike said I should not have done that before I-80 was entirely completed. He made the state-ment, "There's nobody down there in southern Utah but jackrabbits," which alienated the strongest Republican section of the state.

In another instance, somebody had told him we were hav-ing trouble with the off ramps on the freeway in Ogden, and indeed we were. On three different off ramps we'd had some trouble getting rights-of-way, and on one we'd had a particular amount of trouble. Nick asked, "What about the off ramp in Ogden? What have you done to clear up that problem?" The camera was focused on him as I replied, "Which off ramp do you mean, Nick? There are three of them. Do you mean the Thirty-first Street, the Twenty-fourth Street, or the Wilson Lane?" There must have been a pause for thirty seconds while the camera was focused on him, and he had no idea what to answer.

That debate was on Channel 4, and they replayed it several times. I went to the Carmelite Fair the next morning, and the number of people that had seen the program amazed me. We continued to have television debates. Nick became more and more abusive but didn't seem to gain any more facts, and it was obvious to anyone who lis-tened that he was unprepared. On our last television debate I was questioning some of Nick's statements, saying, "This isn't so. You've misunderstood what you've been told on this," and Nick raised up in his chair and in great heat said, "You're questioning my credibility." I waited a moment because I knew the camera was trained on him. Finally I said, "Nick, I'm not questioning your credibility; it's your *ability* that I'm questioning." It was a low blow but it was effective.

I was still concerned about the pull of the presidential candidate because it was obvious that Nixon was going to beat McGovern soundly in Utah and I didn't know how many votes that would cost me. Actually, the polls that were being taken at that time by the newspapers and others showed me with about 75 percent of the vote, compared to Strike's 20 percent, and 5 percent undecided. I knew that couldn't hold because of the effect of the straight ballot. Still, we went into the final week of the campaign feeling rather confident. We ran a few ads, all of them positive, on the record of the administration in the preceding year. And while Nixon did carry the state over McGovern by about 66 percent, I carried the state by 69 percent over Strike.

After I'd appeared on television on the night of the election I tried to call Nick, but he wouldn't come to the phone. However, the next Sunday it was still fairly good weather and I went up to the country club to play golf. Nick was there. He'd overcome his anger and was gracious, and we've continued to be reasonably good friends since.

Early 1973 seemed to be an era of good feeling as far as Utah government was concerned. My inaugural message, which Lucybeth had helped me write, was well received by the public generally and by the two newspapers. At Lucybeth's suggestion I had put in a quotation from a poem, which the *Tribune* and others were unable to identify immediately, and there was some speculation for a day or two as to the source. A note from Lucybeth to Murray Moler of the *Ogden Standard Examiner* cleared that up for them. The line I quoted went "If coins you have but two, with one buy bread and from the dole, buy hyacinths to feed thy soul." The poem was written by Saadi, a medieval Persian poet.

By the time the legislature came in on the second Monday in January, just a week after the inauguration, I was ready with both the state of the state message and the budget message. Neither of these suggested traumatic changes. The Republicans were in control of both houses of the legislature, although their margin of control was not enough that they could have a veto-proof legislature. I got along well that session. Even the typical statements that were made the day following my state of the state message and my budget message were not unduly critical.

I think there were three reasons why I got along so well with the legislature during that year. First, I had just been elected to a third term, the first third term for a Utah governor, and it was evident that I had considerable popular support. This would make the Republicans a little cautious about mounting a partisan attack. The second reason was that the Republican leadership—Warren Pugh, the president of the senate, and Howard Nielson, the speaker of the house—were both good friends with whom I had worked in previous sessions. Both of them were middle-of-the-road Republicans, not unduly conservative, and the suggestions for legislation that I made would meet their political philosophy. The third reason was that we came into the 1973 session with a substantial surplus in the state budget and I was able to propose a reduction of taxes. Of course that was well received. Some of the more conservative Republicans said I hadn't proposed a big enough decrease in taxes, and indeed efforts were made during the session to make greater decreases than I had proposed. However, I was able to head this off and the reductions were pretty much according to my proposals.

During the late 1960s and early 1970s I had a situation going in the state that wasn't available to Governor Matheson during his two terms. Our economy was moving upward quite rapidly and year after year the growth was greater than we had anticipated, with the result that we had surpluses. Another thing that made for a greater than usual increase in revenue in the state government at that time was the fact that increases in the income tax receipts were of a greater percentage than increases in the economy generally. This was because Utah, like the national government, has a graduated income tax which applies successively higher percentages as the income of the individual or family grows.

However, unlike the federal income tax, the Utah income tax quickly peaks out at about $7000 and applies a uniform rate from that point on. Many people were moving through these increased brackets, reaching the $7000 limit during that time, and so in addition to having a greater amount of income to tax, the rate got higher.

That is no longer true, because even a poverty-level family has an income in excess of $7000. Thus as a practical matter the increase in revenue for the income tax now is just about equal in percentage to the increase in income and does not move through those brackets.

Two things that show how noncontroversial the legislature was generally, and which caused the greatest public comment, were proposals to purchase two different tracts of land. One proposal was to establish what was known as the Hardware Ranch near Logan, and another proposal was to purchase the Deseret Livestock Ranch, which was put up for sale by its owners at that time. We bought the Hardware Ranch and made an appropriation to run it, but that was a fairly small expenditure. The purchase of the Deseret Livestock property, on the other hand, would have cost about $10 million, which we had and which many people thought should be expended for this purpose.

However, Morgan and Rich counties, where the Deseret Livestock Ranch was principally located, were opposed because the sale would remove that land from the tax rolls and would put their counties and school districts in a difficult financial position. I expressed my opinion in opposition to the purchase of the Deseret Livestock Ranch, even though many of my friends and political supporters favored it. The bill did not pass the legislature, and a short time later the people who owned the Deseret Livestock Ranch sold it.

Immediately after the 1973 legislative session, the governors had their midwinter conference in Washington. The shadow of Watergate was beginning to be felt when Lucybeth and I went back and, as usual, were invited to dinner at the White House. We were with Ehrlichman and Haldeman at the dinner, and everybody was a little wary of these people because we didn't know whether they were to be charged. The president himself, who was never at ease, was even more ill at ease that night. The Watergate matter was beginning to permeate all aspects of the national scene.

The National Governors' Conference that year elected Dan Evans of Washington as chairman. Dan was in charge of this meeting and although he was a Republican and attempted to steer the governors away from criticism of the president, the critical sentiment was still very strong. It was centered principally on the impoundment of funds that were to go to the states as revenue sharing and for block grants. Congress had appropriated the funds but the president would not spend them. There was also considerable criticism from the governors of the president and his programs in general.

During the spring and summer months of 1973 I was having trouble with the Environmental Protection Agency. There was a built-in potential for conflict between the state governments and the EPA. I, like most of the governors, had some concerns about the federal government going into this field, although I wasn't as opposed as most because I had myself tried to get some reasonable laws and regulations on the Utah state books to meet the problems of both water and air pollution. There was considerable opposition to the EPA's programs in the legislature. Legislators from urban areas were greatly influenced by various industries that didn't want to run the risk of having regulations that would be detrimental to their industries adopted pursuant to statutory authority. The agricultural area legislators tended to be in opposition because one of the principal sources of air pollution was agricultural burning which would have to be controlled if we got a meaningful program. Also, one of the greatest sources of water pollution is animal life—agricultural animal pollution—and so there was further general opposition in the legislature. I was never able to get enough assurance of support that I could put any meaningful pollution control measures on the books. For this reason I welcomed to a degree federal intervention in this field.

There were, however, two things that concerned me. First, it seemed clear to me that under the provisions of the federal constitution, this was an area reserved to the states. Second, each area's problems are different, and when the federal government attacks a problem it tends to follow a uniform procedure throughout the country. At first the EPA didn't even recognize the difference between low-altitude and high-altitude problems as far as automobile emission was concerned. Furthermore, each area has its own water drainage problems, and ours in the Great Basin is certainly different from anywhere else. We drain into the Great Salt Lake, a great sump.

In the early years of the state, we had proceeded on the theory that the lake was so salty it would immediately sterilize and render harmless any polluted water put into it. In the forties and fifties we found that that wasn't true. The lake began to get very polluted. The state itself had made reasonable progress in taking care of sewage disposal, but the EPA had entered this field, and during 1973 and 1974 they were being aggressive.

I got along well with the EPA people in Washington because Russell Peterson, a friend of mine and a former governor of Delaware, was director of the EPA. My problem came principally with the people of Denver at the regional office. During the 1973 legislature they came into Utah and got some legislators to introduce bills without even bringing them to me for consideration. The bills didn't pass and I knew they wouldn't. They couldn't have passed with my support and they certainly couldn't pass without it. The struggle with the EPA continues to this day.

Meanwhile, although the 1974 senatorial election was more than a year away, the matter was already heating up. Wayne Owens, who had been elected to the House in 1972, was looking toward the Senate seat. Gunn McKay was also giving it some consideration. On the Republican side, because it was known that Senator Bennett was not going to seek another term, there was some talk of George Romney moving back to Utah, establishing residency here, and running for the U.S. Senate. But the polls were not encouraging for Romney. I think the people felt that although he came from an old Utah family, he had been away so long that he could not adequately represent Utah's interests. The newspaper polls showed that he probably would not do well, and indeed George himself thought better of it and did not attempt the race.

I didn't want either Gunn McKay or Wayne Owens to make the race. We needed them to hold the two House seats we had, and I felt that both of them could be reelected to the House. I thought that a new candidate, a fresh candidate, might do better than either of them in the Senate race. I attempted to head off both Owens and McKay with an early endorsement of Don Holbrook for the Democratic nomination. Ted Moss didn't endorse anybody, but he joined me in opposition to McKay or Owens running and encouraged them to stay where they were. Actually, my endorsement of Holbrook proved to hurt more than help him, as I think there was considerable resentment in the party that I as governor was trying not only to run the state but to select Utah's congressional delegation. But this matter wouldn't actually come to a head until the next summer in the Democratic state convention.

In the summer and fall of 1973, three changes occurred in public offices that would affect the way I did my job. The first one occurred about the end of June when it was announced that Governor John Love of Colorado was considering resigning his position to accept an appointment from President Nixon as the "Energy Czar." I was surprised that John would consider resigning the governorship to go to work for an administration that even then was on the rocks, although I could understand the desire to move on to something different. John had been governor of Colorado for ten and a half years and felt that this was a new challenge.

A day or two before John was to make the decision, Ann, his wife, telephoned me in Salt Lake and asked if I would please call John and urge him not to take this position in Washington, but to serve out his term as governor. I told Ann that if John wouldn't listen to her he certainly wouldn't listen to me, and that I would prefer not to make the call. She said she understood, and so I didn't call him.

A few days later, after John had made the announcement that he was going to take the energy spot, Lucybeth and I went with Judge David Lewis and his wife, Marie, to a Tenth Circuit judicial conference in Colorado Springs. John was there, his resignation not having taken effect yet, and we talked about it. Even though he was committed, he was having second thoughts. He did take the position, but the wraps that were put on him from the White House, the demands that were made, made it almost impossible for him to do the job properly. He was in the job only a few months when he resigned.

Bill Simon, who later became secretary of the treasury, succeeded John as the "Energy Czar." Simon claimed that John hadn't done the job well and that he hadn't worked hard enough. I doubt if that's true. I don't know whether Simon did a better job than John had done, but I think he had more of the confidence of the Nixon administration.

The second change that occurred during this period was in the presidency of the University of Utah. When I became governor, Jim Fletcher had been president for only a few months. Then, sometime in 1971, Jim received an offer to be the head of NASA, and resigned his position as president.

The Board of Regents, which had the duty of selecting the new president on recommendations from the institutional council, decided that they didn't want to move too quickly, and so Fred Emery was appointed interim president. Fred had been a professor at the University of Utah law school. He was a competent fellow, and a good friend of mine, although a few years younger. His father, Ralph Emery, had been Republican chairman of Salt Lake County, but Fred himself was a devout Democrat. Fred served for two years while the Board of Regents and the institutional council were carrying on a nationwide search for a new president.

As was usually the case in the selection of a college president or the head of a department, I left the selection to a considerable extent up to the board that under the statute had the power to make the appointment. I didn't want to usurp that power. On the other hand, a president of the university or the head of a major department of state government has got to have reasonable rapport with the governor if he or she is going to get on well. And so I told the Board of Regents that they should narrow the field down to around five people and then let me interview them. I would not indicate which one of the five I would prefer. I would merely indicate to them if there was any one of those under consideration with whom I couldn't work. Thus the last five people being considered came to my office for conversations.

The Board of Regents selected David Gardner. I got along well with David. He was a man of great ability, though not a warm person. He was ambitious and I continually had to rein him in and tell him that some of the things he wanted were just not to be. He never did sulk but went on and did his job and was always militant in the cause of the university. I thought that his tenure was highly beneficial to the state and to the school. He remained president for ten years, and later he accepted a position as president of the University of California, one of the most highly regarded educational positions in the country.

On the national scene, almost all of the governors, Democrats and Republicans alike, were pleased with the nomination of Gerald Ford by Nixon to be the new vice-president after Agnew's resignation. This was a new thing in the country. I don't believe a vice-president had ever resigned before; but the new Succession Act had been passed a few years previously and provided that in the event of a vacancy in the vice-presidency, the president would nominate a successor who would have to be approved by Congress. Most governors had known Jerry Ford for many years and liked him very much.

He had been the minority leader of the House of Representatives, and he'd performed his chore of being critical of the Democratic presidents during much of that time. He and Johnson used to engage in verbal battles, but Johnson's responses were often more vicious than Ford's attack.

The Democratic governors knew that Ford had done the job that he was required to do, and they had a certain confidence in him and respect for his kindness and fairness. All of us realized when he was confirmed by Congress, months before Nixon's resignation, that the Nixon presidency was flawed and that Jerry Ford might well turn out to be the next president of the United States.

A few days after Christmas 1973, Harold B. Lee of the LDS Church died suddenly, apparently of a heart attack. This came as a great shock because although President Lee was seventy-four years old, he was young by the standards of previous church leaders. As far as the general populace knew, he had been in good health. I had had some concerns about Lee's health, however. He'd only been president of the church about eighteen months at the time of his death, but he had worked very hard. He had seemed to drive himself.

Around Thanksgiving he and I had appeared jointly in a program on the west side of Salt Lake City. He looked gray and drawn to me, and I asked him if he wasn't pushing too hard. He said he was tired but not overly so. He'd had some colds but thought everything was going to be all right. I hadn't seen him again when I learned of his death. This was a shock to me because a relationship has to exist in Utah between the governor and the president of the church. Neither one seeks concurrence from the other in anything that is done unless it is properly a joint program, but nonetheless they are both in positions of authority and that requires a certain coordination.

I worked well with President Lee. I had known him since I was a young man. A friend named Howard Anderson, who was to be the best man at my wedding, had been a scout leader in the ward and later in the stake which Lee headed up in the late 1930s. Through Howard, I'd gotten to know Lee very well. When he was elected city commissioner of Salt Lake City sometime later, I was active in civic affairs and came to know him even better. In addition, his first wife had died, and his second wife, Joan, was a sister of Edna Cazier. Edna had served as a Democrat in the state legislature from Juab County. I had remained close to Edna through all the years since I'd been assistant attorney general, and getting to know Joan helped President Lee and me to get along a little better.

In the late 1950s or early 1960s I had been defending a man against criminal tax evasion charges in Judge Ritter's court. I badly needed a character witness and my client said he had been a friend of Apostle Lee, but he didn't think I should approach him. I said I was going to anyway, and I went to see Elder Lee to ask him if he'd be willing to appear in court and testify for this man. He said he certainly would even though at that time he was a senior apostle. He was that kind of a man, a good man. I was able to talk affairs of state with him as well because he himself had been in the political world, and although he was a dedicated Republican, he was not an ultraconservative. I think we saw eye to eye on many issues.

I was now concerned about what sort of relationship I might have with Spencer Kimball, who was the senior apostle and the heir apparent to the presidency of the church. I didn't know Kimball well. I had met him on a number of occasions, almost all of them after I had become governor, but our relationship had not been close. He hadn't spent his earlier years in Salt Lake, but came up from Arizona at the time he was made an apostle. Nor did he have a background in the Salt Lake business community.

But we did have a few points of contact. His son, Spencer, Jr., had been dean of the law school at the University of Utah and then went on to another deanship in another state. When we were living in the little white house on University Street, Spencer, Jr., lived nearby. Barbara, his eldest daughter and President Kimball's eldest granddaughter, was Meg's close friend, and we remembered them over the years. Also, Mrs. Kimball, Camilla Eyring, was a close friend of Lucybeth's Aunt Augusta Wells. That friendship dated back to the time when the Ivins family and the Eyring family were in the Mexican Mormon colonies, somewhere around 1905.

But I really didn't need any points of contact with Spencer Kimball; he went more than halfway to meet me. He always seemed glad to see me. Whenever I wanted to see him, he'd make the time available and it proved to be a pleasant and easy relationship.

In the 1974 budget session we were faced with a situation I had not encountered since my first term. The country appeared to be heading into a recession, brought on to a great extent by energy shortages. We were expecting to have a gasoline shortage, and the president ordered the speed limit reduced to fifty-five miles an hour, which I'm sure helped. He had also put the country on daylight saving time for the full year, which I doubt was really an energy conserving measure. While I did not expect there to be a gasoline shortage in Utah, I did expect that tourism would be down in the summer of 1974 because of the nationwide shortage.

Tourism is a very important factor in the Utah economy, and it was inevitable, if tourism was down, that the economy would suffer. The sales tax would be down, the income tax would be down, and we couldn't look forward in 1974 to the increase in tax revenue that we had experienced for several years in the past. It wasn't only my judgment; those on whom I relied for financial advice and for revenue projections also agreed with the forecast. The demands for money had not diminished at all. In the field of education, both higher education and public education were requesting substantial increases in appropriations over what they'd had in 1973. I therefore budgeted frugally. Fortunately, the legislature went along with me. Although there were some changes in priorities in the legislature that changed my budget slightly, the overall expenditures were just about what I had requested.

There were two nonbudgetary matters on the budget session agenda in which I was interested. The first was land-use planning and the second was the Equal Rights Amendment, which came before the legislature that year for ratification. I felt that the land-use measure was absolutely essential for the state. I had delayed putting it on a legislative agenda until I felt fairly sure that I could get it passed, but when I received reasonable assurance from some of the more foresighted Republican legislative leaders, I felt that we probably could get it by that session. Indeed it did pass, though with some minor modifications which I did not feel crippled the act and which I was willing to accept.

I was amazed, however, when the legislature refused to ratify the Equal Rights Amendment. I had been asked at a press conference earlier how I thought the Equal Rights Amendment would fare before the legislature. I guess I was rather naive because I stated I didn't see how anyone was going to be against it. It seemed to me that it was something that would appeal to everybody. For this reason I hadn't done any work with the legislature—I just assumed it would go through. At that time the LDS Church had not taken their position against the amendment; and in view of the fact that Utah had a similar provision in the state constitution, I could see no reason why Utah legislators wouldn't ratify a similar addition to the federal constitution. Some Republicans voted for it, as did almost all of the Democrats, so it was defeated only narrowly. After that the LDS Church took a position against it, and I'm still appalled at the amount of damage and division that's been done in our state and elsewhere over what I regard as quite an innocuous and desirable change in our federal constitution.

I was, during that time, having more and more trouble with Attorney General Vernon Romney and State Auditor David Monson. Romney had made it clear that he was going to run for governor in 1976, and he was beginning his campaign early. He would not only criticize things which I had done from a legal standpoint, but would criticize them from a policy standpoint, which I felt was none of his affair as attorney general. If he wanted to do it as a citizen, of course, he was entitled to.

Monson, on the other hand, was sort of an innocuous fellow, but if somebody would wind him up and point him in the right direction he would make very damaging statements. I have never believed in what is called a performance audit in the public sector. It works well in the private sector, but an auditor's primary duty is to perform fiscal audits to determine whether money is being spent in the manner in which the legislature appropriated it to be spent. Monson, however, was continually making performance audits—that is, he would issue statements critical of policy that I had adopted and that were being carried out by various departments of state government. Once again, if he wanted to do this as a citizen, that was his right, but I felt because of the political division in the public sector, performance audits could be abused.

Certainly Monson was acting politically. I don't believe that he thought of it himself, though, but was being steered by the Republican party with the hope that if a political criticism could be contained in an audit it would probably be given more credence than if it were just stated in a political speech. Monson was two years behind in his fiscal audits, and there were some departments I wanted to have audited. I used to get Monson in my office and scold him for attending to politics instead of auditing, and he'd look down at the floor without saying anything, just nodding his head. For a day or two he'd be all right, but then he'd issue another one of his performance audits critical of my policy.

Our fear that tourism would be down in the summer of 1974 proved to be well founded. We didn't have a shortage of gasoline in the state, because although Utah is a net importer of crude petroleum, it is also a net exporter of refined gasoline and motor oil. This is because we have a great deal more refinery capacity than is required to furnish ourselves with either heating oil or gasoline. We have pipelines coming in from Wyoming and other places, bringing the crude oil into the Utah refineries, and we have pipelines taking the refined gasoline out to Colorado and other areas that do not have enough refining capacity to meet their needs. Nevertheless, the downturn in tourism that we had expected did occur and it was again necessary for me to reduce state expenditures even below the modest appropriations of the legislature. The revenue realization was less than the reduced forecast which we had made at the time the legislature met.

After an extended official trip to China in 1974, Lucybeth and I returned to find that a reception had been arranged for Vice-President Ford at Tremonton. The reception was arranged by J. D. Harris, a leading citizen in that area — a Republican, but a good supporter of mine. Actually the vice-president was coming to visit with a friend of his named Jim Brown, who also lived in Tremonton, and who was the personnel manager of Thiokol Chemical Company. The Browns and the Fords had become acquainted while Ford was in Congress, because each of them would vacation in the wintertime at Vail, Colorado. The Brown children called Ford "Uncle Gerry" and the Ford children, when they came to Utah, would stay with the Browns.

When Ford arrived in Tremonton there was a downpour. So many people had come to the reception that they couldn't all get inside J. D.'s house. The tables in the garden where they were going to serve food were drenched, but everybody took it in good humor. Somebody brought out a whole load of umbrellas. We had a good time and Ford was very gracious and seemed genuinely pleased to see me.

In June 1974, the National Governors' Conference meeting was held in Seattle. Dan Evans was the outgoing chairman of the conference and it was a year for the Democrats to elect the new chairman. I had let it be known that because I probably wouldn't get another chance and had passed up at least one chance before, I would like to be elected chairman of the conference for the 1974–75 year. The Democratic caucus endorsed me, and, as there was no other candidate, I was elected to the chairmanship. This pleased me a great deal, although it would give me considerable extra work to do. The conference that year authorized the chairman to have a staff person in his state, paid by the national conference, in addition to staff people who were resident at the head office in Washington.

In July the state conventions of both political parties were held, the Democratic convention being held one or two weeks prior to the Republican convention. During the early sessions it began to appear that while Wayne Owens would certainly be the high man in the Democratic race for the U.S. Senate, Don Holbrook would probably be able to come through the convention and be a candidate in the primary. However, the polls showed Owens, as we neared the convention, pulling further and further ahead. The proceedings of the House Judiciary Committee, which would eventually lead to the resignation of President Nixon, were going on and Owens was a committee member. These were nationally televised meetings, so Owens was getting a great deal of publicity. Nonetheless, I still felt that Don would qualify. I had even been asked to nominate him. I advised his supporters against this but they seemed to want me to, and Don wanted me to, so I gave the nominating speech for him. This resulted in considerable booing of my position from the delegates, which surprised me, because I felt they should give me the same right that they claimed for themselves to indicate who they wanted for the senatorial nominee.

Whether my doing that helped or hurt, no one knows, but the fact is that Don failed by six votes to get 30 percent, and Owens automatically became the nominee because he received over 70 percent of the vote. In the Republican convention it was almost a foregone conclusion that Jake Garn would win, as he was the choice of the party hierarchy. Since both George Romney and Vernon Romney had dropped out, Garn was being challenged only by my brother, Byron, who had announced his candidacy earlier in the year, and by a Weber State College professor named Hawkins. Garn won the 70 percent vote, so there was to be no Republican Senate primary in the state that year, either.

The newspaper polls that ran in the weeks prior to the convention claimed that in the race for Democratic congressman from the Second District, Salt Lake County Commissioner Ralph McClure was running far ahead, with Daryl McCarty, the executive secretary of the Utah Education Association, running somewhat behind him. In third place, with no more than about 10 percent of the vote, was Allan Howe. Allan, nevertheless, came out high among the three candidates at the convention, as he had done better work with the delegates than had the others. There was also some unfavorable publicity about McClure at that time concerning a messy divorce, among other things, and Daryl McCarty took second place while McClure received only a small percentage of the votes. This eliminated McClure from the race and really marked his end in Utah politics.

Gunn McKay had been nominated by the Democrats without opposition to run from the First Congressional District.

The Republicans had placed two people on the ballot for the Second District: Stephen Harmsen, who had been a Salt Lake City commissioner, and Austin Belnap, who was an insurance man. Belnap was the brother of a law school classmate of mine, and an ultraconservative. The Republicans had also placed two people on the ballot for the First District: a fine young legislator named Ronald Inkley, and Dorothy Clark, who had held a number of positions in the Republican party.

In the September primaries Ron Inkley barely beat Dorothy Clark for the Republican House nomination in the First District, while Stephen Harmsen handily defeated Austin Belnap. Allan Howe had a good margin over Daryl McCarty for the Democratic nomination in the Second District.

Another interesting race that year was for the Utah Supreme Court. Richard Callister, who had been attorney general of the state, had been appointed to the court by Governor Clyde. He had then run and been elected in his own right, and was now coming up for another term. He had a considerable advantage in the election because he was designated as the incumbent and listed first on the ballot. But Callister had a serious problem. He had been arrested one night with a prostitute, and there was a great deal made of it in the press, as there should have been. The result was that three people filed against Callister, so he had to run in the nonpartisan primary. Callister did come out high in the primary, but not high enough to win without a runoff against second-place finisher Richard Maughan, a Salt Lake City lawyer I had appointed earlier to the State Board of Higher Education.

Dick Maughan didn't run too far behind Callister in the primary, and it soon became evident that he stood a good chance of beating Callister in the general election in spite of the incumbent's advantage on the ballot. And indeed, that's what happened. Dick Callister became the only supreme court incumbent in the history of Utah to be defeated. Unquestionably, it was because of the morality issue plaguing him. After he left office, Callister worked for a period as an assistant attorney general. Maughan himself was not to serve through his full ten-year term as justice of the supreme court, because in his sixth or seventh year he developed cancer and died.

Looking back at the Watergate affair, it appears to me almost impossible that this simple burglary should have grown into a national problem. It seems ridiculous that it should have occurred in the first place. They broke into the office of the Democratic National Committee in the Watergate office complex in Washington, supposedly to find secret documents that the Democrats might use in the 1972 campaign. It was a silly thing to do, first, because it was highly unlikely that any secrets, if there were such, would be left around where burglars could find them; and second, because even at that time, several months before the election, it appeared that McGovern would be no problem at all to Nixon in the election. For those two reasons it was a useless and futile thing to do.

Although the Watergate scandal had been breaking, it had not gained much momentum by the fall of 1972 as we went into the elections. Charges had been made on the technical matter of the break-in. But after the 1972 election when Nixon had assumed office for the new term, the thing began to unwind. This was brought about by a number of factors. One was the investigative delving into the affair by the two young *Washington Post* reporters, Robert Woodward and Carl Bernstein. Another was the fact that Judge John Sirica, to whom the Watergate matter had been assigned, and who had heard the cases on which the convictions of Gordon Liddy and the Cubans had been returned in 1973, felt that the affair had to be followed to a logical conclusion.

I think Sirica felt badly about sentencing those who had just carried out someone else's orders, and he wasn't going to let the matter die. He kept pushing the grand juries and the prosecutors to make sure that the investigation exposed all who were culpable. The more it was followed, however, the more effort was made to divert anybody from following it into the White House, and particularly to the presidency. Nixon's men adopted means of suppression and cover-up that were illegal and immoral beyond anything that had occurred in the original break-in.

I knew many of the people involved—some of them very well, and some not so well. I had come to know the president, of course, although I had not come to like him over the four years that he had been in office. John Ehrlichman, who was a domestic counselor for the president, I liked quite well. I would see John every time I went to Washington. We were friendly and on many occasions I sat with him and chatted. I also knew H. R. Haldeman, the chief of staff in the White House, although I didn't like him, not because I felt that he was doing anything wrong, but simply because his was a very austere personality. I remember seeing John Dean around the White House before he was dismissed, but he was a quiet young man and I didn't form much of an impression of him one way or another.

Watergate continued to build all during 1973. Charges were made in Congress that a cover-up was occurring at a very high level. A special prosecutor was appointed for the purpose of carrying on the investigation. I knew Special Prosecutor Archibald Cox only slightly. I had met him a number of times and was on panels with him on two occasions. He was a charming man, rather academic in his approach to things, but, nonetheless, events were to prove he was a very strong person. The attorney general at the time was Elliott Richardson, whom I had known since our meeting at the Daniel Webster Inn some eight years before. Assistant Attorney General William Ruckleshaus I had known from the time he first came to Washington, I believe with the Environmental Protection Agency. He and his wife, Jill, were people that Lucybeth and I saw on occasion.

As the Watergate investigation continued, the discovery was made quite accidentally, through a statement by a man named Butterfield at a congressional hearing, that there was a taping machine in the Oval Office at the White House and that tapes existed of many conversations involving the president and others that might be relevant to the question of who knew what and who ordered what in regard to the Watergate break-in. Cox went before Judge Sirica and got an order to make Nixon turn over those tapes. The order was appealed to the U.S. Supreme Court and was sustained.

Still, Nixon did not turn over the tapes. He proposed that he would turn them over to Senator John Stennis, who was a senior Democratic senator, and let Stennis hear them and decide which ones were relevant to the case. It was a ridiculous proposal because it was a clear violation of the separation of powers in government. Cox rejected the proposal and told the president that he wanted all of the tapes and he wanted them delivered according to the order. On Saturday, October 20, 1973, Nixon ordered Elliott Richardson to fire Cox as special prosecutor. Richardson refused to do so and resigned his office as attorney general. Nixon then ordered William Ruckleshaus to make the firing. Ruckleshaus refused and was fired. The third ranking officer in the Justice Department was Robert Bork, the solicitor general, and Bork did fire Cox. This was unquestionably the turning point.

The tapes were turned over to Cox and played before the congressional committee and the American people. From then on it was all downhill. Nixon himself became almost a prisoner in the White House. He canceled news conferences, he avoided reporters and seemed to avoid public appearances. His statements became more strident and shrill and you could almost see the man disintegrating.

In February 1974, during the midwinter meeting of the National Governors' Conference in Washington, we were invited as usual to the White House for dinner. And as was always the case, we had dinner in the big west dining room where there were big round tables which seated ten people. By custom, President Nixon would sit at one table and Mrs. Nixon at another, and following the same pattern the governors would be seated in order of seniority at one table or the other, while their wives were seated at different tables. I sat with Mrs. Nixon and Lucybeth sat with the president. Also at the president's table were Dan Evans of Washington, John West of South Carolina, and two other governors. The wives of those men were sitting with me at Mrs. Nixon's table.

During the meal the president carried on, according to Lucybeth, a rambling, incoherent conversation with the people at his table. He talked all the time, even with his mouth full, and was a thoroughly unpleasant dinner companion. He had a very hard time appearing to be coherent and rational. It was obvious that the man was coming apart. And yet later in the evening, after the dinner was over, he got up and gave a ten-minute extemporaneous speech on foreign policy which was articulate, almost eloquent. It was hard to believe it was the same man. Mrs. Nixon said little during the dinner that night, and when she did speak, it was in such a low voice that it was hard to hear her. After dinner was over, we went into the East Room to be entertained by Pearl Bailey. She, in her irresistible way, succeeded in lightening the occasion and leading everybody away from the pall of Watergate for a delightful hour.

The tension continued to build during the spring and summer months, with the House considering an impeachment resolution and the tapes revealing that the president had taken an active part very early. On August 9, 1974, I was scheduled to give a talk to the Lions Club in Bountiful. I had gone out there for this purpose when the early news commentator said that the president would be making a statement on television that evening. Everybody expected it would be his resignation speech because of the way things had been going for the past few weeks. We brought a television into the Lions' meeting and all listened to the president's resignation speech. The reaction of the audience almost universally was one of relief, whether they were Democrats or Republicans. They were glad to have this over. Indeed it had, for more than two years, been a national nightmare.

And so Jerry Ford took the oath as president. One of the controversial matters that continued after Nixon's resignation was what should be done about him. It was evident that he was fully as culpable as Ehrlichman and Haldeman and others who had gone to jail, but I believe that the American people did not want to see a president in jail. Certainly what had happened to him—being the only president in history to be forced from office—was much more punishment than jail would have been.

There has been speculation as to whether President Ford, prior to the time of the resignation, had made an agreement that he would pardon Nixon once he became president. Ford denies that there was any agreement and I believe him. Nevertheless, he did grant a pardon to Nixon, and he received a great deal of criticism after that. Pardoning Nixon was one of the major factors that cost Ford his reelection to the presidency in 1976. After a few weeks, Ford selected Nelson

Rockefeller as vice-president. I think it was a reasonably good selection. Certainly if something had happened to Ford, Nelson would have been able to step in. Although I never felt very warm or close to Nelson, I always respected him, and I think his appointment as vice-president, which was unanimously endorsed by the Congress, was also approved of by most of the people.

After Ford assumed the presidency I went to the White House more often. As chairman of the National Governors' Conference I was also ex officio head of two other organizations. One of these was the Council of State Governments, an umbrella organization for ten or eleven associations of various kinds of state government officials. The other was a loosely knit group called the New Coalition, which had been brought into being by Dan Evans while he was chairman the year before. We gathered in the White House at least once a month to discuss projects for revenue sharing and for the block and categorical grants that were to go to state and local governments. We often met with the president, the vice-president, and various members of the cabinet and of the White House staff.

In addition to the meetings that were held in the White House and in the various departments with the New Coalition, the president also looked to the National Governors' Conference for direction in many things. Even when I wasn't in Washington, scarcely a day would go by that I would not get a call from somebody in the White House—often the president himself or a member of the cabinet. It was certainly a good thing that I had staff for the National Governors' Conference in Salt Lake because the work was very heavy at that time.

In the election of 1974, Jake Garn beat Wayne Owens for the U.S. Senate. Allan Howe won the congressional seat that Owens had vacated, and Gunn McKay handily won reelection in his district. I was greatly disturbed in this election by the defeat of the Land Use Bill which was before the electorate as the result of a referendum. The modifications I had made to get it through the legislature may have been mistakes, although I didn't initially believe that the compromise features would hurt the bill. However, some of the more aggressive supporters of the bill, principally the environmental groups, felt that the bill was gutted and so they gave it only slight support in the election. Of course the conservative groups were as much against the bill as they had been before it was amended. It may well be that the bill would have fared better had we never made the tempering amendments. On the other hand, had I not made those amendments, I doubt that I would have been able to get it through the legislature.

That defeat was the biggest disappointment that I had in my twelve years as governor. During the elections both political parties were supporting the bill. I supported it heavily, as did Senator Bennett and Jake Garn—but the staunch conservative groups were able to get enough of their own support to defeat it. It was a shame, because we've never been able to get a satisfactory land-use bill through the legislature since that time, and I feel that our state has suffered greatly from it. For example, in the spring of 1983, we had some disastrous floods and mud slides that destroyed homes. We couldn't have prevented the floods and mud slides by proper land-use planning, but we would not have permitted homes and other public facilities to be built in the floodplains and slide areas where they don't belong in the first place. So while the floods and slides would still have occurred, their destructive effects would have been held to a minimum had we had adequate land-use planning during those years.

In the 1974 election the Democrats had carried both houses of the Utah legislature, which was the first time that had occurred since my initial legislature in 1965. My first two years and my last two years were with Democratic legislatures. The Democratic majorities in the 1975 session were not great, but enough that we could organize and I could expect reasonable backing. In addition, Ronald Rencher, a young lawyer from Weber County who had been in the legislature for about two terms, was selected as speaker of the house, which pleased me greatly. He and I were good friends and I felt that we could work well together.

Ernest Dean, who had been speaker of the house of representatives in 1962, had in the interim been elected to the senate. He had become one of the senior senators and was elected as president of the senate for the 1975 session. This worried me a bit. Ernest really had never forgiven me for defeating him in the gubernatorial primary in 1964. Although he was courteous enough when we met, tales were always coming back to me from people who had talked with Ernest, telling of his bitterness over that campaign. However, during the term that he served as the president of the senate, Ernest was fair and he made every effort to get administration bills through the senate.

Although the legislative session was a general session in 1975, it was evident that our principal problem was going to be the budget. The economy was still in a rather depressed state. Unemployment was fairly high, although it was two percentage points under the national average. The gasoline shortage was hurting tourism. I already had the state under an administratively imposed budget reduction of 3 percent for the fiscal year which would end in July 1975, so it was obvious that we were going to have problems with the budget.

I worked hard getting the budget ready and got the cooperation of the leadership in both houses. They generally agreed that it was going to have to be a lean budget, but that we'd probably also have to make some increases in taxes. Several years before we had, as I have mentioned, eliminated the property tax imposed on a state level. Not only was the state in bad fiscal condition as a result, but the cities and counties in the state were also in a dreadful financial situation. They were just unable to meet the demands for services. The legislative leadership and I therefore agreed that we would support a local option of .5 percent on the sales tax. This was the subject of a great deal of controversy, but it passed. We were also able to pass a budget for the state that saw only a small increase over the preceding year. This was much to the disappointment of the institutions of higher learning and to the state school board, but there was no help for it. Aside from the sales tax issue, this, my last general legislative session, was not controversial and things went well. We got the budget adopted, but we passed no great new social programs. It was, as far as substantive legislation goes, another housekeeping session.

In the fall of 1974, spurred largely by the attorney general's office, there began an investigation of the liquor control system and of the Liquor Commission itself which took up much of 1975. This was pushed by Vernon Romney and certain members of what was known as the Liquor Control Advisory Council. The matter centered largely on sample bottles of liquor that were sent to the Liquor Commission for promotional purposes—all perfectly legally—and also on what had been done with liquor that was not usable because of leakage or other defects. The law said these defective items were to be destroyed, and periodically they were. But the charge was made that liquor samples and liquor bottles that were defective but still usable were being used for political purposes or being sold. There was a great hue and cry in the press, particularly in the *Deseret News*, demanding a full investigation.

As soon as this thing began I called a press conference and said, "If you want to know where the liquor samples went, many of them came up to the governor's residence. We used them there for entertainment and personal purposes. It's been done by all of my predecessors. There's no law against it. If the legislature sees fit to change the law, of course we will stop." This didn't seem to slow the matter down much, although there was never any suggestion in the press that my use of the liquor samples for this purpose was illegal or should be subject to any criminal investigation. Still, the investigation went on. Actually it was two investigations running parallel, as one was conducted by the attorney general's office and another by the Citizen's Advisory Council.

Often these two groups were at odds with one another. But fired up by *Deseret News* editorials saying, "We've seen only the tip of the iceberg," and so forth, a grand jury was called just about the time the legislature adjourned in 1975. This grand jury indicted two of the liquor commissioners. At that time we had three full-time commissioners and one director. This was a jerry-built arrangement. Prior to the time I had been in the governorship there had been three full-time directors who ran the Liquor Commission. This was, in my opinion, an inefficient way to do it, so during my first term in office the legislature passed a bill providing for a five-member part-time policy commission, with a full-time director. This went on for several years and seemed to work fairly well. Then about 1971 the legislature, while under the control of the Republicans, abolished this commission and reinstalled the three full-time commissioners, although they didn't remove the position of director.

The law, however, was unclear on the delineation of the respective duties of the commissioners and the director. I issued several administrative edicts trying to straighten this out, and they worked well except when we had personality conflicts. For a while a man named Ira Hearn was the director. The commissioners were Gerald Hulbert, Norma Thomas, and Gerald Irvine. I finally had to remove Hearn from the directorship simply because the dissension was getting too great in the commission. For a period of time following Hearn's removal, the job of director was held by Grove Cook, who had been an executive in a baking company. Grove held it for about a year, but his health wasn't good. I then appointed Sharp Larson, a man who had been the state auditor, and before that, the Salt Lake County auditor. He and Norma didn't get along and there were soon bad feelings at the commission among the personnel. Morale was low.

The grand jury indicted both Norma Thomas and Gerald Hulbert. Of course the indictment didn't come to trial for some time. I was rather at a loss as to what to do in the meantime because of the sensitivity of the liquor situation. I didn't want two people who were under indictment running the commission. I thought of trying to put Gerry Irvine in as director, but I didn't think that would work either. I therefore asked both Thomas and Hulbert to take leaves of absence pending their trials, and I asked Sharp to give me his resignation. I then asked Paul Holt, a well-known Republican who had long been a respected auditor with the State Tax Commission, to take a leave of absence and run the Liquor Commission. This was entirely outside the law. I should have had three commissioners, but I had only Gerry Irvine left. The thing built up and built up. The attorney general apparently had resolved that he was going to try to get me implicated in some way if he could, and at one time he came up to the residence and took my deposition, which I didn't like at all.

The cases of Norma Thomas and Gerald Hulbert came to separate jury trials, and both of them were acquitted—as indeed they should have been. However, I really did not want them back in the Liquor Commission because I wanted to get a fresh start. Paul Holt didn't want to go on as director much longer, so I asked for resignations all around. I got them and made a new start in the Liquor Commission that carried through for the remainder of my term.

In the late spring and early summer of 1975, even though it was almost a year and a half before the next election, there was once again considerable political activity. Various Republicans were trying to position themselves for the run at the Republican nomination for governor in 1976, and there was a great deal of speculation as to what I was going to do. I was unsure at that time as to whether I would run for a fourth term. Lucybeth and the children felt I should not. I felt that I had an obligation to the Democratic party to run again if it appeared that that was the only reasonable opportunity we would have for holding the governorship. But I felt, as I had in 1972, that I did not want to make an announcement until after the budget session of the legislature in the spring of 1976. I decided to avoid even making the decision until that time. If I'd made up my mind earlier, I'm sure I would have told somebody, and when you tell one person a secret, it's no longer a secret. The campaign would have started early in 1975, a year before it should have, and so even though I was asked the question at almost every press conference I had during the summer and fall of 1975, I gave the same answer – that I had not yet decided.

Sometime in mid-April I received a call from the State Department saying that this year it was the turn of the delegation of U.S. governors to visit the Soviet Union. The two countries alternated: one year a delegation of governors from the Soviet Union came here and the next year a delegation of governors from the United States went there.

This was the first trip in many years in which the governors were permitted to take their wives along. The State Department wanted me, as chairman of the National Governors' Conference, to select a number of senior governors to go. Lucybeth and I had known this trip was coming up and we were looking forward to it. As quickly as I got the invitation I circularized the senior governors to see which of them would be able to join us. Dan Evans, my immediate predecessor as chairman, had been to the Soviet Union only the year before on a trade mission for his state and decided he didn't want to go. However, three of the governors who had been in China with us the year before wanted to go: Marvin Mandel of Maryland, Bob Ray of Iowa, and Arch Moore of West Virginia. Since the China trip, Marvin had remarried and his wife Jeanne went with us, as did Billie Ray and Shelley Moore. Lucybeth and I consider this trip and the one to China to be among our most valuable experiences.

By mid-July I was beginning to tire of the job of governor. The work that I had to do as chairman of the National Governors' Conference was behind me, there were no pressing issues before the state, and I began to get a bit restless. The day-to-day operation of the state took a great deal of time, but most of this work was not very inspiring. It wasn't yet time for me to get involved in the budget process in preparation for the 1976 budget session, and I began to think more and more that I did not want to do this for another four years.

However, I still was not prepared to make an announcement to that effect, or even to make up my mind definitely on what I wanted to do.

When the Salt Palace was constructed early in my first term, it had been necessary because of cost overruns and in order to bring the project within budget to eliminate a proposed concert hall and art center. This had been a big disappointment to the Utah Symphony and the other arts groups. We had attempted to do something about it on a number of occasions and it appeared at one time that probably there was something we could do. A proposal had been made by the Nixon administration to appropriate $1 billion to be divided among the states to construct halls for the observance of the Bicentennial in 1976. We thought that we could get a concert hall from this money. However, the appropriations were never made and so we were left with only the plans and no money.

In the late summer of 1975 Obert Tanner, who was chairman of our Bicentennial Commission, and I got together and discussed the possibility of getting the county to support a bond issue to build a new concert hall and art center. We contacted the county officials because it would have to be primarily a county project—the county being the owners and operators of the Salt Palace. They would have to be favorable to the concert hall proposal for the bond issue to be recommended, and indeed they were. Commissioner Bill Dunn, especially, was a strong supporter. So Obert and I met with Jack Gallivan and I asked Jack if he would take on the chairmanship of a committee to get the concert hall started and make it a reality, if we could arrange to do it by means of appropriations from the state and a bond issue by the county.

At first the proposal for a bond issue didn't take well with the citizens. Early polls showed that a bond would be defeated quite decisively. However, the arts groups did a good job, and both Jack Gallivan as the publisher of the *Tribune* and Wendell Ashton as the publisher of the *Deseret News* pushed it. The bond issue came up in the fall of the year and passed. Between the money from the bond issue and the money that the state was willing to commit, we had enough to go ahead, although escalating costs were worrisome. During the period when we were getting the plans drawn, somebody came to Jack Gallivan with a proposal that we have two halls. We would build a new, large hall for the symphony, and renovate the Capitol

Theater for the opera, the ballet, and other performing companies that required a smaller facility.

This seemed like a poor idea to me at first because I thought it would increase the cost. However, we had some cost estimates run and found that by spending about $4 million we had available on the acquisition and renovation of the Capitol Theater, and by changing the plan for the concert hall so it wouldn't be a multipurpose facility, we could reduce the costs so the two halls would actually cost less than one. This was a difficult concept to sell to the people, even though we had some architectural backing for it. But we were able to sell it and we proceeded with the construction of Symphony Hall and the Art Center and with the renovation of the Capitol Theater. These projects were not completed when I left office in January 1977, although both were well along.

Symphony Hall is indeed something to be proud of. Lucybeth and I have seen concert halls all over the world, including the Sydney Opera House, and none of them is as beautiful as ours. It's marvelous as far as acoustics go, and a fine asset to the city. A great deal of the credit has to go to Jack Gallivan for the project's success.

The mayoralty election in Salt Lake City in the fall of 1975 had me on the spot. When Jake Garn was elected to the U.S. Senate the previous year, he had to resign his position as mayor of Salt Lake City, and a city commissioner named Conrad Harrison was appointed mayor for the interim. Con had been a friend of mine for many years. His wife, Ruth, was a high school friend as well. In 1975, however, Con was challenged by Ted Wilson, an active Democrat who had the support of the Democratic organization in Salt Lake City.

Con had never been identified prominently with either political party. Prior to his appointment as city commissioner, he was a newspaperman and had to maintain neutrality. The commission position was also nonpartisan, and so Con really didn't have a campaign organization. I suppose he got some support from the Republican committee, but not much because they really didn't know whether he was a Democrat or a Republican. In spite of the fact that he did not have a political organization behind him, it was generally expected that because of his exposure as city commissioner and mayor, Con would be able to win, and the early polls showed him doing fairly well.

Ted Wilson, however, was an attractive young candidate. He campaigned hard and began to close the gap on Harrison as the campaign went on. Many of the Democrats wanted me to come out and support Wilson, which I declined to do. I was asked at one of my KUED press conferences where I stood and I explained that while I certainly would like to see a man identified as a Democrat as the mayor of Salt Lake City, I had a long-standing friendship with Conrad Harrison and I intended to vote for him even though I would not campaign either way. As the election approached Wilson began to pull ahead, and he defeated Con for the mayorship by a comfortable margin. Immediately after the election was over I asked Wilson to come up to see me. He did, and we had a good talk. He understood fully my position on the matter, and we got along well.

During November and December, I was preparing for the budget session of the legislature which would meet on the second Monday in January 1976. I prepared a budget which, as had been the case every year, was record breaking. When I first started getting requests from the departments, it appeared that the budget would probably reach $1 billion for the fiscal year that was to begin on July 1. However, a consideration of the revenues available to the state made it appear that a budget of that size was unrealistic and couldn't be met without substantial increases in taxes, which I did not want to propose to the legislature. I was able to reduce budget requests in various areas and prepared a budget that fell about $85 million short of the billion mark, but it was a far cry from the first budget that I had prepared for the legislature some eleven years previously.

Back in 1933, by contrast, when Henry Blood first became governor, the budget of the state for an entire biennium had been only about $35 million. That shows the effect of two things: the growth of the state, and the tremendous inflation that had occurred. Individual salaries of state employees in 1976 were more than six times the level of individual salaries in 1933.

The year ended on a good note for me and my administration. With the city elections over, state and national politics began to attract substantial attention. Seldom would a day go by without some newspaper reporter asking me if I had made up my mind as to whether I would run for a fourth term. Despite pressure from the party, I still hadn't made up my mind. The polls were showing that the Democratic administration of the state was well received, however, and I was beginning to feel more all the time that it was not essential, in order to hold the position for the Democratic party, that I run for the governorship for a fourth time.

CHAPTER SEVEN

BEYOND THE PUBLIC YEARS

Âs we entered the year 1976, the pressure on me to announce my intentions increased even more. Both the news media and the people in the Democratic party pointed out, quite logically I'm sure from their viewpoint, that if I were not going to run then I should give the Democratic candidates, whomever they might be, the maximum opportunity to become known to the people of Utah. I was not sure that was absolutely necessary. I had felt for a long time that campaigns went on too long and that even a new and able candidate could make himself or herself known in a rather short period of time. Furthermore, I had to do the job of governor for another year, whether or not I ran for reelection. Announcing early, whichever way I decided, would give me a problem. The legislature was going to meet in a budget session on the second Monday in January 1976, and although it did not purport to be a momentous one, any session of the legislature is still important. I did not want to have the session turned into a political campaign. Lucybeth and I therefore decided between us that I would stay with the plan not to announce my intentions, or even reach a final decision, until the legislature was finished.

The legislative session was calm and the budget was adopted fairly near to what I had suggested. Few nonbudgetary items were placed on the agenda, and the session passed with little controversy.

Shortly after the session ended, Lucybeth and I, together with the former governor of Wyoming, Stan Hathaway, and his wife, Bobbie, and the former governor of Colorado, John Love, and his wife, Ann, went up for a weekend of ice fishing at the National Park Service's Brinkerhoff House on Jackson Lake. During the evenings the six of us sat around the big grate fire and talked about how it was to leave the governorship, and the pains of decompression. Both Bobbie Hathaway and Ann Love said there was no problem at all, that everything was fine. That was true for them because they did not want their husbands to run for additional terms, as I think Lucybeth did not want me to run for another term.

Both Stan and John had done well after they left the governorship. Stan had that unfortunate experience of his illness while he was secretary of the interior, but after that was over he returned to Wyoming to practice law. John, after he left his position as "Energy Czar," entered a successful career as president and chairman of the board of Ideal Basic Industries, a national cement company. Knowing that both John and Stan were successful after leaving office calmed whatever fears I had as to whether I could make a living after I quit. Whether Lucybeth and I made up our minds while we were at the Brinkerhoff House or on our way back to Salt Lake, I'm not sure, but we did decide against running for a fourth term. We came home and told the children. I had a regularly scheduled press conference with KUED coming up later that week and we decided to hold the announcement until then.

Normally those press conferences had been at 10:00 in the morning, but for some reason KUED could not film this particular press conference until 2:00 in the afternoon. It was generally felt in the news areas that I was going to make an announcement one way or another, and Bill Smart, the editor of *Deseret News*, was very disturbed by the fact that this news conference would be at 2:00 in the afternoon, after his publication time. Bill called me up and remonstrated with me, but I assured him it was none of my doing. He then asked, in view of the fact that I wasn't going to make the announcement in time to permit the *Deseret News* to get it in their afternoon edition, if I would tell him what my announcement was going to be. I declined to do that, because KUED had been good to me over the years and I didn't want to give anybody a scoop on one of their news stories. I'm not sure Bill has ever forgiven me for that.

Lucybeth came with me to the news conference, and we had in the audience as many as thirty people from the local and national press. Generally at a news conference I would draw no more than ten reporters from both the electronic and print media, but this time they were all there. Quite obviously they were expecting me to announce that I would run for a fourth term, and the reporters were primed with questions regarding what my problems would be and what I thought my chances were of winning a fourth term. At the very beginning of the news conference, however, I announced that I would not run, and Lucybeth followed it up with a statement that we just wanted to return to private life. The reporters were left with many questions on their clipboards that couldn't be asked, and the news conference from that time forward was anticlimactic.

Prior to the time that my intention not to run was made known, only one candidate—former county commissioner John Preston Creer—had announced on the Democratic side. Within a short time after I made my announcement, two other men stated that they would run: Desmond Anderson, the mayor of Logan, and Steve Dirks, the mayor of Ogden. Ernest Dean, who had been my opponent in the 1964 primary and who was at this time president of the senate, said that he was considering running for the position, as did John Klas, who had been state Democratic chairman during several of the years while I was governor.

It appeared certain that Vernon Romney was going to be the nominee in the Republican primary. Several others had announced against him, principally Dixie Leavitt, a very able state senator from Cedar City, but the Brahmins of the Republican party appeared to have laid their hands on the head of Vernon and anointed him as their nominee. Prior to the final date for filing in May, I had felt that Vernon would be the nominee and that any articulate and obviously capable Democratic candidate could beat him in the election.

I don't remember who first mentioned to me the possibility of Scott Matheson becoming a candidate. I had known both Scott and his father well. His father had been U.S. attorney for the district of Utah and was a good friend of mine. I was about halfway in age between the two: about fifteen years younger than Scott, Sr., and fifteen years older than Scott, Jr. I had known Scott, Jr., from the time he was in high school, and I regarded him highly. I had appointed him to a number of positions in state government and relied heavily on his advice. He was a member of the original group of young Democratic lawyers that helped me prepare a program for the first session of the legislature in 1965. So when I was first approached with the idea of having Scott as a candidate, I stated that I thought he would make a good governor. I was certain he would make a good candidate because he was attractive and articulate.

In the press Scott had indicated that he had some interest in running, and one day Dan Berman called me and said, "I think it would be a good idea if you and Lucybeth were to ask Scott and Norma to come up and talk to you about what this job entails." I don't recall whether I called Scott or he called me, but one Sunday morning they came over for breakfast and the four of us talked for about two hours. They were uncertain as to what they wanted to do. They wanted to know what the demands of the job were, how much pressure it put on the governor. They also wanted to know about the demands on the governor's wife.

I made it clear to Scott that I was not going to take a position in the Democratic convention or in the Democratic primary even if he chose to run. Particularly, I was not going to take a position while John Klas was still running, although I felt he would fall out early. Scott said he understood that and didn't expect me to take a position. It was a free and open and very enjoyable discussion that Sunday morning. When they left Scott still hadn't definitely decided to run, although his decision was announced not long after that.

In the meantime I had become more deeply involved in Democratic presidential politics than I really cared to be. In February 1976 the National Governors' Conference had its midwinter meeting in Washington, D.C. The New Hampshire primary had been held the day before we met. In that primary Jimmy Carter had been the high vote getter. During the early stages of the competition for the Democratic nomination, the leading contenders were Scoop Jackson and Hubert Humphrey. Ed Muskie made an early attempt, but had finally decided that he wouldn't run. I talked to Ed about it and he said that he had been engaged in presidential politics for eight years now, and it was very difficult. He and Jane had decided that they just didn't want to do it anymore.Other candidates were Jerry Brown, Pat Brown's son, who was then governor of California; Frank Church, a senator from Idaho; and Mo Udall, a congressman from Arizona.

Jimmy Carter had not run well in any of the polls before now, but at that time the New Hampshire primary was very important in the selection of the nominees of political parties, and Jimmy zeroed in on it. He didn't have enough money to make a nationwide race and concentrated almost all his money, almost all his staff, and almost all his personal time for several months in New Hampshire. As a result he did emerge the winner, and quite a decisive one.

The morning after the primary Carter flew down to Washington. Bob Strauss, the chairman of the Democratic National Committee, was a bit uncertain as to how to deal with the phenomenon of Jimmy Carter, and he called an off-the-record meeting of the Democratic governors—there were about thirty-two of us at that time. I chaired the meeting as the senior governor. Bob went around the room and asked each of us how we felt about the Democratic presidential race at that point. No one had anything very good to say about Carter.

I was the last one questioned. Bob asked, "How do you feel about it, Cal?" And I said, "Jimmy's all right with me. I've had some problems with him, but if he gets the nomination, I can support him. If I were going to choose the most able of the hundred and forty-six men and women I've served with as governor, though, he wouldn't be among them." Then Phil Noel, the governor of Rhode Island and a big bluff extroverted sort of guy, asked, "Where would you rate me, Cal?" In a spirit of fun I said, "I'd rate you number forty, Phil, just behind Jimmy." It was a light-hearted joke and nobody thought anything about it.

We left the meeting and went into the general session, and about an hour and a half later they brought in the late-morning edition of the *Washington Star*. There on the front page in a box outlined in black was an article headlined, "Governors' Chief Rates Carter #39." Of course that wasn't accurate. I was no longer the governors' chief and the rating had been just a joke. Furthermore, I thought it was confidential; I didn't know anybody would leak what had happened at the meeting. I suppose that's no excuse for not having been more careful, but, at any rate, the meeting let out just before noon and I went back to my hotel room. Jimmy was already on the phone and in high dudgeon. "Did you say that?" he demanded.

"Well now, just a minute," I answered. "Let me tell you how it happened."

"I don't want to know how it happened. Did you say it?"

"Jimmy, there were extenuating circumstances."

"Did you say it?" he insisted.

"Yes, I said it. Now do you want to know why?"

"I don't want to know anything more about it."

"All right," I concluded, "I said it, and that's it." And that ended that conversation.

When the Democrats met in the regular midsummer meeting, which was on July 4 that year at Hershey, Pennsylvania, Jimmy was there. He didn't have the nomination yet, but it was obvious that he would get it. Of course he attempted to mend all his fences with the Democratic governors, including me. And I did what I was supposed to do as a Democratic governor when he came to Utah. I appeared with him at a number of political meetings, including one in the Salt Lake Tabernacle. I did everything I could for him, but I was never quite forgiven for that faux pas.

After the election, in December 1976, Jimmy had his transition team in Plains, Georgia. I called him on the phone to urge him to appoint Ted Moss to a high position, preferably secretary of the interior. Jimmy answered the phone rather promptly and I was surprised at that. He seemed quite pleasant and I told him I would appreciate it if he would appoint Ted. He said, "Well, I don't know. We are considering him." And then he said, "Would you consider a position in my administration?"

"Jimmy, you really don't mean that," I replied. "You wouldn't appoint me. You're just asking me to apply so you can turn me down."

"Now, why would you say that?" he asked.

"In the first place, you and I haven't always gotten along very well."

He said, "Oh, yes, but that's all behind us."

"In the second place," I continued, "the state of Utah gave you next to the lowest percentage of any state in the Union."

"Next to the lowest? Next to the lowest? The *very* lowest!"

I didn't get an appointment with the Carter administration, nor did Ted Moss.

A sequel to that story occurred the next February. Lucybeth and I were in Palm Springs as guests of Grace and Obert Tanner. Obert and I had gone out to play on the Thunderbird Golf Course, and as we were approaching the number one tee somebody shouted behind me, "Hey, Cal." I turned around and saw that it was Gerry Ford, who had been practicing in a sand bunker. He came over and shook my hand and said, "Do you know that even though you had nothing to do with it, I'm sure I got the highest percentage vote in Utah of any state in the Union?" I said, "Mr. President, somebody else told me that not more than two months ago."

After the legislature adjourned, I seemed to have a letdown. Since I had announced I wasn't going to run again, there were no great projects I felt I could undertake. Then I began receiving requests that

I entertain this or that proposal for my employment after I left office. I was pretty sure that I wanted to return to the practice of law.

The only offer that I received from the commercial sector that really interested me came from Sam Skaggs. Sam had been a friend and supporter of mine for a long time, and he sent Scott Bergeson, who had at one time worked for me, to see if I would consider taking a position as general counsel in the Skaggs organization. I was told that the Skaggs company was contemplating expanding substantially, which they have done in the years since. The thing that turned me against this proposal, although it intrigued me a great deal, was that Skaggs had a rather rigid rule that its executives had to retire at age sixty-five. They assured me the rule could be waived if I were interested in the position; however, I did not know how long beyond sixty-five I would be permitted to go even if the requirement were waived, and if it were not waived I would have only two years in the job before I reached retirement age. I therefore declined the offer.

Invitations came from several of the largest law firms in Salt Lake City as well. The three that interested me most were from what is now called Watkiss and Campbell, the firm that I had left twelve years earlier; from VanCott, Bagley, Cornwall & McCarthy; and from Jones, Waldo, Holbrook & McDonough—the offer that I subsequently accepted. I would have enjoyed going back to my old firm for nostalgia's sake, but it had changed very much since I left, growing from a five-man firm to one of about twenty persons. Harry Pugsley and Zar Hayes were no longer in the firm name: Harry had retired entirely and Zar had gone to an "of counsel" status. Most of the new lawyers I knew very little, if at all, and it didn't seem to be a place in which I would naturally fit. The VanCott firm was also one of the largest and best in Salt Lake City. Many years before I had received and declined an offer from Marr VanCott to join that firm, and I was pleased that they would reconsider me as I left office.

But what really influenced me in favor of Jones, Waldo, Holbrook & McDonough was the fact that in the last year I was in the governorship Hal Waldo had died of cancer, leaving a void in the senior partnership that needed to be filled by an experienced lawyer. This appeared to be a place into which I could naturally fit. In addition to that, Don Holbrook, by the time I joined the firm, was really the senior member, as Joe Jones had become "of counsel." I have never had reason to regret the decision I made.

Early in 1976 a project which had been a source of controversy during the entire time I was in the governorship was terminated.
This was the proposed coal-fired electrical power plant on the
Kaiparowits plateau in southern Utah. During the midsixties there
was little opposition to the project and it appeared to be moving along
well in the planning stage. By 1968, however, opposition to the plant
began growing in environmental circles. The project was delayed time
after time by various factors. At one time the proposing companies
themselves, which were Southern California Edison, San Diego Gas
and Electric, and Arizona Public Service Company, deferred the plant
in favor of the Navajo plant, which they were also building. After a
few years planning for Kaiparowits got moving again, but the need for
environmental impact statements and other matters slowed it down.

I engaged in many debates on this project with various environmental groups. At one time the argument was featured on the television program "60 Minutes" with Robert Redford opposing the project
and I being the principal spokesman for it. Then one day in February
1976 I was called by Bill Gould, the president of Southern California
Edison, who told me that his company had decided that escalating
costs had priced the project out of the market and that it would not
be built. This was a great disappointment to me, as I had envisioned
this not only as a project that would bring a tax base and employment
to some of the poor southern Utah counties, but also as a market for
Utah coal.

Lucybeth and I decided that although it would probably
serve no great public purpose, we would in this last year repeat our
county trips. I'm not sure whether it was nostalgia that made us do it
or if I was just getting bored staying in the Capitol. Things were running so smoothly in the state at that time that my absence would
scarcely be noticed.

During our visit to the St. George area, we stayed in
Rockville with Donna and Bud Kastler. My plane was to pick us up at
the St. George airport the next morning. We had almost a full
planeload, as Ted and Phyllis Moss and another couple were with us.
Just as we were about to leave the airport, Allan Howe came into the
terminal, said he had to get to Salt Lake, and asked if he could ride up
with us. It made the plane crowded, but I couldn't see how I could
refuse him. The conversation on the way up dealt with what was happening in Congress, particularly with Wayne Hayes and Wilbur Mills,

whose sexual exploits were placing Congress in a bad light. Allan was very vocal in condemning his colleagues' conduct.

We arrived in Salt Lake Saturday about noon. Early the next morning one of the newspapers called to ask me about Allan Howe, who had been arrested Saturday night on the west side of Salt Lake City for soliciting sex for hire. This was the beginning of a disturbing period in Democratic party affairs. Nobody was willing to condemn Allan before he was convicted, but I knew something about the reality of the affair from Gunn McKay and Ted Moss. Allan had returned to Washington almost immediately after he had been released on bond following a not guilty plea. I talked to both Ted and Gunn on Sunday afternoon and told them we had to find out what had happened. If the facts and circumstances were such that Allan was going to be convicted at his trial, we'd better see if we could get him out as a Democratic candidate. He was the only person who had filed for the Democratic nomination for Congress from the Second Congressional District, so there was nothing that could be done legally to prevent him from getting the nomination automatically. Nobody else could file, and the party had no mechanism by which he could be removed as a candidate unless he voluntarily withdrew.

I talked with Allan, who had returned to Washington, on Monday or Tuesday by telephone and told him that I wanted him to talk to Gunn and Ted and to be frank with them, tell them what the facts were, and if he were not guilty then we'd stand by him and see him through. But if he faced the prospect, the probability, of conviction during the campaign, then he should withdraw as a candidate so that the Democrats could select someone else in his place. Allan met with Gunn and Ted at Ted's house, and it appeared that he was going to withdraw since he was of the opinion that he would probably be convicted.

While they were discussing the matter a telephone call came for Allan, and from hearing one side of the conversation, Ted and Gunn concluded that this was a staff person calling Allan to tell him that, contrary to what he had supposed, the police did not have his voice on the tape recorder. They had only one side of a conversation between the police decoy who was posing as a prostitute and Allan, as the recording had not picked up Allan's voice. Immediately Allan's position changed. He said he was not going to withdraw and that he would proceed to run for reelection.

We in the Democratic party knew he could not win. An attempt was made to get an opposing candidate at the convention, but that was ruled illegal, and Allan was the nominee in the general election. Daryl McCarty, the chief executive officer of the Utah Education Association, got a campaign going to have himself named a write-in candidate on the ballot, and actually received about 20 percent of the vote; but it wasn't enough. Allan was defeated very badly by Dan Marriott, a newcomer to politics who would not have stood a chance of defeating Howe had it not been for what had happened. Later Allan went to trial and was convicted.

During the late spring and summer of 1976, as I traveled around the state, I was cautious to avoid any involvement with the Democratic convention and the Democratic primary. I did not want to be seen as taking a position among the Democratic candidates, even though I felt that Matheson was the strongest. At our state convention, which was held early in July, Scott Matheson and John Preston Creer emerged as the two high vote getters. They were to run in the primary election to be held on the second Tuesday in September.

The primary campaign was a difficult time for me because of my resolve to remain uninvolved, even though I wanted to see Matheson beat Creer. However, something happened during the closing days that just about forced my hand. Creer ran a big ad in the weekend newspaper advocating an immediate repeal of the sales tax on food. This was a matter I had debated many times with the more liberal Democratic legislators. They had wanted for several years to repeal this portion of the sales tax; and I had told them that I agreed it was a regressive tax but it couldn't be repealed until some other way was found to replace the substantial money, about $40 million, that would be lost. And then Creer came out and proposed the repeal without making any suggestions as to how we would go about making up the lost revenues.

This appeared to me as a challenge, though I met it rather mildly. I issued a statement repeating what I had told the legislators: if any candidate or legislator was going to advocate the repeal of the sales tax on food, in order to be responsible he would have to suggest at the same time a source of revenue to make up the difference. This Creer had not done as I pointed out. The Creer people felt that was unfair of me, but I felt that they had thrown down the gauntlet.

When the primary election was held, the Democratic nomination went to Scott Matheson by a comfortable majority. Vernon Romney beat Dixie Leavitt on the Republican side, as had been expected, although Dixie made a respectable showing. Ted Moss had no opposition in the Democratic primary, and Orrin Hatch beat Jack Carlson for the Republican nomination for the Senate. The stage was set for the general election. I now felt it was not only my right but my duty to involve myself vigorously in the campaign. I went out with Scott Matheson and Ted Moss to various meetings. We also went into supermarkets and shopping centers, where generally people recognized Ted and me, but almost none of them recognized Scott; it was therefore a good way for Scott to get exposure. We went into most of the counties together as well. I tried to get back to the Capitol almost every day, and was able to do so because campaign headquarters had hired an airplane.

I wanted at some appropriate time to say just how I felt about Vernon Romney and his capability, because the thought of having him as governor depressed me greatly. I knew Vernon to be a mediocre lawyer. He seldom showed up on time to the board of examiners meetings. Although he certainly didn't have to punch a time clock as far as I was concerned, I doubt that he put in twenty-five hours a week while he was attorney general. If you were going to try to be governor on that basis, you were bound to be a failure. Furthermore, Vernon was opposed philosophically to many of the things that I supported. Over almost eight years I had borne the indignity of his constant sniping, and so I was looking for an opportunity to let the people know how I felt about Romney as a candidate.

The opportunity came at a banquet at the Hotel Utah. It was October 16, 1976, far enough ahead of the election that I couldn't be accused of a last-minute slander campaign. Jerry Brown, the governor of California, was the principal speaker, and I was asked for some preliminary remarks. Keeping my voice down, and without becoming dramatic, I said that so far as the ability to be governor was concerned, Vernon Romney was not the equal of Scott Matheson in either the energy or the intellectual capacity required. There was some stirring in the crowd as I spoke. The next morning the *Tribune* didn't play it up too much, although they gave that statement of mine the headline rather than Jerry Brown's speech. Jerry has told me many times since that he'd never been more effectively upstaged in all his political career. The *Deseret News* on Monday ran a big article and an editorial highly critical of me for what I'd said. I immediately prepared a long letter to the *Deseret News* and suggested they print it in full, which they did. In this letter I gave details of what I regarded as Romney's shortcomings.

The debate went on right up until the time of the election. Soon the debate no longer focused on me, but on Romney. The Republican party had a big caucus in Salt Lake where many of the state senators and representatives of that party demanded that I make a retraction. I calmly said, "I've nothing to retract. I've stated the facts as I see them." I don't know whether that was a turning point in the campaign, but I'm sure that for the next three weeks of the campaign the voters watched Romney very closely to see if they perceived him as I did. Evidently a sufficient number perceived him that way, as he lost the election. Scott won with about 52 percent. Unfortunately Ted Moss, who had been leading in the polls, fell short in his bid for reelection and lost his seat to Orrin Hatch.

The election being over and my term having only two more months to run, there was little to do except housekeeping jobs. But there was a budget to put together, and although it was going to be Scott's budget that had to be presented to the legislature, he asked me if I would make it and let him sit in on the sessions. Scott took a short vacation, and after he got back he sat in almost every day with me and Herb Smart as we listened to the heads of the various departments of the state government present their requests for funding. I would make my recommendations and pass them on to Scott, and, where he accepted them, he put them in the budget. It was basically his budget, and as it went to the legislature that year, it was a good budget. It was accepted by the legislature mostly as it was presented.

A series of disquieting events occurred in the last months of 1976, concerning a prison inmate named Gary Gilmore. Gilmore had committed an atrocious murder, was tried and convicted in the district courts of Utah of first degree murder, and was sentenced to be executed. There had not been a sentence of capital punishment carried out in the United States for eleven years. During that time the U.S. Supreme Court had been, in various decisions, refining the limit of the power of capital punishment. After his conviction, Gilmore refused to let his attorneys appeal the case to the Utah Supreme Court, saying that he wanted to die.

Most states had an automatic appeal provision which required their supreme courts to review death sentences, whether or not an appeal was taken by the defendant in such cases. Utah didn't have that provision in its laws at the time, and as Gilmore wouldn't make an appeal, various other people tried to appeal for him. The Utah Supreme Court, however, held that those people had no legal standing. It appeared that Gilmore was headed for a firing squad at the Utah State Prison sometime early in December.

I didn't feel it was right that the ultimate decision of whether a man was to live or die should rest with the man himself, and although no procedure was outlined in our law, I wanted some other review. I personally felt that Gilmore should be executed. However, I exercised the governor's limited power to commute a death sentence until the board of pardons could meet, at which time they would consider whether to commute the sentence. The governor of Utah has pardon or commutation power only to this extent. The board of pardons met and decided that Gilmore should die. He was executed by firing squad on January 17, 1977.

Two days before New Year's we moved back into our own home, which had been rented for twelve years. The last tenants had left in time to enable us to repair and redecorate, so the house was ready for us. Coming back revived many memories. None of the children had been married when we left the home, now three of them were married and Vince was about to be. Lucybeth and I spent the first day at home just reminiscing.

Inauguration Day was the first Monday in January 1977. Once again a breakfast was held in the boardroom for state officers, former governors, and other people that either the new governor or the past governor wanted to invite. The group gathered there that morning was similar to the group that had been gathered twelve years before, except Scott and Norma were there and George Clyde was missing because he had died. Mrs. Clyde attended, however, as did the Maws, the Lees, and various friends of ours and the Mathesons.

It came time for the ceremonies to begin. The stand on which the oath was to be administered and the guests were to sit was again erected on the east end of the rotunda in front of the supreme court. The rotunda was full of people. There was an aisle from the boardroom up through the rotunda to the steps leading to the platform, and the various guests went up on the arms of military officers.

Lucybeth and I were last, except for Scott. We came into the rotunda where the people could see us, the band struck up "Try to Remember," and we were greeted by a wonderful ovation. It made us feel very good because the outpouring of affection was obvious. We took our seats and then Scott was brought in.

I sat there thinking, "In ten minutes I will no longer be governor of Utah. I've held this position for twelve years and I'm running out of time right now." Scott had asked me to speak before he spoke. I had difficulty talking. It was an emotional time, and I'm sure I choked up, but I merely wanted to express my thanks to the people of Utah. I also wanted to express my appreciation that I was being succeeded by a man in whom I had confidence. I kept thinking, as that ceremony was going on, how I would have felt had Vernon Romney been the newly elected governor. I suppose I would have gone through with the ceremony, but it would have been almost unbearable.

When the ceremony was over, we left the stand to another march—I believe it was "Recessional." After twelve years in office, I was a private citizen again.

After a month's vacation in Hawaii, we returned to Salt Lake and I began to work at the law firm of Jones, Waldo, Holbrook & McDonough, where I have continued practice since. My time at the law firm has been pleasant and it has provided Lucybeth and me with an adequate income. A few years after I joined the firm I began cutting back on my hours, at the rate of about 10 percent per year, and I now work about half time.

I have handled a variety of cases in the years that I have been with the firm, including some very large ones. Among these was *National League of Cities and Towns vs. Usary* before the U.S. Supreme Court. In this action we succeeded in having declared unconstitutional an act of Congress which I felt encroached upon the powers of the state and local government. My opponent in that case was Robert Bork, whose nomination by President Reagan to be a justice of the U.S. Supreme Court in 1987 was so fiercely debated before the Senate Judiciary Committee, before ultimately being rejected by Congress.

We argued the *Usary* case twice, as Justice Douglas had become ill after the first argument and the remaining judges were equally divided. In the book published several years ago called *The Brethren*, which is a history of the Supreme Court, several pages are devoted to the discussion of the Court in reaching its decision in this hotly contested case. Justice Burger later told me that the case had caused him as much trouble as any case he had ever decided. Seventeen college law review articles had been written on the decision, all of them critical. The case was later overruled.

In 1979, Lucybeth and I bought a condominium in St. George. We stay there about a week of every month except in midsummer. I dictated the contents of this book on tapes over a period of some two years as Lucybeth and I were driving to and from St. George. Our firm has a branch office there with six lawyers, so I am able to work in St. George whenever I am so inclined.

Lucybeth and I have traveled extensively since I left office. We vacation outside of the United States each year for about thirty days, having been several times to England, and to France, Italy, and Spain. We have also taken trips to the South Pacific and the Far East, including Burma, and we once spent a month in the Balkans. In the next year or two we hope to go back to China and the Soviet Union.

Three years ago a great sadness came to us. Our daughter Meg died of cancer. This has been a hard blow to bear, but has probably brought our other three children and their children even closer to us. All of them live in Salt Lake, and we are visited frequently by Meg's husband, Russell, and their three children.

We look back on the public years with nostalgia. They were hard years, but they were also rewarding years. We got to meet the great and near-great people in this country and other countries and to view at close range their strengths and their weaknesses. We also got to know the state of Utah and its people in a manner that no other position would have afforded.

I learned as a political figure what I already knew as a trial lawyer—you should not underestimate the average juror or the average voter. If you have a good case and present it fairly, you will be listened to and will receive a fair verdict. However, if you attempt to deceive jurors or citizens or to patronize them, your cause is certain to be lost.

I have found men and women who are employed by government at all levels to be no more or less honest, able, and dedicated than their counterparts in the private sector of our economy. I believe that government is generally somewhat less efficient than business and industry. This is because democracy is inherently less efficient. The division of powers concept found in government, which is necessary for the preservation of our freedoms, often makes government cumbersome—but it also tends to guard against abuses. On the other hand, I believe there is less outright corruption in government than in business and industry simply because of the greater degree of scrutiny. A minor embezzlement which in industry might rate a paragraph on the inside page of a paper will command headlines if it occurs in government. The press is a watchdog of our public servants. While sometimes the press abuses its power, it offers the best protection against the greater danger of abuse of power and position by public officials. I believe that next to the ministry, government service, and particularly service in elective offices, offers the greatest opportunity for public service available to our people. I tell my children and my grandchildren that they owe it to themselves and to their neighbors to be involved in public affairs. Those who disdain such involvement are doing a disservice to our society.

If coins you have but two, with one buy bread and from the dole, buy hyacinths to feed thy soul.

—Saadi, medieval Persian poet

Governor and Lucybeth Rampton, circa 1970.

Lucybeth C. Rampton, as first lady.

*The Ramptons at the Western Governors' Conference,
West Yellowstone, Montana, June 1967.*

The Rampton family, 1968. Front, left to right, Vince, Lucybeth,
Janet and husband Robert Warburton; back, left to right, the governor,
Anthony, Meg and husband Russell Munk.

Being awarded an Honorary Doctor of Laws degree, 1970, University of Utah.
Left to right, Edward W. Clyde, Calvin L. Rampton,
W. Averell Harriman, and university president, James C. Fletcher.

*Secretary of the Interior Stewart L. Udall signing the transfer of land
to create the Research Park at the University of Utah, October 1968.
Standing, left to right, are University of Utah President
James C. Fletcher, Senator Frank Moss, Governor Rampton, and
Robert D. Nielson, State Director, Bureau of Land Management.*

The governor at an EIMCO Corporation promotion for new mining equipment.

Michael Dukakis, Calvin Rampton, and Jimmy Carter at the governor's conference at Hershey, Pennsylvania, 1976.

USSR Supreme Soviet President Nicolai V. Podgorny, third from the left, and his colleagues meet a delegation from the United States, 1975. Seated across the table from the president are, right to left, Governor Wendell Anderson of Minnesota, Governor Richard Kneip of South Dakota, Governor Rampton, Governor Thomas Salmon of Vermont, and Governor Robert Ray of Iowa.

Four former governors of Utah, left to right, J. Bracken Lee,
Scott M. Matheson, Herbert B. Maw, and Calvin L. Rampton, 1986.

INDEX

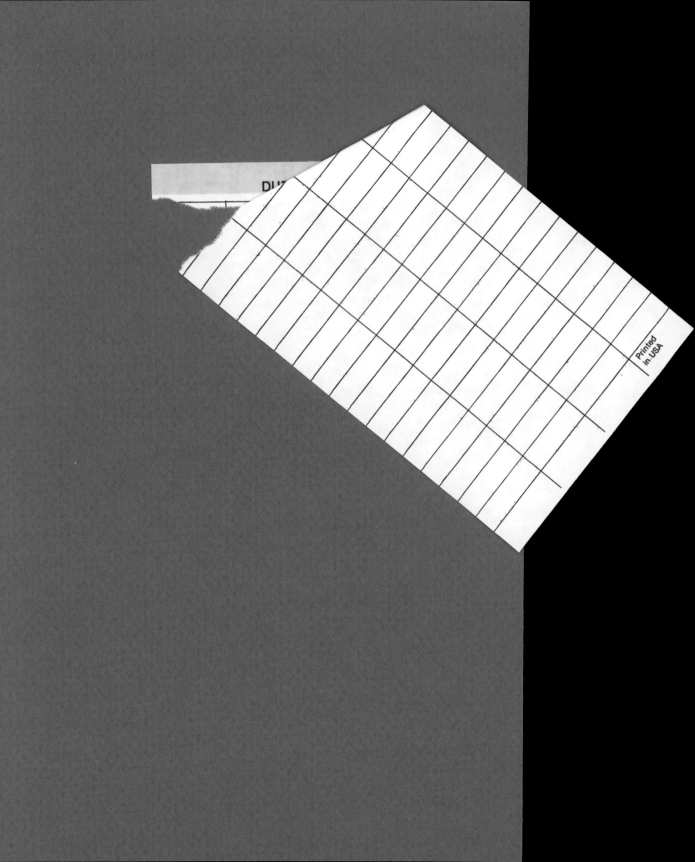